# GREATEST AMERICAN SPEECHES

**First Published 2025**

**FiNGERPRINT! CLASSICS**
**Prakash Books**

Fingerprint Publishing
@FingerprintP
@fingerprintpublishingbooks
www.fingerprintpublishing.com



ISBN: 978 93 6214 707 3

*"If you talk to a man in a language he understands, that goes to his head. If you talk to him in his language, that goes to his heart."*

—Nelson Mandela

# *About This Edition*

*This edition brings together 35 of the most defining speeches in U.S. history, capturing the ideals, struggles, and triumphs that shaped the nation. From Patrick Henry's call for liberty to Franklin D. Roosevelt's Four Freedoms, this collection showcases the words of leaders who inspired change. Spanning revolution, war, and progress, these speeches reflect the enduring spirit of democracy, courage, and the American dream.*

# CONTENTS

# 1

## Give Me Liberty or Give Me Death

★ ★ ★ ★ ★ ★ ★

Patrick Henry
Richmond, Virginia, U.S.A.
23 March 1775

*Fighting for independence for the state of Virginia, Henry addressed the people at the Virginia House of Burgesses. He espoused in his speech that Britain had been treating Virginians not as equals but as subordinates. It was time to fight to overthrow the British to gain their freedom, or die trying.*

*A month after this speech, the Battle of Lexington and Concord had started. This was the first event that marked the start of the Revolutionary War from 1775 to 1783.*

No man thinks more highly than I do of the patriotism, as well as abilities, of the very worthy gentlemen who have just addressed the House. But different men often see the same subject in different lights; and, therefore, I hope that it will not be thought disrespectful to those gentlemen, if, entertaining as I do opinions of a character very opposite to theirs, I shall speak forth my sentiments freely and without reserve. This is no time for ceremony. The question before the House is one of awful moment to this country. For my own part I consider it as nothing less than a question of freedom or slavery; and in proportion to the magnitude of the subject ought to be the freedom of the debate. It is only in this way that we can hope to arrive at truth, and fulfil the great responsibility which we hold to God and our country. Should I keep back my opinions at such a time, through fear of giving offense, I should consider myself as guilty of treason towards my country, and of an act of disloyalty towards the majesty of heaven, which I revere above all earthly kings.

Mr. President, it is natural to man to indulge in the illusions of hope. We are apt to shut our eyes against a painful truth, and listen to the song of that siren, till she transforms us into beasts. Is this the part of wise men, engaged in a great and arduous struggle for liberty? Are we disposed to be of the number of those who, having eyes, see not, and having ears, hear not, the things which so nearly concern their temporal salvation? For my part, whatever anguish of spirit it may cost, I am willing to know the whole truth—to know the worst and to provide for it.

I have but one lamp by which my feet are guided; and that is the lamp of experience. I know of no way of judging of the future but by the past. And judging by the past, I wish to know what there has been in the conduct of the British ministry for the last ten years, to justify those hopes with which gentlemen have been pleased to solace themselves and the House.

Is it that insidious smile with which our petition has been lately received? Trust it not, sir; it will prove a snare to your feet. Suffer not yourselves to be betrayed with a kiss. Ask yourselves how this gracious reception of our petition comports with these warlike preparations which cover our waters and darken our land. Are fleets and armies necessary to a work of love and reconciliation? Have we shown ourselves so unwilling to be reconciled that force must be called in to win back our love? Let us not deceive ourselves, sir. These are the implements of war and subjugation—the last arguments to which kings resort. I ask gentlemen, sir, what means this martial array, if its purpose be not to force us to submission? Can gentlemen assign any other possible motives for it? Has Great Britain any enemy, in this quarter of the world, to call for all this accumulation of navies and armies?

No, sir, she has none. They are meant for us; they can be meant for no other. They are sent over to bind and rivet upon us those chains which the British ministry have been so long forging. And what have we to oppose to them? Shall we try argument? Sir, we have been trying that for the last ten years. Have we anything new to offer on the subject? Nothing.

We have held the subject up in every light of which it is capable; but it has been all in vain. Shall we resort to entreaty and humble supplication? What terms shall we find which have not been already exhausted? Let us not, I beseech you, sir, deceive ourselves longer.

Sir, we have done everything that could be done to avert the storm which is now coming on. We have petitioned; we have remonstrated; we have supplicated; we have prostrated ourselves before the throne, and have implored its interposition to arrest the tyrannical hands of the ministry and parliament.

Our petitions have been slighted; our remonstrances have produced additional violence and insult; our supplications have been disregarded; and we have been spurned, with contempt, from the foot of the throne. In vain, after these things, may we indulge the fond hope of peace and reconciliation. There is no longer any room for hope.

If we wish to be free—if we mean to preserve inviolate those inestimable privileges for which we have been so long contending—if we mean not basely to abandon the noble struggle in which we have been so long engaged, and which we have pledged ourselves never to abandon until the glorious object of our contest shall be obtained—we must fight! I repeat it, sir, we must fight! An appeal to arms and to the God of Hosts is all that is left us!

They tell us, sir, that we are weak; unable to cope with so formidable an adversary. But when shall we be stronger? Will it be the next week, or the next year? Will it be when we are totally disarmed, and when a British guard shall be stationed in every house? Shall we gather strength by irresolution and inaction? Shall we acquire the means of effectual resistance, by lying supinely on our backs, and hugging the delusive phantom of hope, until our enemies shall have bound us hand and foot?

Sir, we are not weak if we make a proper use of the means which the God of nature hath placed in our power. Three millions of people, armed in the holy cause of liberty, and in such a country as that which we possess, are invincible by any force which our enemy can send against us. Besides, sir, we shall not fight our battles alone. There is a just God who presides over the destinies of nations, and who will raise up friends to fight our battles for us.

The battle, sir, is not to the strong alone; it is to the vigilant, the active, the brave. Besides, sir, we have no election. If we were base enough to desire it, it is now too late to retire from the contest. There is no retreat but in submission and slavery! Our chains are forged! Their clanking may be heard on the plains of Boston! The war is inevitable—and let it come! I repeat it, sir, let it come!

It is in vain, sir, to extenuate the matter. Gentlemen may cry, Peace, Peace—but there is no peace. The war is actually begun! The next gale that sweeps from the north will bring to our ears the clash of resounding arms! Our brethren are already in the field! Why stand we here idle? What is it that gentlemen wish? What would they have? Is life so dear, or peace so sweet, as to be purchased at the price of chains and slavery? Forbid it, Almighty God! I know not what course others may take; but as for me, give me liberty or give me death!

*Note: There is no written record of this speech. Henry's biographer, William Wirt, reconstructed the speech many years later from reminiscences of men who were present when it was delivered.*

# 2

## The Newburgh Address

★ ★ ★ ★ ★ ★ ★

George Washington
Newburgh, New York, U.S.A.
15 March 1783

*The soldiers of the Continental Army were getting agitated since they had not been paid for their service in the war. The Congress was bankrupt. The army was deliberating on whether they should revolt—if the war continued, they would refuse to participate, and if the war ended they would march to the Congress and demand what they were owed.*

*Washington had come to know the severity of the situation and addressed the soldiers to defuse the growing unrest. He voiced that while he understood their suffering and sympathized with their demands, he disapproved of the way they wanted to achieve them.*

Gentlemen:

By an anonymous summons, an attempt has been made to convene you together; how inconsistent with the rules of propriety, how unmilitary, and how subversive of all order and discipline, let the good sense of the army decide . . .

Thus much, gentlemen, I have thought it incumbent on me to observe to you, to show upon what principles I opposed the irregular and hasty meeting which was proposed to have been held on Tuesday last—and not because I wanted a disposition to give you every opportunity consistent with your own honour, and the dignity of the army, to make known your grievances. If my conduct heretofore has not evinced to you that I have been a faithful friend to the army, my declaration of it at this time would be equally unavailing and improper. But as I was among the first who embarked in the cause of our common country. As I have never left your side one moment, but when called from you on public duty. As I have been the constant companion and witness of your distresses, and not among the last to feel and acknowledge your merits. As I have ever considered my own military reputation as inseparably connected with that of the army. As my heart has ever expanded with joy, when I have heard its praises, and my indignation has arisen, when the mouth of detraction has been opened against it, it can scarcely be supposed, at this late stage of the war, that I am indifferent to its interests.

But how are they to be promoted? The way is plain, says the anonymous addresser. If war continues, remove into the unsettled country, there establish yourselves, and leave an ungrateful country to defend itself. But who are they to defend? Our wives, our children, our farms, and other property which we leave behind us. Or, in this state of hostile separation, are we to take the two first (the latter cannot be removed) to perish in a wilderness, with hunger, cold, and nakedness? If peace takes place, never sheathe your swords, says he, until you have obtained full and ample justice; this dreadful alternative, of either deserting our country in the extremest hour of her distress or turning our arms against it (which is the apparent object, unless Congress can be compelled into instant compliance), has something so shocking in it that humanity revolts at the idea. My God! What can this writer have in view, by recommending such measures? Can he be a friend to the army? Can he be a friend to this country? Rather, is he not an insidious foe? Some emissary, perhaps, from New York, plotting the ruin of both, by sowing the seeds of discord and separation between the civil and military powers of the continent? And what a compliment does he pay to our understandings when he recommends measures in either alternative, impracticable in their nature?

I cannot, in justice to my own belief, and what I have great reason to conceive is the intention of Congress, conclude this address, without giving it as my decided opinion, that that honourable body entertain exalted sentiments of the services of the army; and, from a full conviction of its merits and sufferings, will do it complete justice. That their endeavours to discover and establish funds for this purpose have been unwearied, and will not cease till they have succeeded, I have not a doubt. But, like all other large bodies, where there is a variety of different interests to reconcile, their deliberations are slow. Why, then, should we distrust them? And, in consequence of that distrust, adopt measures which may cast a shade over that glory which has been so justly acquired; and tarnish the reputation of an army which is celebrated through all Europe, for its fortitude and patriotism? And for what is this done? To bring the object we seek nearer? No! Most certainly, in my opinion, it will cast it at a greater distance.

For myself (and I take no merit in giving the assurance, being induced to it from principles of gratitude, veracity, and justice), a grateful sense of the confidence you have ever placed in me, a recollection of the cheerful assistance and prompt obedience I have experienced from you, under every vicissitude of fortune, and the sincere affection I feel for an army I have so long had the honour to command will oblige me to declare, in this public and solemn manner, that, in the attainment of complete justice for all your toils and dangers, and in the gratification of every wish, so far as may be done consistently with the great duty I owe my country and those powers we are bound to respect, you may freely command my services to the utmost of my abilities.

While I give you these assurances, and pledge myself in the most unequivocal manner to exert whatever ability I am possessed of in your favour, let me entreat you, gentlemen, on your part, not to take any measures which, viewed in the calm light of reason, will lessen the dignity and sully the glory you have hitherto maintained; let me request you to rely on the plighted faith of your country, and place a full confidence in the purity of the intentions of Congress; that, previous to your dissolution as an army, they will cause all your accounts to be fairly liquidated, as directed in their resolutions, which were published to you two days ago, and that they will adopt the most effectual measures in their power to render ample justice to you, for your faithful and meritorious services. And let me conjure you, in the name of our common country, as you value your own sacred honour, as you respect the rights of humanity, and as you regard the military and national character of America, to express your utmost horror and detestation of the man who wishes, under any specious pretences, to overturn the liberties of our country, and who wickedly attempts to open the floodgates of civil discord and deluge our rising empire in blood.

By thus determining and thus acting, you will pursue the plain and direct road to the attainment of your wishes. You will defeat the insidious designs of our enemies, who are compelled to resort from open force to secret artifice. You will give one more distinguished proof of unexampled patriotism and patient virtue, rising superior to the pressure of the most complicated sufferings. And you will, by the dignity of your conduct, afford occasion for posterity to say, when speaking of the glorious example you have exhibited to mankind, 'Had this day been wanting, the world had never seen the last stage of perfection to which human nature is capable of attaining.'

# 3

# Resignation Speech

★ ★ ★ ★ ★ ★ ★

George Washington
Annapolis, Maryland, U.S.A.
23 December 1783

*The Continental Army had been formed in 1775, after the outbreak of the American Revolution. Washington was chosen to lead the army since he had prior military experience and had proved to be an able leader.*

*After the Treaty of Paris had been signed, George Washington addressed the congress and relinquished his post of commander-in-chief of the Continental Army, giving the military authority over to the civilians.*

The great events on which my resignation depended having at length taken place; I have now the honour of offering my sincere Congratulations to Congress and of presenting myself before them to surrender into their hands the trust committed to me, and to claim the indulgence of retiring from the service of my country.

Happy in the confirmation of our Independence and Sovereignty, and pleased with the opportunity afforded the United States of becoming a respectable Nation, I resign with satisfaction the Appointment I accepted with diffidence. A diffidence in my abilities to accomplish so arduous a task, which however was superseded by a confidence in the rectitude of our Cause, the support of the Supreme Power of the Union, and the patronage of Heaven.

The successful termination of the War has verified the most sanguine expectations, and my gratitude for the interposition of Providence, and the assistance I have received from my countrymen, increases with every review of the momentous contest.

While I repeat my obligations to the Army in general, I should do injustice to my own feelings not to acknowledge in this place the peculiar services and distinguished merits of the gentlemen who have been attached to my person during the war. It was impossible the choice of confidential officers to compose my family should have been more fortunate. Permit me, sir, to recommend in particular those, who have continued in service to the present moment, as worthy of the favourable notice and patronage of Congress.

I consider it an indispensable duty to close this last solemn act of my official life, by commending the interests of our dearest country to the protection of Almighty God, and those who have the superintendence of them, to his holy keeping.

Having now finished the work assigned me, I retire from the great theatre of action; and bidding an affectionate farewell to this August body under whose orders I have so long acted, I here offer my commission, and take my leave of all the employments of public life.

# 4

# Disapproving and Accepting the Constitution

★ ★ ★ ★ ★ ★ ★

Benjamin Franklin
Philadelphia, U.S.A.
17 September 1787

*Benjamin Franklin was one of the people who signed the final draft of the Constitution, and he had something to say about it. There were some aspects of the Constitution that he lauded, and some he thought were flawed—and he was sure that he will never approve of them. But, he accepted its problems with its benefits.*

I confess that I do not entirely approve of this Constitution at present; but, sir, I am not sure I shall never approve it, for, having lived long, I have experienced many instances of being obliged, by better information or fuller consideration, to change opinions even on important subjects, which I once thought right, but found to be otherwise. It is therefore that, the older I grow, the more apt I am to doubt my own judgment of others. Most men, indeed, as well as most sects in religion, think themselves in possession of all truth, and that wherever others differ from them, it is so far error. Steele, a Protestant, in a dedication, tells the Pope that the only difference between our two churches in their opinions of the certainty of their doctrine is, the Romish Church is infallible, and the Church of England is never in the wrong. But, though many private persons think almost as highly of their own infallibility as of that of their sect, few express it so naturally as a certain French lady, who, in a little dispute with her sister, said: 'But I meet with nobody but myself that is always in the right.'

In these sentiments, sir, I agree to this Constitution, with all its faults—if they are such—because I think a general government necessary for us, and there is no form of government but what may be a blessing to the people, if well administered; and I believe, further, that this is likely to be well administered for a course of years, and can only end in despotism, as other forms have done before it, when the people shall become so corrupted as to need despotic government, being incapable of any other. I doubt, too, whether any other convention we can obtain may be able to make a better Constitution; for, when you assemble a number of men, to have the advantage of their joint wisdom, you inevitably assemble with those men all their prejudices, their passions, their errors of opinion, their local interests, and their selfish views. From such an assembly can a perfect production be expected? It therefore astonishes me, sir, to find this system approaching so near to perfection as it does; and I think it will astonish our enemies, who are waiting with confidence to hear that our counsels are confounded like those of the builders of Babel, and that our States are on the point of separation, only to meet hereafter for the purpose of cutting one another's throats. Thus I consent, sir, to this Constitution, because I expect no better, and because I am not sure that it is not the best. The opinions I have had of its errors I sacrifice to the public good. I have never whispered a syllable of them abroad. Within these walls they were born, and here they shall die. If every one of us, in returning to our constituents, were to report the objections he has had to it, and endeavour to gain partisans in support of them, we might prevent its being generally received, and thereby lose all the salutary effects and great advantages resulting naturally in our favour among foreign nations, as well as among ourselves, from our real or apparent unanimity. Much of the strength and efficiency of any government, in procuring and securing happiness to the people, depends on opinion, on the general opinion of the goodness of that government, as well as of the wisdom and integrity of its governors. I hope, therefore, for our own sakes, as a part of the people, and for the sake of our posterity, that we shall act heartily and unanimously in recommending this Constitution wherever our influence may extend, and turn our future thoughts and endeavours to the means of having it well administered.

On the whole, sir, I cannot help expressing a wish that every member of the convention who may still have objections to it, would, with me, on this occasion, doubt a little of his own infallibility, and, to make manifest our unanimity, put his name to this instrument.

*Note: Benjamin Franklin signed three more important documents aside from the American Constitution—The Declaration of Independence, The Treaty of Alliance with France, and The Treaty of Paris.*

# 5

## First Inaugural Speech

★ ★ ★ ★ ★ ★ ★

George Washington
New York, U.S.A.
30 April 1789

*George Washington delivered the very first inaugural address to a joint session of Congress at the Federal Hall on Wall Street. From then, it became a tradition and all the presidents after him have followed it.*

*This address garnered a favourable response from the Senate and the House, both of which promised to consider the president's recommendations.*

Fellow citizens of the Senate and of the House of Representatives:

Among the vicissitudes incident to life no event could have filled me with greater anxieties than that of which the notification was transmitted by your order, and received on the fourteenth day of the present month. On the one hand, I was summoned by my Country, whose voice I can never hear but with veneration and love, from a retreat which I had chosen with the fondest predilection, and, in my flattering hopes, with an immutable decision, as the asylum of my declining years—a retreat which was rendered every day more necessary as well as more dear to me by the addition of habit to inclination, and of frequent interruptions in my health to the gradual waste committed on it by time. On the other hand, the magnitude and difficulty of the trust to which the voice of my country called me, being sufficient to awaken in the wisest and most experienced of her citizens a distrustful scrutiny into his qualifications, could not but overwhelm with despondence one who (inheriting inferior endowments from nature and unpractised in the duties of civil administration) ought to be peculiarly conscious of his own deficiencies. In this conflict of emotions all I dare aver is that it has been my faithful study to collect my duty from a just appreciation of every circumstance by which it might be affected. All I dare hope is that if, in executing this task, I have been too much swayed by a grateful remembrance of former instances, or by an affectionate sensibility to this transcendent proof of the confidence of my fellow citizens, and have thence too little consulted my incapacity as well as disinclination for the weighty and untried cares before me, my error will be palliated by the motives which mislead me, and its consequences be judged by my country with some share of the partiality in which they originated.

Such being the impressions under which I have, in obedience to the public summons, repaired to the present station, it would be peculiarly improper to omit in this first official act my fervent supplications to that Almighty Being who rules over the universe, who presides in the councils of nations, and whose providential aids can supply every human defect, that His benediction may consecrate to the liberties and happiness of the people of the United States a government instituted by themselves for these essential purposes, and may enable every instrument employed in its administration to execute with success the functions allotted to his charge. In tendering this homage to the Great Author of every public and private good, I assure myself that it expresses your sentiments not less than my own, nor those of my fellow citizens at large less than either. No people can be bound to acknowledge and adore the Invisible Hand which conducts the affairs of men more than those of the United States. Every step by which they have advanced to the character of an independent nation seems to have been distinguished by some token of providential agency; and in the important revolution just accomplished in the system of their united government the tranquil deliberations and voluntary consent of so many distinct communities from which the event has resulted cannot be compared with the means by which most governments have been established without some return of pious gratitude, along with an humble anticipation of the future blessings which the past seem to presage. These reflections, arising out of the present crisis, have forced themselves too strongly on my mind to be suppressed. You will join with me, I trust, in thinking that there are none under the influence of which the proceedings of a new and free government can more auspiciously commence.

By the article establishing the executive department it is made the duty of the president 'to recommend to your consideration such measures as he shall judge necessary and expedient.' The circumstances under which I now meet you will acquit me from entering into that subject further than to refer to the great constitutional charter under which you are assembled, and which, in defining your powers, designates the objects to which your attention is to be given. It will be more consistent with those circumstances, and far more congenial with the feelings which actuate me, to substitute, in place of a recommendation of particular measures, the tribute that is due to the talents, the rectitude, and the patriotism which adorn the characters selected to devise and adopt them. In these honourable qualifications I behold the surest pledges that as on one side no local prejudices or attachments, no separate views nor party animosities, will misdirect the comprehensive and equal eye which ought to watch over this great assemblage of communities and interests, so, on another, that the foundation of our national policy will be laid in the pure and immutable principles of private morality, and the pre-eminence of free government be exemplified by all the attributes which can win the affections of its citizens and command the respect of the world. I dwell on this prospect with every satisfaction which an ardent love for my country can inspire, since there is no truth more thoroughly established than that there exists in the economy and course of nature an indissoluble union between virtue and happiness; between duty and advantage; between the genuine maxims of an honest and magnanimous policy and the solid rewards of public prosperity and felicity; since we ought to be no less persuaded that the propitious smiles of Heaven can never be expected on a nation that disregards the eternal rules of order and right which Heaven itself has ordained; and since the preservation of the sacred fire of liberty and the destiny of the republican model of government are justly considered, perhaps, as deeply, as finally, staked on the experiment entrusted to the hands of the American people.

Besides the ordinary objects submitted to your care, it will remain with your judgment to decide how far an exercise of the occasional power delegated by the fifth article of the Constitution is rendered expedient at the present juncture by the nature of objections which have been urged against the system, or by the degree of in quietude which has given birth to them. Instead of undertaking particular recommendations on this subject, in which I could be guided by no lights derived from official opportunities, I shall again give way to my entire confidence in your discernment and pursuit of the public good; for I assure myself that whilst you carefully avoid every alteration which might endanger the benefits of an united and effective government, or which ought to await the future lessons of experience, a reverence for the characteristic rights of freemen and a regard for the public harmony will sufficiently influence your deliberations on the question how far the former can be impregnably fortified or the latter be safely and advantageously promoted. To the foregoing observations I have one to add, which will be most properly addressed to the House of Representatives. It concerns myself, and will therefore be as brief as possible. When I was first honoured with a call into the service of my country, then on the eve of an arduous struggle for its liberties, the light in which I contemplated my duty required that I should renounce every pecuniary compensation. From this resolution I have in no instance departed; and being still under the impressions which produced it, I must decline as inapplicable to myself any share in the personal emoluments which may be indispensably included in a permanent provision for the executive department, and must accordingly pray that the pecuniary estimates for the station in which I am placed may during my continuance in it be limited to such actual expenditures as the public good may be thought to require.

Having thus imparted to you my sentiments as they have been awakened by the occasion which brings us together, I shall take my present leave; but not without resorting once more to the benign Parent of the Human Race in humble supplication that, since He has been pleased to favour the American people with opportunities for deliberating in perfect tranquillity, and dispositions for deciding with unparalleled unanimity on a form of government for the security of their union and the advancement of their happiness, so His divine blessing may be equally conspicuous in the enlarged views, the temperate consultations, and the wise measures on which the success of this government must depend.

# 6

## Farewell Address

★ ★ ★ ★ ★ ★ ★

George Washington
Philadelphia, U.S.A.
17 September 1796

*George Washington was the first President of the United States. In 1796, nearing the end of his second term, he chose to step down from his post. He addressed the American masses for the last time, most of which wanted him to run for another term as president.*

*The following speech was not spoken but published in Philadelphia's newspaper American Daily Advertiser. Washington advised his people to be wary of geographical sectionalism, political factionalism, and interference by foreign powers.*

Friends and Citizens:

The period for a new election of a citizen to administer the executive Government of the United States being not far distant, and the time actually arrived when your thoughts must be employed in designating the person who is to be clothed with that important trust, it appears to me proper, especially as it may conduce to a more distinct expression of the public voice, that I should now apprise you of the resolution I have formed to decline being considered among the number of those out of whom a choice is to be made.

I beg you, at the same time, to do me the justice to be assured that this resolution has not been taken without a strict regard to all the considerations appertaining to the relation which binds a dutiful citizen to his country; and that, in withdrawing the tender of service, which silence in my situation might imply, I am influenced by no diminution of zeal for your future interest, no deficiency of grateful respect for your past kindness, but am supported by a full conviction that the step is compatible with both.

The acceptance of, and continuance hitherto in, the office to which your suffrages have twice called me, have been a uniform sacrifice of inclination to the opinion of duty, and to a deference for what appeared to be your desire. I constantly hoped that it would have been much earlier in my power, consistently with motives which I was not at liberty to disregard, to return to that retirement from which I had been reluctantly drawn. The strength of my inclination to do this, previous to the last election, had even led to the preparation of an address to declare it to you; but mature reflection on the then perplexed and critical posture of our affairs with foreign nation, and the unanimous advice of persons entitled to my confidence, impelled me to abandon the idea.

I rejoice that the state of your concerns, external as well as internal, no longer renders the pursuit of inclination incompatible with the sentiment of duty or propriety; and am persuaded, whatever partiality may be retained for my services, that, in the present circumstances of our country, you will not disapprove my determination to retire.

The impressions with which I first undertook the arduous trust were explained on the proper occasion. In the discharge of this trust, I will only say that I have, with good intentions, contributed towards the organization and administration of the government the best exertions of which a very fallible judgement was capable. Not unconscious in the outset of the inferiority of my qualifications, experience in my own eyes, perhaps still more in the eyes of others, has strengthened the motives to diffidence of myself; and every day the increasing weight of years admonishes me more and more that the shade of retirement is as necessary to me as it will be welcome. Satisfied that if any circumstances have given peculiar value to my services, they were temporary, I have the consolation to believe that, while choice and prudence invite me to quit the political scene, patriotism does not forbid it.

In looking forward to the moment which is intended to terminate the career of my public life, my feelings do not permit me to suspend the deep acknowledgment of that debt of gratitude which I owe to my beloved country for the many honours it has conferred upon me; still more for the steadfast confidence with which it has supported me, and for the opportunities I have thence enjoyed of manifesting my inviolable attachment by services faithful and persevering, though in usefulness unequal to my zeal. If benefits have resulted to our country from these services let it always be remembered to your praise, and as an instructive example in our annals, that, under circumstances in which the passions, agitated in every direction, were liable to mislead, amid appearances sometimes dubious, vicissitudes of fortune often discouraging, in situations in which not unfrequently want of success has countenanced the spirit of criticism, the constancy of your support was the essential prop of the efforts and a guaranty of the plans by which they were effected. Profoundly penetrated with this idea, I shall carry it with me to my grave as a strong incitement to unceasing vows that heaven may continue to you the choicest tokens of its beneficence; that your union and brotherly affection may be perpetual; that the free Constitution, which is the work of your hands, may be sacredly maintained; that its administration in every department may be stamped with wisdom and virtue; that, in fine, the happiness of the people of these States, under the auspices of liberty, may be made complete by so careful a preservation and so prudent a use of this blessing as will acquire to them the glory of recommending it to the applause, the affection, and adoption of every nation which is yet a stranger to it.

Here, perhaps, I ought to stop. But a solicitude for your welfare which cannot end but with my life, and the apprehension of danger natural to that solicitude, urge me, on an occasion like the present, to offer to your solemn contemplation and to recommend to your frequent review some sentiments which are the result of much reflection of no inconsiderable observation, and which appear to me all-important to the permanency of your felicity as a people. These will be offered to you with the more freedom as you can only see in them the disinterested warnings of a parting friend who can possibly have no personal motive to bias his counsel. Nor can I forget, as an encouragement to it, your indulgent reception of my sentiments on a former and not dissimilar occasion.

Interwoven as is the love of liberty with every ligament of your hearts, no recommendation of mine is necessary to fortify or confirm the attachment.

The unity of government which constitutes you one people is also now dear to you. It is justly so, for it is a main pillar in the edifice of your real independence; the support of your tranquillity at home, your peace abroad; of your safety; of your prosperity; of that very liberty which you so highly prize. But as it is easy to foresee that from different causes and from different quarters much pains will be taken, many artifices employed, to weaken in your minds the conviction of this truth; as this is the point in your political fortress against which the batteries of internal and external enemies will be most constantly and actively (though often covertly and insidiously) directed, it is of infinite moment that you should properly estimate the immense value of your national Union to your collective and individual happiness; that you should cherish a cordial, habitual, and immovable attachment to it; accustoming yourselves to think and speak of it as the palladium of your political safety and prosperity; watching for its preservation with jealous anxiety; discountenancing whatever may suggest even a suspicion that it can in any event be abandoned; and indignantly frowning upon the first dawning of every attempt to alienate any portion of our country from the rest, or to enfeeble the sacred ties which now link together the various parts.

For this you have every inducement of sympathy and of interest. Citizens, either by birth or choice, of a common country, that country has a right to concentrate your affections. The name of American which belongs to you in your national capacity must always exalt the just pride of patriotism more than any appellation derived from local discriminations. With slight shades of difference you have the same religion, manners, habits, and political principles. You have in a common cause fought and triumphed together; the independence and liberty you possess are the work of joint counsels and joint efforts, of common dangers, sufferings, and successes.

But these considerations, however powerfully they address themselves to your sensibility, are greatly outweighed by those which apply more immediately to your interest. Here every portion of our country finds the most commanding motives for carefully guarding and preserving the union of the whole.

The North, in an unrestrained intercourse with the South, protected by the equal laws of a common government, finds in the productions of the latter great additional resources of maritime and commercial enterprise and precious materials of manufacturing industry. The South, in the same intercourse, benefiting by the agency of the North, sees its agriculture grow and its commerce expand. Turning partly into its own channels the seamen of the North, it finds its particular navigation invigorated, and while it contributes, in different ways, to nourish and increase the general mass of the national navigation, it looks forward to the protection of a maritime strength, to which itself is unequally adapted. The East, in a like intercourse with the West, already finds—and in a progressive improvement of interior communications by land and water will more and more find—a valuable vent for the commodities which it brings from abroad or manufactures at home.

The West derives from the East supplies requisite to its growth and comfort, and what is perhaps of still greater consequence, it must of necessity owe the secure enjoyment of indispensable outlets for its own productions to the weight, influence, and the future maritime strength of the Atlantic side of the Union, directed by an indissoluble community of interest as one nation. Any other tenure by which the West can hold this essential advantage, whether derived from its own separate strength or from an apostate and unnatural connection with any foreign power, must be intrinsically precarious.

While, then, every part of our country thus feels an immediate and particular interest in union, all the parts combined cannot fail to find in the united mass of means and efforts greater strength, greater resource, proportionably greater security from external danger, a less frequent interruption of their peace by foreign nations; and, what is of inestimable value, they must derive from union an exemption from those broils and wars between themselves which so frequently afflict neighbouring countries not tied together by the same governments, which their own rivalships alone would be sufficient to produce, but which opposite foreign alliances, attachments, and intrigues would stimulate and embitter. Hence, likewise, they will avoid the necessity of those overgrown military establishments, which, under any form of government, are inauspicious to liberty, and which are to be regarded as particularly hostile to republican liberty. In this sense it is that your union ought to be considered as a main prop of your liberty, and that the love of the one ought to endear to you the preservation of the other.

These considerations speak a persuasive language to every reflecting and virtuous mind, and exhibit the continuance of the Union as a primary object of patriotic desire. Is there a doubt whether a common government can embrace so large a sphere? Let experience solve it. To listen to mere speculation in such a case were criminal. We are authorized to hope that a proper organization of the whole, with the auxiliary agency of governments for the respective subdivisions, will afford a happy issue to the experiment. It is well worth a fair and full experiment. With such powerful and obvious motives to union affecting all parts of our country, while experience shall not have demonstrated its impracticability, there will always be reason to distrust the patriotism of those who in any quarter may endeavour to weaken its bands.

In contemplating the causes which may disturb our Union it occurs as a matter of serious concern that any ground should have been furnished for characterizing parties by geographical discriminations, Northern and Southern, Atlantic and Western; whence designing men may endeavour to excite a belief that there is a real difference of local interests and views. One of the expedients of party to acquire influence within particular districts is to misrepresent the opinions and aims of other districts. You cannot shield yourselves too much against the jealousies and heartburnings which spring from these misrepresentations; they tend to render alien to each other those who ought to be bound together by fraternal affection. The inhabitants of our Western country have lately had a useful lesson on this head; they have seen, in the negotiation by the executive, and in the unanimous ratification by the Senate, of the treaty with Spain, and in the universal satisfaction at that event throughout the United States, a decisive proof how unfounded were the suspicions propagated among them of a policy in the general government and in the Atlantic States unfriendly to their interests in regard to the Mississippi; they have been witnesses to the formation of two treaties, that with Great Britain and that with Spain, which secure to them everything they could desire, in respect to our foreign relations, toward confirming their prosperity. Will it not be their wisdom to rely for the preservation of these advantages on the Union by which they were procured? Will they not henceforth be deaf to those advisers, if such there are, who would sever them from their brethren, and connect them with aliens?

To the efficacy and permanency of your Union a government for the whole is indispensable. No alliances, however strict, between the parts can be an adequate substitute; they must inevitably experience the infractions and interruptions which all alliances in all times have experienced. Sensible of this momentous truth, you have improved upon your first essay by the adoption of a constitution of government better calculated than your former for an intimate union and for the efficacious management of your common concerns. This government, the offspring of your own choice, uninfluenced and unawed, adopted upon full investigation and mature deliberation, completely free in its principles, in the distribution of its powers, uniting security with energy, and containing within itself a provision for its own amendment, has a just claim to your confidence and your support. Respect for its authority, compliance with its laws, acquiescence in its measures, are duties enjoined by the fundamental maxims of true liberty. The basis of our political systems is the right of the people to make and to alter their constitutions of government. But the constitution which at any time exists till changed by an explicit and authentic act of the whole people is sacredly obligatory upon all. The very idea of the power and the right of the people to establish government presupposes the duty of every individual to obey the established government.

All obstructions to the execution of the laws, all combinations and associations, under whatever plausible character, with the real design to direct, control, counteract, or awe the regular deliberation and action of the constituted authorities, are destructive of this fundamental principle, and of fatal tendency. They serve to organize faction, to give it an artificial and extraordinary force; to put, in the place of the delegated will of the nation, the will of a party, often a small but artful and enterprising minority of the community; and, according to the alternate triumphs of different parties, to make the public administration the mirror of the ill-concerted and incongruous projects of fashion, rather than the organs of consistent and wholesome plans digested by common councils, and modified by mutual interests.

However, combinations or associations of the above description may now and then answer popular ends, they are likely, in the course of time and things, to become potent engines, by which cunning, ambitious, and unprincipled men will be enabled to subvert the power of the people, and to usurp for themselves the reins of government, destroying afterward the very engines which have lifted them to unjust dominion.

Towards the preservation of your government, and the permanency of your present happy state, it is requisite, not only that you steadily discountenance irregular oppositions to its acknowledged authority, but also that you resist with care the spirit of innovation upon its principles, however specious the pretexts. One method of assault may be to affect, in the forms of the Constitution, alterations which will impair the energy of the system, and thus to undermine what cannot be directly overthrown. In all the changes to which you may be invited, remember that time and habit are at least as necessary to fix the true character of governments as of other human institutions; that experience is the surest standard by which to test the real tendency of the existing constitution of a country; that facility in changes, upon the credit of mere hypothesis and opinion, exposes to perpetual change, from the endless variety of hypothesis and opinion; and remember especially that for the efficient management of your common interests, in a country so extensive as ours, a government of as much vigour as is consistent with the perfect security of liberty is indispensable. Liberty itself will find in such a government, with powers properly distributed and adjusted, its surest guardian. It is, indeed, little else than a name where the government is too feeble to withstand the enterprises of faction, to confine each member of the society within the limits prescribed by the laws, and to maintain all in the secure and tranquil enjoyment of the rights of person and property.

I have already intimated to you the danger of parties in the State, with particular reference to the founding of them on geographical discrimination. Let me now take a more comprehensive view, and warn you in the most solemn manner against the baneful effects of the spirit of party generally.

This spirit, unfortunately, is inseparable from our nature, having its root in the strongest passions of the human mind. It exists under different shapes in all governments, more or less stifled, controlled, or repressed; but in those of the popular form it is seen in its greatest rankness, and is truly their worst enemy.

The alternate domination of one faction over another, sharpened by the spirit of revenge, natural to party dissension, which in different ages and countries has perpetrated the most horrid enormities, is itself a frightful despotism. But this leads at length to a more formal and permanent despotism. The disorders and miseries which result gradually incline the minds of men to seek security and repose in the absolute power of an individual, and sooner or later the chief of some prevailing faction, more able or more fortunate than his competitors, turns this disposition to the purposes of his own elevation, on the ruins of public liberty.

Without looking forward to an extremity of this kind (which nevertheless ought not to be entirely out of sight), the common and continued mischiefs of the spirit of party are sufficient to make it the interest and duty of a wise people to discourage and restrain it. It serves always to distract the public councils and enfeeble the public administration. It agitates the community with ill-founded jealousies and false alarms; kindles the animosity of one part against another; foments, occasionally, riot and insurrection. It opens the doors to foreign influence and corruption, which find a facilitated access to the government itself through the channels of party passions. Thus the policy and the will of one country are subjected to the policy and will of another.

There is an opinion that parties in free countries are useful checks upon the administration of the government and serve to keep alive the spirit of liberty. This within certain limits is probably true, and in governments of a monarchical cast, patriotism may look with indulgence, if not with favour, upon the spirit of party. But in those of the popular character, in governments purely elective, it is a spirit not to be encouraged. From their natural tendency it is certain there will always be enough of that spirit for every salutary purpose. And there being constant danger of excess, the effort ought to be by force of

public opinion to mitigate and assuage it. A fire not to be quenched, it demands a uniform vigilance to prevent its bursting into a flame, lest, instead of warming, it should consume.

It is important, likewise, that the habits of thinking in a free country should inspire caution, in those entrusted with its administration, to confine themselves within their respective constitutional spheres, avoiding in the exercise of the powers of one department to encroach upon another. The spirit of encroachment tends to consolidate the powers of all the departments in one, and thus to create, whatever the form of government, a real despotism. A just estimate of that love of power and proneness to abuse it which predominates in the human heart is sufficient to satisfy us of the truth of this position. The necessity of reciprocal checks in the exercise of political power by dividing and distributing it into different depositories, and constituting each the guardian of the public weal against invasions by the others, has been evinced by experiments, ancient and modern, some of them in our country and under our own eyes. To preserve them must be as necessary as to institute them. If, in the opinion of the people, the distribution or modification of the constitutional powers be in any particular wrong, let it be corrected by an amendment in the way which the Constitution designates. But let there be no change by usurpation; for though this, in one instance, may be the instrument of good, it is the customary weapon by which free governments are destroyed. The precedent must always greatly overbalance in permanent evil any partial or transient benefit which the use can at any time yield.

Of all the dispositions and habits which lead to political prosperity, religion and morality are indispensable supports. In vain would that man claim the tribute of patriotism who should labour to subvert these great pillars of human happiness, these firmest props of the duties of men and citizens. The mere politician, equally with the pious man, ought to respect and to cherish them. A volume could not trace all their connections with private and public felicity. Let it simply be asked, Where is the security for property,

for reputation, for life, if the sense of religious obligation desert the oaths, which are the instruments of investigation in courts of justice? And let us with caution indulge the supposition that morality can be maintained without religion. Whatever may be conceded to the influence of refined education on minds of peculiar structure, reason and experience both forbid us to expect that national morality can prevail in exclusion of religious principle.

It is substantially true that virtue or morality is a necessary spring of popular government. The rule, indeed, extends with more or less force to every species of free government. Who that is a sincere friend to it can look with indifference upon attempts to shake the foundation of the fabric?

Promote, then, as an object of primary importance, institutions for the general diffusion of knowledge. In proportion as the structure of a government gives force to public opinion it is essential that public opinion should be enlightened.

As a very important source of strength and security, cherish public credit. One method of preserving it is to use it as sparingly as possible; avoiding occasions of expense by cultivating peace, but remembering also that timely disbursements to prepare for danger frequently prevent much greater disbursements to repel it; avoiding likewise the accumulation of debt, not only by shunning occasions of expense, but by vigorous exertion in time of peace to discharge the debts, which unavoidable wars may have occasioned, not ungenerously throwing upon posterity the burden which we ourselves ought to bear. The execution of these maxims belongs to your representatives, but it is necessary that public opinion should cooperate. To facilitate to them the performance of their duty it is essential that you should practically bear in mind that toward the payment of debts there must be revenue; that to have revenue there must be taxes; that no taxes can be devised which are not more or less inconvenient and unpleasant; that the intrinsic embarrassment, inseparable from the selection of the proper objects (which is always a choice of difficulties), ought to be a decisive motive for a candid construction of the conduct of

the government in making it, and for a spirit of acquiescence in the measures for obtaining revenue which the public exigencies may at any time dictate.

Observe good faith and justice toward all nations; cultivate peace and harmony with all. Religion and morality enjoin this conduct, and can it be that good policy does not equally enjoin it? It will be worthy of a free, enlightened, and, at no distant period, a great nation, to give to mankind the magnanimous and novel example of a people always guided by an exalted justice and benevolence. Who can doubt that, in the course of time and things, the fruits of such a plan would richly repay any temporary advantages which might be lost by a steady adherence to it? Can it be that providence has not connected the permanent felicity of a nation with its virtue? The experiment, at least, is recommended by every sentiment which ennobles human nature. Alas! Is it rendered impossible by its vices?

In the execution of such a plan nothing is more essential than that permanent, inveterate antipathies against particular nations and passionate attachments for others should be excluded, and that, in place of them, just and amicable feelings toward all should be cultivated. The nation which indulges toward another an habitual hatred or an habitual fondness is in some degree a slave. It is a slave to its animosity or to its affection, either of which is sufficient to lead it astray from its duty and its interest. Antipathy in one nation against another disposes each more readily to offer insult and injury, to lay hold of slight causes of umbrage, and to be haughty and intractable, when accidental or trifling occasions of dispute occur. Hence, frequent collisions; obstinate, envenomed, and bloody contests. The nation, prompted by ill will and resentment, sometimes impels to war the government, contrary to the best calculations of policy. The government sometimes participates in the national propensity, and adopts through passion what reason would reject; at other times it makes the animosity of the nation subservient to projects of hostility instigated by pride, ambition, and other sinister and pernicious motives. The peace often, sometimes perhaps the liberty, of nations has been the victim.

So, likewise, a passionate attachment of one nation for another produces a variety of evils. Sympathy for the favourite nation, facilitating the illusion of an imaginary common interest in cases where no real common interest exists, and infusing into one the enmities of the other, betrays the former into a participation in the quarrels and wars of the latter, without adequate inducement or justification. It leads also to concessions to the favourite nation of privileges denied to others, which is apt doubly to injure the nation making the concessions by unnecessarily parting with what ought to have been retained, and by exciting jealousy, ill will, and a disposition to retaliate, in the parties from whom equal privileges are withheld. And it gives to ambitious, corrupted, or deluded citizens (who devote themselves to the favourite nation), facility to betray or sacrifice the interests of their own country without odium, sometimes even with popularity; gilding with the appearances of a virtuous sense of obligation, a commendable deference for public opinion, or a laudable zeal for public good, the base or foolish compliances of ambition, corruption, or infatuation.

As avenues to foreign influence in innumerable ways, such attachments are particularly alarming to the truly enlightened and independent patriot. How many opportunities do they afford to tamper with domestic factions, to practise the arts of seduction, to mislead public opinion, to influence or awe the public councils! Such an attachment of a small or weak toward a great and powerful nation dooms the former to be the satellite of the latter.

Against the insidious wiles of foreign influence (I conjure you to believe me, fellow citizens), the jealousy of a free people ought to be constantly awake, since history and experience prove that foreign influence is one of the most baneful foes of republican government. But that jealousy, to be useful, must be impartial, else it becomes the instrument of the very influence to be avoided, instead of a defence against it. Excessive partiality for one foreign nation and excessive dislike of another cause those whom they actuate to see danger only on one side, and serve to veil and even second the arts

of influence on the other. Real patriots, who may resist the intrigues of the favourite, are liable to become suspected and odious; while its tools and dupes usurp the applause and confidence of the people, to surrender their interests.

The great rule of conduct for us, in regard to foreign nations, is, in extending our commercial relations, to have with them as little political connection as possible. So far as we have already formed engagements, let them be fulfilled with perfect good faith. Here let us stop. Europe has a set of primary interests which to us have none, or a very remote, relation. Hence she must be engaged in frequent controversies, the causes of which are essentially foreign to our concerns. Hence, therefore, it must be unwise in us to implicate ourselves, by artificial ties, in the ordinary vicissitudes of her politics or the ordinary combinations and collisions of her friendships or enmities.

Our detached and distant situation invites and enables us to pursue a different course. If we remain one people, under an efficient government the period is not far off when we may defy material injury from external annoyance; when we may take such an attitude as will cause the neutrality we may at any time resolve upon to be scrupulously respected; when belligerent nations, under the impossibility of making acquisitions upon us, will not lightly hazard the giving us provocation; when we may choose peace or war, as our interest, guided by justice, shall counsel.

Why forego the advantages of so peculiar a situation? Why quit our own to stand upon foreign ground? Why, by interweaving our destiny with that of any part of Europe, entangle our peace and prosperity in the toils of European ambition, rivalship, interest, humour, or caprice?

It is our true policy to steer clear of permanent alliances with any portion of the foreign world—so far, I mean, as we are now at liberty to do it; for let me not be understood as capable of patronizing infidelity to existing engagements. I hold the maxim no less applicable to public than to private affairs, that honesty is always the best policy.

I repeat it, therefore, let those engagements be observed in their genuine sense. But, in my opinion, it is unnecessary and would be unwise to extend them.

Taking care always to keep ourselves, by suitable establishments, on a respectable defensive posture, we may safely trust to temporary alliances for extraordinary emergencies.

Harmony, liberal intercourse with all nations, are recommended by policy, humanity, and interest. But even our commercial policy should hold an equal and impartial hand; neither seeking nor granting exclusive favours or preferences; consulting the natural course of things; diffusing and diversifying by gentle means the streams of commerce, but forcing nothing; establishing, with powers so disposed, in order to give trade a stable course, to define the rights of our merchants, and to enable the government to support them, conventional rules of intercourse, the best that present circumstances and mutual opinion will permit, but temporary, and liable to be from time to time abandoned or varied, as experience and circumstances shall dictate; constantly keeping in view that it is folly in one nation to look for disinterested favours from another; that it must pay with a portion of its independence for whatever it may accept under that character; that, by such acceptance, it may place itself in the condition of having given equivalents for nominal favours, and yet of being reproached with ingratitude for not giving more. There can be no greater error than to expect or calculate upon real favours from nation to nation. It is an illusion which experience must cure, which a just pride ought to discard.

In offering to you, my countrymen, these counsels of an old and affectionate friend, I dare not hope they will make the strong and lasting impression I could wish; that they will control the usual current of the passions, or prevent our nation from running the course which has hitherto marked the destiny of nations. But if I may even flatter myself that they may be productive of some partial benefit, some occasional good; that they may now and then recur to moderate the fury of party spirit, to warn against the mischiefs of foreign intrigue, to guard against the impostures of pretended patriotism: this hope will be a full recompense for the solicitude for your welfare by which they have been dictated.

How far in the discharge of my official duties I have been guided by the principles which have been delineated, the public records and other evidences of my conduct must witness to you and to the world. To myself, the assurance of my own conscience is, that I have at least believed myself to be guided by them.

In relation to the still subsisting war in Europe, my proclamation of the twenty-second of April 1793, is the index of my plan. Sanctioned by your approving voice, and by that of your representatives in both houses of Congress, the spirit of that measure has continually governed me, uninfluenced by any attempts to deter or divert me from it.

After deliberate examination, with the aid of the best lights I could obtain, I was well satisfied that our country, under all the circumstances of the case, had a right to take, and was bound in duty and interest to take, a neutral position. Having taken it, I determined, as far as should depend upon me, to maintain it, with moderation, perseverance, and firmness.

The considerations which respect the right to hold this conduct, it is not necessary on this occasion to detail. I will only observe that, according to my understanding of the matter, that right, so far from being denied by any of the belligerent powers, has been virtually admitted by all.

The duty of holding a neutral conduct may be inferred, without anything more, from the obligation which justice and humanity impose on every nation, in cases in which it is free to act, to maintain inviolate the relations of peace and amity towards other nations.

The inducements of interest for observing that conduct will best be referred to your own reflections and experience. With me a predominant motive has been to endeavour to gain time to our country to settle and mature its yet recent institutions, and to progress without interruption to that degree of strength and consistency which is necessary to give it, humanly speaking, the command of its own fortunes.

Though in reviewing the incidents of my administration I am unconscious of intentional error, I am nevertheless too sensible of my defects not to think it probable that I may have committed many errors. Whatever they may be, I fervently beseech the Almighty to avert or mitigate the evils to which they may tend. I shall also carry with me the hope that my country will never cease to view them with indulgence; and that, after forty-five years of my life dedicated to its service with an upright zeal, the faults of incompetent abilities will be consigned to oblivion, as myself must soon be to the mansions of rest.

Relying on its kindness in this as in other things, and actuated by that fervent love toward it which is so natural to a man who views in it the native soil of himself and his progenitors for several generations, I anticipate with pleasing expectation that retreat in which I promise myself to realize, without alloy, the sweet enjoyment of partaking in the midst of my fellow citizens the benign influence of good laws under a free government, the ever favourite object of my heart, and the happy reward, as I trust, of our mutual cares, labours, and dangers.

*Note: The handwritten draft of this speech was thirty-two pages long.*

# 7

## Sixth Annual Message

★ ★ ★ ★ ★ ★ ★

Thomas Jefferson
Washington, D.C., U.S.A.
2 December 1806

*Article II, section three of the United States Constitution stated 'He shall from time to time give to the Congress information of the state of the union, and recommend to their consideration such measures as he shall judge necessary and expedient.' Taking it as an instruction, the presidents gave oral messages while Jefferson preferred not to give speeches.*

*The following text was Jefferson's sixth annual message to the Congress. It was a written report. In one of Jefferson's letters, he admitted that giving a speech was inconvenient—'it takes more time than reading and it robs legislators the ability to think before responding.'*

To the Senate and House of Representatives of the United States of America in Congress assembled: It would have given me, fellow citizens, great satisfaction to announce in the moment of your meeting that the difficulties in our foreign relations existing at the time of your last separation had been amicably and justly terminated. I lost no time in taking those measures which were most likely to bring them to such a termination by special missions charged with such powers and instructions as in the event of failure could leave no imputation on either our moderation or forbearance. The delays which have since taken place in our negotiations with the British Government appear to have proceeded from causes which do not forbid the expectation that during the course of the session I may be enabled to lay before you their final issue. What will be that of the negotiations for settling our differences with Spain nothing which had taken place at the date of the last dispatches enables us to pronounce. On the western side of the Mississippi she advanced in considerable force, and took post at the settlement of Bayou Pierre, on the Red River. This village was originally settled by France, was held by her as long as she held Louisiana, and was delivered to Spain only as a part of Louisiana. Being small, insulated, and distant, it was not observed at the moment of redelivery to France and the United States that she continued a guard of half a dozen men which had been stationed there. A proposition, however, having been lately made by our commander in chief to assume the Sabine River as a temporary line of separation between the troops of the two nations until the issue of our negotiations shall be known, this has been referred by the Spanish commandant to his superior, and in the meantime he has withdrawn his force to the western side of the Sabine River. The correspondence on this subject now communicated will exhibit more particularly the present state of things in that quarter.

The nature of that country requires indispensably that an unusual proportion of the force employed there should be cavalry or mounted infantry. In order, therefore, that the commanding officer might be enabled to act with effect, I had authorized him to call on the governors of Orleans and Mississippi for a corps of five hundred volunteer cavalry. The temporary arrangement he has proposed may perhaps render this unnecessary; but I inform you with great pleasure of the promptitude with which the inhabitants of those Territories have tendered their services in defence of their country. It has done honour to themselves, entitled them to the confidence of their fellow citizens in every part of the Union, and must strengthen the general determination to protect them efficaciously under all circumstances which may occur.

Having received information that in another part of the United States a great number of private individuals were combining together, arming and organizing themselves contrary to law, to carry on a military expedition against the territories of Spain, I thought it necessary, by proclamation as well as by special orders, to take measures for preventing and suppressing this enterprise, for seizing the vessels, arms, and other means provided for it, and for arresting and bringing to justice its authors and abettors. It was due to that good faith which ought ever to be the rule of action in public as well as in private transactions, it was due to good order and regular government, that while the public force was acting strictly on defensive and merely to protect our citizens from aggression the criminal attempts of private individuals to decide for their country the question of peace or war by commencing active and unauthorized hostilities should be promptly and efficaciously suppressed.

Whether it will be necessary to enlarge our regular forces will depend on the result of our negotiations with Spain; but as it is uncertain when that result will be known, the provisional measures requisite for that, and to meet any pressure intervening in that quarter, will be a subject for your early consideration.

The possession of both banks of the Mississippi reducing to a single point the defence of that river, its waters, and the country adjacent, it becomes highly necessary to provide for that point a more adequate security. Some position above its mouth, commanding the passage of the river, should be rendered sufficiently strong to cover the armed vessels which may be stationed there for defence, and in conjunction with them to present an insuperable obstacle to any force attempting to pass. The approaches to the city of New Orleans from the eastern quarter also will require to be examined and more effectually guarded. For the internal support of the country the encouragement of a strong settlement on the western side of the Mississippi, within reach of New Orleans, will be worthy the consideration of the legislature.

The gun boats authorized by an act of the last session are so advanced that they will be ready for service in the ensuing spring. Circumstances permitted us to allow the time necessary for their more solid construction. As a much larger number will still be wanting to place our sea port towns and waters in that state of defence to which we are competent and they entitled, a similar appropriation for a further provision for them is recommended for the ensuing year.

A further appropriation will also be necessary for repairing fortifications already established and the erection of such other works as may have real effect in obstructing the approach of an enemy to our sea port towns, or their remaining before them.

In a country whose constitution is derived from the will of the people, directly expressed by their free suffrages; where the principal executive functionaries and those of the legislature are renewed by them at short periods; where under the character of jurors they exercise in person the greatest portion of the judiciary powers; where the laws are consequently so formed and administered as to bear with equal weight and favour on all, restraining no man in the pursuits of honest industry and securing to everyone the property which that acquires, it would not be supposed that any safe-guards could be needed against insurrection or enterprise on the public peace or authority. The laws, however, aware that these should not be trusted to moral restraints only, have wisely provided punishment for these crimes when committed. But would it not be salutary to give also the means of preventing their commission? Where an enterprise is meditated by private individuals against a foreign nation in amity with the United States, powers of prevention to a certain extent are given by the laws. Would they not be as reasonable and useful where the enterprise preparing is against the United States? While adverting to this branch of law it is proper to observe that in enterprises meditated against foreign nations the ordinary process of binding to the observance of the peace and good behaviour, could it be extended to acts to be done out of the jurisdiction of the United States, would be effectual in some cases where the offender is able to keep out of sight every indication of his purpose which could draw on him the exercise of the powers now given by law.

The states on the coast of Barbary seem generally disposed at present to respect our peace and friendship; with Tunis alone some uncertainty remains. Persuaded that it is our interest to maintain our peace with them on equal terms or not at all, I propose to send in due time a reinforcement into the Mediterranean unless previous information shall show it to be unnecessary.

We continue to receive proofs of the growing attachment of our Indian neighbours and of their dispositions to place all their interests under the patronage of the United States. These dispositions are inspired by their confidence in our justice and in the sincere concern we feel for their welfare; and as long as we discharge these high and honourable functions with the integrity and good faith which alone can entitle us to their continuance we may expect to reap the just reward in their peace and friendship.

The expedition of Messrs Lewis and Clarke, for exploring the river Missouri and the best communication from that to the Pacific Ocean has had all the success which could have been expected. They have traced the Missouri nearly to its source, descended the Columbia to the Pacific Ocean, ascertained with accuracy the geography of that interesting communication across our continent, learnt the character of the country, of its commerce and inhabitants; and it is but justice to say that Messrs Lewis and Clarke and their brave companions have by this arduous service deserved well of their country.

The attempt to explore the Red River, under the direction of Mr. Freeman, though conducted with a zeal and prudence meriting entire approbation, has not been equally successful. After proceeding up it about six hundred miles, nearly as far as the French settlements had extended while the country was in their possession, our geographers were obliged to return without completing their work.

Very useful additions have also been made to our knowledge of the Mississippi by Lieutenant Pike, who has ascended it to its source, and whose journal and map, giving the details of his journey, will shortly be ready for communication to both Houses of Congress. Those of Messrs. Lewis, Clarke, and Freeman will require further time to be digested and prepared. These important surveys, in addition to those before possessed, furnish materials for commencing an accurate map of the Mississippi and its western waters. Some principal rivers, however, remain still to be explored, toward which the authorization of Congress by moderate appropriations will be requisite.

I congratulate you, fellow citizens, on the approach of the period at which you may interpose your authority constitutionally to withdraw the citizens of the United States from all further participation in those violations of human rights which have been so long continued on the unoffending inhabitants of Africa, and which the morality, the reputation, and the best of our country have long been eager to proscribe. Although no law you may pass can take prohibitory effect till the first day of the year 1808, yet the intervening period is not too long to prevent by timely notice expeditions which cannot be completed before that day.

The receipts at the Treasury during the year ending on the 30th day of September last have amounted to near $15 million, which have enabled us, after meeting the current demands, to pay $2.7 million of the American claims in part of the price of Louisiana; to pay of the funded debt upward of $3 million of principal and nearly $4 million of interest, and, in addition, to reimburse in the course of the present month near $2 million of 5.5% stock. These payments and reimbursements of the funded debt, with those which had been made in the four years and a half preceding, will at the close of the present year have extinguished upward of twenty-three millions of principal.

The duties composing the Mediterranean fund will cease by law at the end of the present session. Considering, however, that they are levied chiefly on luxuries and that we have an impost on salt, a necessary of life, the free use of which otherwise is so important, I recommend to your consideration the suppression of the duties on salt and the continuation of the Mediterranean fund instead thereof for a short time, after which that also will become unnecessary for any purpose now within contemplation.

When both of these branches of revenue shall in this way be relinquished there will still ere long be an accumulation of moneys in the Treasury beyond the instalments of public debt which we are permitted by contract to pay. They cannot then, without a modification assented to by the public creditors, be applied to the extinguishment of this debt and the complete liberation of our revenues, the most desirable of all objects. Nor, if our peace continues, will they be wanting for any other existing purpose. The question therefore now comes forward, To what other objects shall these surpluses be appropriated, and the whole surplus of impost, after the entire discharge of the public debt, and during those intervals when the purposes of war shall not call for them? Shall we suppress the impost and give that advantage to foreign over domestic manufactures? On a few articles of more general and necessary use the suppression in due season will doubtless be right, but the great mass of the articles on which impost is paid are foreign luxuries, purchased by those only who are rich enough to afford themselves the use of them.

Their patriotism would certainly prefer its continuance and application to the great purposes of the public education, roads, rivers, canals, and such other objects of public improvement as it may be thought proper to add to the constitutional enumeration of Federal powers. By these operations new channels of communications will be opened between the States, the lines of separation will disappear, their interests will be identified, and their union cemented by new and indissoluble ties. Education is here placed among the articles of public care, not that it would be proposed to take its ordinary branches out of the hands of private enterprise, which manages so much better all the concerns to which it is equal, but a public institution can alone supply those sciences which though rarely called for are yet necessary to complete the circle, all the parts of which contribute to the improvement of the country and some of them to its preservation.

The subject is now proposed for the consideration of Congress, because if approved by the time the State legislatures shall have deliberated on this extension of the Federal trusts, and the laws shall be passed and other arrangements made for their execution, the necessary funds will be on hand and without employment.

I suppose an amendment to the Constitution, by consent of the States, necessary, because the objects now recommended are not among those enumerated in the Constitution, and to which it permits the public moneys to be applied.

The present consideration of a national establishment for education particularly is rendered proper by this circumstance also, that if Congress, approving the proposition, shall yet think it more eligible to found it on a donation of lands, they have it now in their power to endow it with those which will be among the earliest to produce the necessary income. This foundation would have the advantage of being independent of war, which may suspend other improvements by requiring for its own purposes the resources destined for them.

This, fellow citizens, is the state of the public interests at the present moment and according to the information now possessed. But such is the situation of the nations of Europe and such, too, the predicament is which we stand with some of them that we cannot rely with certainty on the present aspect of our affairs, that may change from moment to moment during the course of your session or after you shall have separated.

Our duty is, therefore, to act upon things as they are and to make a reasonable provision for whatever they may be. Were armies to be raised whenever a speck of war is visible in our horizon, we never should have been without them. Our resources would have been exhausted on dangers which have never happened, instead of being reserved for what is really to take place. A steady, perhaps a quickened, pace in preparation for the defence of our sea port towns and waters; an early settlement of the most exposed and vulnerable parts of our country; a militia so organized that its effective portions can be called to any point in the Union, or volunteers instead of them to serve a sufficient time, are means which may always be ready, yet never preying on our resources until actually called into use. They will maintain the public interests while a more permanent force shall be in course of preparation. But much will depend on the promptitude with which these means can be brought into activity. If war be forced upon us, in spite of our long and vain appeals to the justice of nations, rapid and vigorous movements in its outset will go far toward securing us in its course and issue, and toward throwing its burthens on those who render necessary the resort from reason to force.

The result of our negotiations, or such incidents in their course as may enable us to infer their probably issue; such further movements also on our western frontiers as may shew whether war is to be pressed there while negotiation is protracted elsewhere, shall be communicated to you from time to time as they become known to me, with whatever other information I possess or may receive, which may aid your deliberations on the great national interests committed to your charge.

# 8

# The Hypocrisy of American Slavery

★ ★ ★ ★ ★ ★ ★

Frederick Douglass
Rochester, New York, U.S.A.
4 July 1852

*Frederick Douglass had experienced the horrors of American slavery since he was a child. An illegitimate son of a white man and a black woman, he was separated from his mother and made to work on the southern plantations from a young age.*

*Douglass gave a speech denouncing slavery as the 'greatest sin and shame of America.' Right from the beginning of the speech, he voices the irony of calling a black man, a former slave, a man with virtually no freedom, to speak at the Fourth of July festivities.*

Fellow citizens, pardon me, and allow me to ask, why am I called upon to speak here today? What have I or those I represent to do with your national independence? Are the great principles of political freedom and of natural justice, embodied in that Declaration of

Independence, extended to us? And am I, therefore, called upon to bring our humble offering to the national altar, and to confess the benefits, and express devout gratitude for the blessings resulting from your independence to us?

Would to God, both for your sakes and ours, that an affirmative answer could be truthfully returned to these questions. Then would my task be light, and my burden easy and delightful. For who is there so cold that a nation's sympathy could not warm him? Who so obdurate and dead to the claims of gratitude, that would not thankfully acknowledge such priceless benefits? Who so stolid and selfish that would not give his voice to swell the hallelujahs of a nation's jubilee, when the chains of servitude had been torn from his limbs? I am not that man. In a case like that, the dumb might eloquently speak, and the 'lame man leap as an hart.'

But such is not the state of the case. I say it with a sad sense of disparity between us. I am not included within the pale of this glorious anniversary! Your high independence only reveals the immeasurable distance between us. The blessings in which you this day rejoice are not enjoyed in common. The rich inheritance of justice, liberty, prosperity, and independence bequeathed by your fathers is shared by you, not by me. The sunlight that brought life and healing to you has brought stripes and death to me. This Fourth of July is yours, not mine. You may rejoice, I must mourn. To drag a man in fetters into the grand illuminated temple of liberty, and call upon him to join you in joyous anthems, were inhuman mockery and sacrilegious irony. Do you mean, citizens, to mock me, by asking me to speak today? If so, there is a parallel to your conduct. And let me warn you, that it is dangerous to copy the example of a nation (Babylon) whose crimes, towering up to heaven, were thrown down by the breath of the Almighty, burying that nation in irrecoverable ruin.

Fellow citizens, above your national, tumultuous joy, I hear the mournful wail of millions, whose chains, heavy and grievous yesterday, are today rendered more intolerable by the jubilant shouts that reach them. If I do forget, if I do not remember those bleeding children of sorrow this day, 'may my right hand forget her cunning, and may my tongue cleave to the roof of my mouth!'

To forget them, to pass lightly over their wrongs and to chime in with the popular theme would be treason most scandalous and shocking, and would make me a reproach before God and the world.

My subject, then, fellow citizens, is 'American Slavery.' I shall see this day and its popular characteristics from the slave's point of view. Standing here, identified with the American bondman, making his wrongs mine, I do not hesitate to declare, with all my soul, that the character and conduct of this nation never looked blacker to me than on this Fourth of July.

Whether we turn to the declarations of the past, or to the professions of the present, the conduct of the nation seems equally hideous and revolting. America is false to the past, false to the present, and solemnly binds herself to be false to the future. Standing with God and the crushed and bleeding slave on this occasion, I will, in the name of humanity, which is outraged, in the name of liberty, which is fettered, in the name of the Constitution and the Bible, which are disregarded and trampled upon, dare to call in question and to denounce, with all the emphasis I can command, everything that serves to perpetuate slavery—the great sin and shame of America! 'I will not equivocate—I will not excuse.' I will use the severest language I can command, and yet not one word shall escape me that any man, whose judgment is not blinded by prejudice, or who is not at heart a slave-holder, shall not confess to be right and just.

But I fancy I hear some of my audience say it is just in this circumstance that you and your brother Abolitionists fail to make a favourable impression on the public mind. Would you argue more and denounce less, would you persuade more and rebuke less, your cause would be much more likely to succeed. But, I submit, where all is plain there is nothing to be argued. What point in the anti-slavery creed would you have me argue? On what branch of the subject do the people of this country need light? Must I undertake to prove that the slave is a man? That point is conceded already. Nobody doubts it. The slave-holders themselves acknowledge it in the enactment of laws for their government. They acknowledge it when they punish disobedience on the part of the slave. There are seventy-two crimes in the State of Virginia, which, if committed by a black man (no matter how ignorant he be), subject him to the punishment of death; while only two of these same crimes will subject a white man to like punishment.

What is this but the acknowledgment that the slave is a moral, intellectual, and responsible being? The manhood of the slave is conceded. It is admitted in the fact that Southern statute books are covered with enactments, forbidding, under severe fines and penalties, the teaching of the slave to read and write. When you can point to any such laws in reference to the beasts of the field, then I may consent to argue the manhood of the slave. When the dogs in your streets, when the fowls of the air, when the cattle on your hills, when the fish of the sea, and the reptiles that crawl, shall be unable to distinguish the slave from a brute, then I will argue with you that the slave is a man!

For the present it is enough to affirm the equal manhood of the Negro race. Is it not astonishing that, while we are plowing, planting, and reaping, using all kinds of mechanical tools, erecting houses, constructing bridges, building ships, working in metals of brass, iron, copper, silver, and gold; that while we are reading, writing, and ciphering, acting as clerks, merchants, and secretaries, having among us lawyers, doctors, ministers, poets, authors, editors, orators, and teachers; that we are engaged in all the enterprises common to other men—digging gold in California, capturing the whale in the Pacific, feeding sheep and cattle on the hillside, living, moving, acting, thinking, planning, living in families as husbands, wives, and children, and above all, confessing and worshipping the Christian God, and looking hopefully for life and immortality beyond the grave—we are called upon to prove that we are men?

Would you have me argue that man is entitled to liberty? That he is the rightful owner of his own body? You have already declared it. Must I argue the wrongfulness of slavery? Is that a question for republicans?

Is it to be settled by the rules of logic and argumentation, as a matter beset with great difficulty, involving a doubtful application of the principle of justice, hard to understand? How should I look today in the presence of Americans, dividing and subdividing a discourse, to show that men have a natural right to freedom, speaking of it relatively and positively, negatively and affirmatively? To do so would be to make myself ridiculous, and to offer an insult to your understanding. There is not a man beneath the canopy of heaven who does not know that slavery is wrong for him.

What am I to argue that it is wrong to make men brutes, to rob them of their liberty, to work them without wages, to keep them ignorant of their relations to their fellow men, to beat them with sticks, to flay their flesh with the lash, to load their limbs with irons, to hunt them with dogs, to sell them at auction, to sunder their families, to knock out their teeth, to burn their flesh, to starve them into obedience and submission to their masters? Must I argue that a system thus marked with blood and stained with pollution is wrong? No—I will not. I have better employment for my time and strength than such arguments would imply.

What, then, remains to be argued? Is it that slavery is not divine; that God did not establish it; that our doctors of divinity are mistaken? There is blasphemy in the thought. That which is inhuman cannot be divine. Who can reason on such a proposition? They that can, may—I cannot. The time for such argument is past.

At a time like this, scorching irony, not convincing argument, is needed. Oh! had I the ability, and could I reach the nation's ear, I would today pour out a fiery stream of biting ridicule, blasting reproach, withering sarcasm, and stern rebuke. For it is not light that is needed, but fire; it is not the gentle shower, but thunder. We need the storm, the whirlwind, and the earthquake. The feeling of the nation must be quickened; the conscience of the nation must be roused; the propriety of the nation must be startled; the hypocrisy of the nation must be exposed; and its crimes against God and man must be denounced.

What to the American slave is your Fourth of July? I answer, a day that reveals to him more than all other days of the year, the gross injustice and cruelty to which he is the constant victim. To him your celebration is a sham; your boasted liberty an unholy license; your national greatness, swelling vanity; your sounds of rejoicing are empty and heartless; your shouts of liberty and equality, hollow mock; your prayers and hymns, your sermons and thanksgivings, with all your religious parade and solemnity, are to him mere bombast, fraud, deception, impiety, and hypocrisy—a thin veil to cover up crimes which would disgrace a nation of savages. There is not a nation of the earth guilty of practices more shocking and bloody than are the people of these United States at this very hour.

Go search where you will, roam through all the monarchies and despotisms of the Old World, travel through South America, search out every abuse and when you have found the last, lay your facts by the side of the everyday practices of this nation, and you will say with me that, for revolting barbarity and shameless hypocrisy, America reigns without a rival.

# 9

# The Gettysburg Address

★ ★ ★ ★ ★ ★ ★

Abraham Lincoln
Gettysburg, Pennsylvania, U.S.A.
19 November 1863

*Lincoln delivered this speech to the American public four months after the Battle of Gettysburg during the Civil War. This battle had been a turning point for America as the Union army had emerged victorious over the Confederate forces.*

*This speech honours the soldiers slain in the battle at Gettysburg and addresses the importance of national unity to better combat the Civil War.*

Four score and seven years ago our fathers brought forth on this continent, a new nation, conceived in liberty, and dedicated to the proposition that all men are created equal.

Now we are engaged in a great civil war, testing whether that nation, or any nation so conceived and so dedicated, can long endure. We are met on a great battlefield of that war. We have come to dedicate a portion of that field, as a final resting place for those who here gave their lives that that nation might live. It is altogether fitting and proper that we should do this.

But in a larger sense, we cannot dedicate—we cannot consecrate—we cannot hallow—this ground. The brave men, living and dead, who struggled here, have consecrated it, far above our poor power to add or detract. The world will little note, nor long remember, what we say here, but it can never forget what they did here. It is for us the living, rather, to be dedicated here to the unfinished work which they who fought here have thus far so nobly advanced. It is rather for us to be here dedicated to the great task remaining before us—that from these honoured dead we take increased devotion to that cause for which they gave the last full measure of devotion—that we here highly resolve that these dead shall not have died in vain—that this nation, under God, shall have a new birth of freedom—and that government of the people, by the people, for the people, shall not perish from the earth.

*Note: The main speaker of the day had been Edward Everett, not Lincoln. Everett delivered his two-hour-long speech but Lincoln's two-minute speech is more famous than his.*

# 10

## Second Inaugural Address

★ ★ ★ ★ ★ ★ ★

Abraham Lincoln
Pennsylvania Avenue, U.S.A.
4 March 1865

*America had grown weary after being involved in a Civil War for four years. Lincoln, in this speech, assured the public that the war was drawing to a close as the North stood on the brink of victory. He admitted that the nation bore guilt for the sin of slavery, the practice of which had been the cause of the war.*

*The dispute between abolitionists and slaveholders had been at the heart of the Civil War. Lincoln called for the North and South to reconcile at the end of his speech. Slavery was rampant in South America and the North had openly opposed this.*

*Lincoln was assassinated a month after delivering this speech.*

Fellow countrymen:

At this second appearing to take the oath of the presidential office there is less occasion for an extended address than there was at the first. Then a statement, somewhat in detail, of a course to be pursued seemed fitting and proper. Now, at the expiration of four years, during which public declarations have been constantly called forth on every point and phase of the great contest which still absorbs the attention and engrosses the energies of the nation, little that is new could be presented. The progress of our arms, upon which all else chiefly depends, is as well known to the public as to myself, and it is, I trust, reasonably satisfactory and encouraging to all. With high hope for the future, no prediction in regard to it is ventured.

On the occasion corresponding to this four years ago all thoughts were anxiously directed to an impending civil war. All dreaded it; all sought to avert it. While the inaugural address was being delivered from this place, devoted altogether to saving the Union without war, insurgent agents were in the city seeking to destroy it without war—seeking to dissolve the Union and divide effects by negotiation. Both parties deprecated war, but one of them would make war rather than let the nation survive, and the other would accept war rather than let it perish, and the war came.

One-eighth of the whole population were coloured slaves, not distributed generally over the Union, but localized in the southern part of it. These slaves constituted a peculiar and powerful interest. All knew that this interest was somehow the cause of war. To strengthen, perpetuate, and extend this interest was the object for which the insurgents would rend the Union even by war, while the government claimed no right to do more than to restrict the territorial enlargement of it. Neither party expected for the war the magnitude or the duration which it has already attained.

Neither anticipated that the cause of the conflict might cease with or even before the conflict itself should cease. Each looked for an easier triumph, and a result less fundamental and astounding. Both read the same Bible and pray to the same God, and each invokes His aid against the other. It may seem strange that any men should dare to ask a just God's assistance in wringing their bread from the sweat of other men's faces, but let us judge not, that we be not judged. The prayers of both could not be answered. That of neither has been answered fully. The Almighty has His own purposes. 'Woe unto the world because of offenses; for it must needs be that offenses come, but woe to that man by whom the offense cometh.' If we shall suppose that American slavery is one of those offenses which, in the providence of God, must needs come, but which, having continued through His appointed time, He now wills to remove, and that He gives to both North and South this terrible war as the woe due to those by whom the offense came, shall we discern therein any departure from those divine attributes which the believers in a living God always ascribe to Him? Fondly do we hope, fervently do we pray, that this mighty scourge of war may speedily pass away. Yet, if God wills that it continue until all the wealth piled by the bondsman's two hundred and fifty years of unrequited toil shall be sunk, and until every drop of blood drawn with the lash shall be paid by another drawn with the sword, as was said three thousand years ago, so still it must be said 'the judgments of the Lord are true and righteous altogether.'

With malice toward none, with charity for all, with firmness in the right as God gives us to see the right, let us strive on to finish the work we are in, to bind up the nation's wounds, to care for him who shall have borne the battle and for his widow and his orphan, to do all which may achieve and cherish a just and lasting peace among ourselves and with all nations.

*Note: The abolitionist, Frederick Douglass, was in the crowd listening to Lincoln's speech. He later stated that the speech sounded more like a sermon than a state paper.*

# 11

## Duties of American Citizenship

★ ★ ★ ★ ★ ★ ★

Theodore Roosevelt
Buffalo, New York, U.S.A.
26 January 1883

*The last four words summarize the purpose of Roosevelt's speech—'a good American citizen.' Roosevelt addressed his countrymen and educated them on their roles and responsibilities.*

*One of the American citizen's duties is active participation in politics, in doing something other than choosing a leader. Roosevelt criticized intellectuals who discuss political institutions merely because they are versed in political literature, even though they have no practical knowledge of it.*

Of course, in one sense, the first essential for a man's being a good citizen is his possession of the home virtues of which we think when we call a man by the emphatic adjective of manly. No man can be a good citizen who is not a good husband and a good father, who is not honest in his dealings with other men and women, faithful to his friends and fearless in the presence of his foes, who has not got a sound heart, a sound mind, and a sound body; exactly as no amount of attention to civil duties will save a nation if the domestic life is undermined, or there is lack of the rude military virtues which alone can assure a country's position in the world. In a free republic the ideal citizen must be one willing and able to take arms for the defence of the flag, exactly as the ideal citizen must be the father of many healthy children. A race must be strong and vigorous; it must be a race of good fighters and good breeders, else its wisdom will come to naught and its virtue be ineffective; and no sweetness and delicacy, no love for and appreciation of beauty in art or literature, no capacity for building up material prosperity can possibly atone for the lack of the great virile virtues.

But this is aside from my subject, for what I wish to talk of is the attitude of the American citizen in civic life. It ought to be axiomatic in this country that every man must devote a reasonable share of his time to doing his duty in the Political life of the community. No man has a right to shirk his political duties under whatever plea of pleasure or business; and while such shirking may be pardoned in those of small cleans it is entirely unpardonable in those among whom it is most common—in the people whose circumstances give them freedom in the struggle for life. In so far as the community grows to think rightly, it will likewise grow to regard the young man of means who shirks his duty to the State in time of peace as being only one degree worse than the man who thus shirks it in time of war. A great many of our men in business, or of our young men who are bent on enjoying life (as they have a perfect right to do if only they do not sacrifice other things to enjoyment), rather plume themselves upon being good citizens if they even vote; yet voting is the very least of their duties. Nothing worth gaining is ever gained without effort. You can no more have freedom without striving and suffering for it than you can win success as a banker or a lawyer without labour and effort, without self-denial in youth and the display of a ready and alert intelligence in middle age. The people who say that they have not time to attend to politics are simply saying that they are unfit to live in a free community. Their place is under a despotism; or if they are content to do nothing but vote, you can take despotism tempered by an occasional plebiscite, like that of the second Napoleon. In one of Lowell's magnificent stanzas about the Civil War he speaks of the fact which his countrymen were then learning, that freedom is not a gift that tarries long in the hands of cowards: nor yet does it tarry long in the hands of the sluggard and the idler, in the hands of the man so much absorbed in the pursuit of pleasure or in the pursuit of gain, or so much wrapped up in his own easy home life as to be unable to take his part in the rough struggle with his fellow men for political supremacy. If freedom is worth having, if the right of self-government is a valuable right, then the one and the other must be retained exactly as our forefathers acquired them, by labour, and especially by labour in organization, that is in combination with our fellows who have the same interests and the same principles. We should not accept the excuse of the business man who attributed his failure to the fact that his social duties were so pleasant and engrossing that he had no time left for work in his office; nor would we pay much heed to his further statement that he did not like business anyhow because he thought the morals of the business community by no means what they should be, and saw that the great successes were most often won by men of the Jay Gould stamp. It is just the same way with politics. It makes one feel half angry and half amused, and wholly contemptuous, to find men of high business or social standing in the community saying that they really have not got time to go to ward meetings, to organize political clubs, and to take a personal share in all the important details of practical politics; men who further urge against their going the fact that they think the condition of political morality low, and are afraid that they may be required to do what is not right if they go into politics.

The first duty of an American citizen, then, is that he shall work in politics; his second duty is that he shall do that work in a practical manner; and his third is that it shall be done in accord with the highest principles of honour and justice. Of course, it is not possible to define rigidly just the way in which the work shall be made practical. Each man's individual temper and convictions must be taken into account. To a certain extent his work must be done in accordance with his individual beliefs and theories of right and wrong. To a yet greater extent it must be done in combination with others, he yielding or modifying certain of his own theories and beliefs so as to enable him to stand on a common ground with his fellows, who have likewise yielded or modified certain of their theories and beliefs. There is no need of dogmatizing about independence on the one hand or party allegiance on the other. There are occasions when it may be the highest duty of any man to act outside of parties and against the one with which he has himself been hitherto identified; and there may be many more occasions when his highest duty is to sacrifice some of his own cherished opinions for the sake of the success of the party which he on the whole believes to be right. I do not think that the average citizen, at least in one of our great cities, can very well manage to support his own party all the time on every issue, local and otherwise; at any rate if he can do so he has been more fortunately placed than I have been. On the other hand, I am fully convinced that to do the best work people must be organized; and of course an organization is really a party, whether it be a great organization covering the whole nation and numbering its millions of adherents, or an association of citizens in a particular locality, banded together to win a certain specific victory, as, for instance, that of municipal reform. Somebody has said that a racing-yacht, like a good rifle, is a bundle of incompatibilities; that you must get the utmost possible sail power without sacrificing some other quality if you really do get the utmost sail power, that, in short you have got to make more or less of a compromise on each in order to acquire the dozen things needful; but, of course, in making this compromise you must be very careful for the sake of something unimportant not to sacrifice any of the great principles of successful naval architecture. Well, it is about so with a man's political work. He has got to preserve his independence on the one hand; and on the other, unless he wishes to be a wholly ineffective crank, he has got to have some sense of party allegiance and party responsibility, and he has got to realize that in any given exigency it may be a matter of duty to sacrifice one quality, or it may be a matter of duty to sacrifice the other.

If it is difficult to lay down any fixed rules for party action in the abstract; it would, of course, be wholly impossible to lay them down for party action in the concrete, with reference to the organizations of the present day. I think that we ought to be broad-minded enough to recognize the fact that a good citizen, striving with fearlessness, honesty, and common sense to do his best for the nation, can render service to it in many different ways, and by connection with many different organizations. It is well for a man if he is able conscientiously to feel that his views on the great questions of the day, on such questions as the tariff, finance, immigration, the regulation of the liquor traffic, and others like them, are such as to put him in accord with the bulk of those of his fellow citizens who compose one of the greatest parties: but it is perfectly supposable that he may feel so strongly for or against certain principles held by one party, or certain principles held by the other, that he is unable to give his full adherence to either. In such a case I feel that he has no right to plead this lack of agreement with either party as an excuse for refraining from active political work prior to election. It will, of course, bar him from the primaries of the two leading parties, and preclude him from doing his share in organizing their management; but, unless he is very unfortunate, he can surely find a number of men who are in the same position as himself and who agree with him on some specific piece of political work, and they can turn in practically and effectively long before election to try to do this new piece of work in a practical manner.

One seemingly very necessary caution to utter is, that a man who goes into politics should not expect to reform everything right off, with a jump. I know many excellent young men who, when awakened to the fact that they have neglected their political duties, feel an immediate impulse to form themselves into an organization which shall forthwith purify politics everywhere, national, State, and city alike; and I know of a man who having gone round once to a primary, and having, of course, been unable to accomplish anything in a place where he knew no one and could not combine with anyone, returned saying it was quite useless for a good citizen to try to accomplish anything in such a manner. To these too hopeful or too easily discouraged people I always feel like reading Artemus Ward's article upon the people of his town who came together in a meeting to resolve that the town should support the Union and the Civil War, but were unwilling to take any part in putting down the rebellion unless they could go as brigadier-generals. After the battle of Bull Run there were a good many hundreds of thousands of young men in the North who felt it to be their duty to enter the Northern armies; but no one of them who possessed much intelligence expected to take high place at the outset, or anticipated that individual action would be of decisive importance in any given campaign. He went in as private or sergeant, lieutenant or captain, as the case might be, and did his duty in his company, in his regiment, after a while in his brigade. When Ball's Bluff and Bull Run succeeded the utter failure of the Peninsular campaign, when the terrible defeat of Fredericksburg was followed by the scarcely less disastrous day at Chancellorsville he did not announce (if he had any pluck or manliness about him) that he considered it quite useless for any self-respecting citizen to enter the Army of the Potomac, because he really was not of much weight in its councils, and did not approve of its management; he simply gritted his teeth and went doggedly on with his duty, grieving over, but not disheartened at the innumerable shortcomings and follies committed by those who helped to guide the destinies of the army, recognizing also the bravery, the patience, intelligence, and resolution with which other men in high places offset the follies and shortcomings and persevering with equal mind through triumph and defeat until finally he saw the tide of failure turn at Gettysburg and the full flood of victory come with Appomattox.

I do wish that more of our good citizens would go into politics, and would do it in the same spirit with which their fathers went into the Federal armies. Begin with the little thing, and do not expect to accomplish anything without an effort. Of course, if you go to a primary just once, never having taken the trouble to know any of the other people who go there you will find yourself wholly out of place; but if you keep on attending and try to form associations with other men whom you meet at the political gatherings, or whom you can persuade to attend them, you will very soon find yourself a weight. In the same way, if a man feels that the politics of his city, for instance, are very corrupt and wants to reform them, it would be an excellent idea for him to begin with his district. If he joins with other people, who think as he does, to form a club where abstract political virtue will be discussed he may do a great deal of good. We need such clubs; but he must also get to know his own ward or his own district, put himself in communication with the decent people in that district, of whom we may rest assured there will be many, willing and able to do something practical for the procurance of better government. Let him set to work to procure a better assemblyman or better alderman before he tries his hand at making a mayor, a governor, or a president. If he begins at the top he may make a brilliant temporary success, but the chances are a thousand to one that he will only be defeated eventually; and in no event will the good he does stand on the same broad and permanent foundation as if he had begun at the bottom. Of course, one or two of his efforts may be failures; but if he has the right stuff in him he will go ahead and do his duty irrespective of whether he meets with success or defeat. It is perfectly right to consider the question of failure while shaping one's efforts to succeed in the struggle for the right; but there should be no consideration of it whatsoever when the question is as to whether one should or should not make a struggle for the right. When once a band of one hundred and fifty or two hundred honest, intelligent men, who mean business and know their business, is found in any district, whether in one of the regular organizations or outside, you can guarantee that the local politicians of that district will begin to treat it with a combination of fear, hatred, and respect, and that its influence will be felt; and that while sometimes men will be elected to office in direct defiance of its wishes, more often the successful candidates will feel that they have to pay some regard to its demands for public decency and honesty.

But in advising you to be practical and to work hard, I must not for one moment be understood as advising you to abandon one iota of your self-respect and devotion to principle. It is a bad sign for the country to see one class of our citizens sneer at practical politicians, and another at Sunday-school politics. No man can do both effective and decent work in public life unless he is a practical politician on the one hand, and a sturdy believer in Sunday-school politics on the other. He must always strive manfully for the best, and yet, like Abraham Lincoln, must often resign himself to accept the best possible. Of course when a man verges on to the higher ground of statesmanship, when he becomes a leader, he must very often consult with others and defer to their opinion, and must be continually settling in his mind how far he can go in just deference to the wishes and prejudices of others while yet adhering to his own moral standards: but I speak not so much of men of this stamp as I do of the ordinary citizen, who wants to do his duty as a member of the commonwealth in its civic life; and for this man I feel that the one quality which he ought always to hold most essential is that of disinterestedness. If he once begins to feel that he wants office himself, with a willingness to get it at the cost of his convictions, or to keep it when gotten, at the cost of his convictions, his usefulness is gone. Let him make up his mind to do his duty in politics without regard to holding office at all, and let him know that often the men in this country who have done the best work for our public life have not been the men in office. If, on the other hand, he attains public position, let him not strive to plan out for himself a career. I do not think that any man should let himself regard his political career as a means of livelihood, or as his sole occupation in life; for if he does he immediately becomes most seriously handicapped. The moment that he begins to think how such and such an act will affect the voters in his district, or will affect some great political leader who will have an influence over his destiny, he is hampered and his hands are bound. Not only may it be his duty often to disregard the wishes of politicians, but it may be his clear duty at times to disregard the wishes of the people. The voice of the people is not always the voice of God; and when it happens to be the voice of the devil, then it is a man's clear duty to defy its behests. Different political conditions breed different dangers. The demagogue is as unlovely a creature as the courtier, though one is fostered under republican and the other under monarchical institutions. There is every reason why a man should have an honourable ambition to enter public life, and an honourable ambition to stay there when he is in; but he ought to make up his mind that he cares for it only as long as he can stay in it on his own terms, without sacrifice of his own principles; and if he does thus make up his mind he can really accomplish twice as much for the nation, and can reflect a hundredfold greater honour upon himself, in a short term of service, than can the man who grows grey in the public employment at the cost of sacrificing what he believes to be true and honest. And moreover, when a public servant has definitely made up his mind that he will pay no heed to his own future, but will do what he honestly deems best for the community, without regard to how his actions may affect his prospects, not only does he become infinitely more useful as a public servant, but he has a far better time. He is freed from the harassing care which is inevitably the portion of him who is trying to shape his sails to catch every gust of the wind of political favour.

But let me reiterate, that in being virtuous he must not become ineffective, and that he must not excuse himself for shirking his duties by any false plea that he cannot do his duties and retain his self-respect. This is nonsense, he can; and when he urges such a plea it is a mark of mere laziness and self-indulgence. And again, he should beware how he becomes a critic of the actions of others, rather than a doer of deeds himself; and in so far as he does act as a critic (and of course the critic has a great and necessary function) he must beware of indiscriminate censure even more than of indiscriminate praise.

The screaming vulgarity of the foolish spread-eagle orator who is continually yelling defiance at Europe, praising everything American, good and bad, and resenting the introduction of any reform because it has previously been tried successfully abroad, is offensive and contemptible to the last degree; but after all it is scarcely as harmful as the peevish, fretful, sneering, and continual fault-finding of the refined, well-educated man, who is always attacking good and bad alike, who genuinely distrusts America, and in the true spirit of servile colonialism considers us inferior to the people across the water. It may be taken for granted that the man who is always sneering at our public life and our public men is a thoroughly bad citizen, and that what little influence he wields in the community is wielded for evil. The public speaker or the editorial writer who teaches men of education that their proper attitude toward American politics should be one of dislike or indifference is doing all he can to perpetuate and aggravate the very evils of which he is ostensibly complaining. Exactly as it is generally the case that when a man bewails the decadence of our civilization he is himself physically, mentally, and morally a first-class type of the decadent, so it is usually the case that when a man is perpetually sneering at American politicians, whether worthy or unworthy, he himself is a poor citizen and a friend of the very forces of evil against which he professes to contend. Too often these men seem to care less for attacking bad men, than for ruining the characters of good men with whom they disagree on some pubic question; and while their influence against the bad is almost nil, they are sometimes able to weaken the hands of the good by withdrawing from them support to which they are entitled, and they thus count in the sum total of forces that work for evil. They answer to the political prohibitionist, who, in a close contest between a temperance man and a liquor seller diverts enough votes from the former to elect the liquor seller. Occasionally it is necessary to beat a pretty good man, who is not quite good enough, even at the cost of electing a bad one—but it should be thoroughly recognized that this can be necessary only occasionally and indeed, I may say, only in very exceptional cases, and that as a rule where it is done the effect is thoroughly unwholesome in every way, and those taking part in it deserve the severest censure from all honest men.

Moreover, the very need of denouncing evil makes it all the more wicked to weaken the effect of such denunciations by denouncing also the good. It is the duty of all citizens, irrespective of party, to denounce, and, so far as may be, to punish crimes against the public on the part of politicians or officials. But exactly as the public man who commits a crime against the public is one of the worst of criminals, so, close on his heels in the race for iniquitous distinction, comes the man who falsely charges the public servant with outrageous wrongdoing; whether it is done with foul-mouthed and foolish directness in the vulgar and violent party organ, or with sarcasm, innuendo, and the half-truths that are worse than lies, in some professed organ of independence. Not only should criticism be honest, but it should be intelligent, in order to be effective. I recently read in a religious paper an article railing at the corruption of our public life, in which it stated incidentally that the lobby was recognized as all-powerful in Washington. This is untrue. There was a day when the lobby was very important at Washington, but its influence in Congress is now very small indeed; and from a pretty intimate acquaintance with several Congresses I am entirely satisfied that there is among the members a very small proportion indeed who are corruptible, in the sense that they will let their action be influenced by money or its equivalent. Congressmen are very often demagogues; they are very often blind partisans; they are often exceedingly short-sighted, narrow-minded, and bigoted; but they are not usually corrupt; and to accuse a narrow-minded demagogue of corruption when he is perfectly honest, is merely to set him more firmly in his evil course and to help him with his constituents, who recognize that the charge is entirely unjust, and in repelling it lose sight of the man's real shortcomings. I have known more than one State legislature, more than one board of aldermen against which the charge of corruption could perfectly legitimately be brought, but it cannot be brought against Congress. Moreover these sweeping charges really do very little good. When I was in the New York legislature, one of the things that I used to mind most was the fact that at the close of every session the papers that affect morality invariably said that particular legislature was the worst legislature since the days of tweed. The statement was not true as a rule; and, in any event, to lump all the members, good and bad, in sweeping condemnation simply hurt the good and helped the bad. Criticism should be fearless, but I again reiterate that it should be honest and should be discriminating. When it is sweeping and unintelligent, and directed against good and bad alike, or against the good and bad qualities of any man alike, it is very harmful. It tends steadily to deteriorate the character of our public men; and it tends to produce a very unwholesome spirit among young men of education, and especially among the young men in our colleges.

Against nothing is fearless and specific criticism more urgently needed than against the 'spoils system,' which is the degradation of American politics. And nothing is more effective in thwarting the purposes of the spoilsmen than the civil service reform. To be sure, practical politicians sneer at it. One of them even went so far as to say that civil-service reform is asking a man irrelevant questions. What more irrelevant question could there be than that of the practical politician who asks the aspirant for his political favour—'Whom did you vote for in the last election?' There is certainly nothing more interesting, from a humorous point of view, than the heads of departments urging changes to be made in their underlings, 'on the score of increased efficiency' they say; when as the result of such a change the old incumbent often spends six months teaching the new incumbent how to do the work almost as well as he did himself! Occasionally the civil-service reform has been abused, but not often. Certainly the reform is needed when you contemplate the spectacle of a New York City treasurer who acknowledges his annual fees to be eighty-five thousand dollars, and who pays a deputy one thousand five hundred dollars to do his work when you note the corruptions in the New York legislature, where one man says he has a horror of the

Constitution because it prevents active benevolence, and another says that you should never allow the Constitution to come between friends! All these corruptions and vices are what every good American citizen must fight against.

Finally, the man who wishes to do his duty as a citizen in our country must be imbued through and through with the spirit of Americanism. I am not saying this as a matter of spread-eagle rhetoric: I am saying it quite soberly as a piece of matter-of-fact, common-sense advice, derived from my own experience of others. Of course, the question of Americanism has several sides. If a man is an educated man, he must show his Americanism by not getting misled into following out and trying to apply all the theories of the political thinkers of other countries, such as Germany and France, to our own entirely different conditions. He must not get a fad, for instance, about responsible government; and above all things he must not, merely because he is intelligent, or a college professor well read in political literature, try to discuss our institutions when he has had no practical knowledge of how they are worked. Again, if he is a wealthy man, a man of means and standing, he must really feel, not merely affect to feel, that no social differences obtain save such as a man can in some way himself make by his own actions. People sometimes ask me if there is not a prejudice against a man of wealth and education in ward politics. I do not think that there is, unless the man in turn shows that he regards the facts of his having wealth and education as giving him a claim to superiority aside from the merit he is able to prove himself to have in actual service. Of course, if he feels that he ought to have a little better treatment than a carpenter, a plumber, or a butcher, who happens to stand beside him, he is going to be thrown out of the race very quickly, and probably quite roughly; and if he starts in to patronize and elaborately condescend to these men he will find that they resent this attitude even more. Do not let him think about the matter at all. Let him go into the political contest with no more thought of such matters than a college boy gives to the social standing of the members of his own and rival teams in a hotly contested football match. As soon as he begins to take an interest in politics (and he will speedily not only get interested for the sake of politics, but also take a good healthy interest in playing the game itself—an interest which is perfectly normal and praise-worthy, and to which only a prig would object), he will begin to work up the organization in the way that will be most effective, and he won't care a rap about who is put to work with him, save in so far as he is a good fellow and an efficient worker. There was one time that a number of men who think as we do here tonight (one of the number being myself) got hold of one of the assembly districts of New York, and ran it in really an ideal way, better than any other assembly district has ever been run before or since by either party. We did it by hard work and good organization; by working practically, and yet by being honest and square in motive and method: especially did we do it by all turning in as straight-out Americans without any regard to distinctions of race origin. Among the many men who did a great deal in organizing our victories was the son of a Presbyterian clergyman, the nephew of a Hebrew rabbi, and two well-known Catholic gentlemen. We also had a Columbia College professor (the stroke-oar of a university crew), a noted retail butcher, and the editor of a local German paper, various brokers, bankers, lawyers, bricklayers and a stone-mason who was particularly useful to us, although on questions of theoretic rather than applied politics he had a decidedly socialistic turn of mind.

Again, questions of race origin, like questions of creed, must not be considered: we wish to do good work, and we are all Americans, pure and simple. In the New York legislature, when it fell to my lot to choose a committee—which I always esteemed my most important duty at Albany—no less than three out of the four men I chose were of Irish birth or parentage; and three abler and more fearless and disinterested men never sat in a legislative body; while among my especial political and personal friends in that body was a gentleman from the southern tier of counties, who was, I incidentally found out, a German by birth, but who was just as straight United States as if his ancestors had come over here in the Mayflower or in Henry Hudson's yacht. Of course, none of these men of Irish or German birth would have been worth their salt had they continued to act after coming here as Irishmen or Germans, or as anything but plain straight-out Americans. We have not any room here for a divided allegiance. A man has got to be an American and nothing else; and he has no business to be mixing us up with questions of foreign politics, British or Irish, German or French, and no business to try to perpetuate their language and customs in the land of complete religious toleration and equality. If, however, he does become honestly and in good faith an American, then he is entitled to stand precisely as all other Americans stand, and it is the height of un-Americanism to discriminate against him in any way because of creed or birthplace. No spirit can be more thoroughly alien to American institutions, than the spirit of the Know-Nothings.

In facing the future and in striving, each according to the measure of his individual capacity, to work out the salvation of our land, we should be neither timid pessimists nor foolish optimists. We should recognize the dangers that exist and that threaten us: we should neither overestimate them nor shrink from them, but steadily fronting them should set to work to overcome and beat them down. Grave perils are yet to be encountered in the stormy course of the Republic—perils from political corruption, perils from individual laziness, indolence and timidity, perils springing from the greed of the unscrupulous rich, and from the anarchic violence of the thriftless and turbulent poor. There is every reason why we should recognize them, but there is no reason why we should fear them or doubt our capacity to overcome them, if only each will, according to the measure of his ability, do his full duty, and endeavour so to live as to deserve the high praise of being called a good American citizen.

# 12

## The Man with the Muck Rake

★ ★ ★ ★ ★ ★ ★

Theodore Roosevelt
Washington, D.C., U.S.A.
15 April 1906

*In John Bunyan's Pilgrim's Progress, the man with the muck rake had only focused on the filth on the floor, signifying that he only noticed the vile things in life. Roosevelt compared the journalists of his day with this man in the following speech. In his opinion, American writers, who were protesting about the problems in the country and solely criticizing the dishonest behaviour, crimes, and other misdeeds of individuals, needed to offer constructive criticism instead.*

*This speech started a national debate about the role of the press in the nation. Some people agreed with Roosevelt, others thought that the press was doing much-needed work in exposing the corruption prevalent in the country.*

Over a century ago Washington laid the corner stone of the Capitol in what was then little more than a tract of wooded wilderness here beside the Potomac. We now find it necessary to provide by great additional buildings for the business of the government.

This growth in the need for the housing of the government is but a proof and example of the way in which the nation has grown and the sphere of action of the national government has grown. We now administer the affairs of a nation in which the extraordinary growth of population has been outstripped by the growth of wealth in complex interests. The material problems that face us today are not such as they were in Washington's time, but the underlying facts of human nature are the same now as they were then. Under altered external form we war with the same tendencies toward evil that were evident in Washington's time, and are helped by the same tendencies for good. It is about some of these that I wish to say a word today.

In Bunyan's *Pilgrim's Progress*, you may recall the description of the Man with the Muck Rake, the man who could look no way but downward, with the muck rake in his hand; who was offered a celestial crown for his muck rake, but who would neither look up nor regard the crown he was offered, but continued to rake to himself the filth of the floor.

In *Pilgrim's Progress*, the man with the muck rake is set forth as the example of him whose vision is fixed on carnal instead of spiritual things. Yet he also typifies the man who in this life consistently refuses to see aught that is lofty, and fixes his eyes with solemn intentness only on that which is vile and debasing.

Now, it is very necessary that we should not flinch from seeing what is vile and debasing. There is filth on the floor, and it must be scraped up with the muck rake; and there are times and places where this service is the most needed of all the services that can be performed. But the man who never does anything else, who never thinks or speaks or writes, save of his feats with the muck rake, speedily becomes, not a help but one of the most potent forces for evil.

There are in the body politic, economic and social, many and grave evils, and there is urgent necessity for the sternest war upon them. There should be relentless exposure of and attack upon every evil man, whether politician or business man, every evil practice, whether in politics, business, or social life. I hail as a benefactor every writer or speaker, every man who, on the platform or in a book, magazine, or newspaper, with merciless severity makes such attack, provided always that he in his turn remembers that the attack is of use only if it is absolutely truthful.

The liar is no whit better than the thief, and if his mendacity takes the form of slander he may be worse than most thieves. It puts a premium upon knavery untruthfully to attack an honest man, or even with hysterical exaggeration to assail a bad man with untruth.

An epidemic of indiscriminate assault upon character does no good, but very great harm. The soul of every scoundrel is gladdened whenever an honest man is assailed, or even when a scoundrel is untruthfully assailed.

Now, it is easy to twist out of shape what I have just said, easy to affect to misunderstand it, and if it is slurred over in repetition not difficult really to misunderstand it. Some persons are sincerely incapable of understanding that to denounce mud slinging does not mean the endorsement of whitewashing; and both the interested individuals who need whitewashing and those others who practice mud slinging like to encourage such confusion of ideas.

One of the chief counts against those who make indiscriminate assault upon men in business or men in public life is that they invite a reaction which is sure to tell powerfully in favour of the unscrupulous scoundrel who really ought to be attacked, who ought to be exposed, who ought, if possible, to be put in the penitentiary. If Aristides is praised overmuch as just, people get tired of hearing it; and over-censure of the unjust finally and from similar reasons results in their favour.

Any excess is almost sure to invite a reaction; and, unfortunately, the reactions instead of taking the form of punishment of those guilty of the excess, is apt to take the form either of punishment of the unoffending or of giving immunity, and even strength, to offenders. The effort to make financial or political profit out of the destruction of character can only result in public calamity. Gross and reckless assaults on character, whether on the stump or in newspaper, magazine, or book, create a morbid and vicious public sentiment, and at the same time act as a profound deterrent to able men of normal sensitiveness and tend to prevent them from entering the public service at any price.

As an instance in point, I may mention that one serious difficulty encountered in getting the right type of men to dig the Panama canal is the certainty that they will be exposed, both without, and, I am sorry to say, sometimes within, Congress, to utterly reckless assaults on their character and capacity.

At the risk of repetition let me say again that my plea is not for immunity to, but for the most unsparing exposure of, the politician who betrays his trust, of the big business man who makes or spends his fortune in illegitimate or corrupt ways. There should be a resolute effort to hunt every such man out of the position he has disgraced. Expose the crime, and hunt down the criminal; but remember that even in the case of crime, if it is attacked in sensational, lurid, and untruthful fashion, the attack may do more damage to the public mind than the crime itself.

It is because I feel that there should be no rest in the endless war against the forces of evil that I ask the war be conducted with sanity as well as with resolution. The men with the muck rakes are often indispensable to the well-being of society; but only if they know when to stop raking the muck, and to look upward to the celestial crown above them, to the crown of worthy endeavour. There are beautiful things above and round about them; and if they gradually grow to feel that the whole world is nothing but muck, their power of usefulness is gone.

If the whole picture is painted black there remains no hue whereby to single out the rascals for distinction from their fellows. Such painting finally induces a kind of moral colour blindness; and people affected by it come to the conclusion that no man is really black, and no man really white, but they are all grey.

In other words, they neither believe in the truth of the attack, nor in the honesty of the man who is attacked; they grow as suspicious of the accusation as of the offense; it becomes well-nigh hopeless to stir them either to wrath against wrongdoing or to enthusiasm for what is right; and such a mental attitude in the public gives hope to every knave, and is the despair of honest men. To assail the great and admitted evils of our political and industrial life with such crude and sweeping generalizations as to include decent men in the general condemnation means the searing of the public conscience. There results a general attitude either of cynical belief in and indifference to public corruption or else of a distrustful inability to discriminate between the good and the bad. Either attitude is fraught with untold damage to the country as a whole.

The fool who has not sense to discriminate between what is good and what is bad is well-nigh as dangerous as the man who does discriminate and yet chooses the bad. There is nothing more distressing to every good patriot, to every good American, than the hard, scoffing spirit which treats the allegation of dishonesty in a public man as a cause for laughter. Such laughter is worse than the crackling of thorns under a pot, for it denotes not merely the vacant mind, but the heart in which high emotions have been choked before they could grow to fruition. There is any amount of good in the world, and there never was a time when loftier and more disinterested work for the betterment of mankind was being done than now. The forces that tend for evil are great and terrible, but the forces of truth and love and courage and honesty and generosity and sympathy are also stronger than ever before. It is a foolish and timid, no less than a wicked thing, to blink the fact that the forces of evil are strong, but it is even worse to fail to take into account the strength of the forces that tell for good.

Hysterical sensationalism is the poorest weapon wherewith to fight for lasting righteousness. The men who with stern sobriety and truth assail the many evils of our time, whether in the public press, or in magazines, or in books, are the leaders and allies of all engaged in the work for social and political betterment. But if they give good reason for distrust of what they say, if they chill the ardour of those who demand truth as a primary virtue, they thereby betray the good cause and play into the hands of the very men against whom they are nominally at war.

In his *Ecclesiastical Polity* that fine old Elizabethan divine, Bishop Hooker, wrote:

He that goeth about to persuade a multitude that they are not so well governed as they ought to be shall never want attentive and favourable hearers, because they know the manifold defects whereunto every kind of regimen is subject, but the secret lets and difficulties, which in public proceedings are innumerable and inevitable, they have not ordinarily the judgment to consider.

This truth should be kept constantly in mind by every free people desiring to preserve the sanity and poise indispensable to the permanent success of self-government. Yet, on the other hand, it is vital not to permit this spirit of sanity and self-command to degenerate into mere mental stagnation. Bad though a state of hysterical excitement is, and evil though the results are which come from the violent oscillations such excitement invariably produces, yet a sodden acquiescence in evil is even worse.

At this moment we are passing through a period of great unrest—social, political, and industrial unrest. It is of the utmost importance for our future that this should prove to be not the unrest of mere rebelliousness against life, of mere dissatisfaction with the inevitable inequality of conditions, but the unrest of a resolute and eager ambition to secure the betterment of the individual and the nation.

So far as this movement of agitation throughout the country takes the form of a fierce discontent with evil, of a determination to punish the authors of evil, whether in industry or politics, the feeling is to be heartily welcomed as a sign of healthy life.

If, on the other hand, it turns into a mere crusade of appetite against appetite, of a contest between the brutal greed of the 'have-nots' and the brutal greed of the 'haves,' then it has no significance for good, but only for evil. If it seeks to establish a line of cleavage, not along the line which divides good men from bad, but along that other line, running at right angles thereto, which divides those who are well off from those who are less well off, then it will be fraught with immeasurable harm to the body politic.

We can no more and no less afford to condone evil in the man of capital than evil in the man of no capital. The wealthy man who exults because there is a failure of justice in the effort to bring some trust magnate to account for his misdeeds is as bad as, and no worse than, the so-called labour leader who clamorously strives to excite a foul class feeling on behalf of some other labour leader who is implicated in murder. One attitude is as bad as the other, and no worse; in each case the accused is entitled to exact justice; and in neither case is there need of action by others which can be construed into an expression of sympathy for crime.

It is a prime necessity that if the present unrest is to result in permanent good the emotion shall be translated into action, and that the action shall be marked by honesty, sanity, and self-restraint. There is mighty little good in a mere spasm of reform. The reform that counts is that which comes through steady, continuous growth; violent emotionalism leads to exhaustion.

It is important to this people to grapple with the problems connected with the amassing of enormous fortunes, and the use of those fortunes, both corporate and individual, in business. We should discriminate in the sharpest way between fortunes well won and fortunes ill won; between those gained as an incident to performing great services to the community as a whole and those gained in evil fashion by keeping just within the limits of mere law honesty. Of course, no amount of charity in spending such fortunes in any way compensates for misconduct in making them.

As a matter of personal conviction, and without pretending to discuss the details or formulate the system, I feel that we shall ultimately have to consider the adoption of some such scheme as that of a progressive tax on all fortunes, beyond a certain amount, either given in life or devised or bequeathed upon death to any individual—a tax so framed as to put it out of the power of the owner of one of these enormous fortunes to hand on more than a certain amount to any one individual; the tax of course, to be imposed by the national and not the state government. Such taxation should, of course, be aimed merely at the inheritance or transmission in their entirety of those fortunes swollen beyond all healthy limits. Again, the national government must in some form exercise supervision over corporations engaged in interstate business—and all large corporations engaged in interstate business—whether by license or otherwise, so as to permit us to deal with the far reaching evils of overcapitalization.

This year we are making a beginning in the direction of serious effort to settle some of these economic problems by the railway rate legislation. Such legislation, if so framed, as I am sure it will be, as to secure definite and tangible results, will amount to something of itself; and it will amount to a great deal more in so far as it is taken as a first step in the direction of a policy of superintendence and control over corporate wealth engaged in interstate commerce; this superintendence and control not to be exercised in a spirit of malevolence toward the men who have created the wealth, but with the firm purpose both to do justice to them and to see that they in their turn do justice to the public at large.

The first requisite in the public servants who are to deal in this shape with corporations, whether as legislators or as executives, is honesty. This honesty can be no respecter of persons. There can be no such thing as unilateral honesty. The danger is not really from corrupt corporations; it springs from the corruption itself, whether exercised for or against corporations.

The eighth commandment reads, 'Thou shalt not steal.' It does not read, 'Thou shalt not steal from the rich man.' It does not read, 'Thou shalt not steal from the poor man.' It reads simply and plainly, 'Thou shalt not steal.'

No good whatever will come from that warped and mock morality which denounces the misdeeds of men of wealth and forgets the misdeeds practiced at their expense; which denounces bribery, but blinds itself to blackmail; which foams with rage if a corporation secures favours by improper methods, and merely leers with hideous mirth if the corporation is itself wronged.

The only public servant who can be trusted honestly to protect the rights of the public against the misdeeds of a corporation is that public man who will just as surely protect the corporation itself from wrongful aggression.

If a public man is willing to yield to popular clamour and do wrong to the men of wealth or to rich corporations, it may be set down as certain that if the opportunity comes he will secretly and furtively do wrong to the public in the interest of a corporation.

But in addition to honesty, we need sanity. No honesty will make a public man useful if that man is timid or foolish, if he is a hot-headed zealot or an impracticable visionary. As we strive for reform we find that it is not at all merely the case of a long uphill pull. On the contrary, there is almost as much of breeching work as of collar work. To depend only on traces means that there will soon be a runaway and an upset.

The men of wealth who today are trying to prevent the regulation and control of their business in the interest of the public by the proper government authorities will not succeed, in my judgment, in checking the progress of the movement. But if they did succeed they would find that they had sown the wind and would surely reap the whirlwind, for they would ultimately provoke the violent excesses which accompany a reform coming by convulsion instead of by steady and natural growth.

On the other hand, the wild preachers of unrest and discontent, the wild agitators against the entire existing order, the men who act crookedly, whether because of sinister design or from mere puzzle headedness, the men who preach destruction without proposing any substitute for what they intend to destroy, or who propose a substitute which would be far worse than the existing evils—all these men are the most dangerous opponents of real reform. If they get their way they will lead the people into a deeper pit than any into which they could fall under the present system. If they fail to get their way they will still do incalculable harm by provoking the kind of reaction which in its revolt against the senseless evil of their teaching would enthrone more securely than ever the evils which their misguided followers believe they are attacking.

More important than aught else is the development of the broadest sympathy of man for man. The welfare of the wage worker, the welfare of the tiller of the soil, upon these depend the welfare of the entire country; their good is not to be sought in pulling down others; but their good must be the prime object of all our statesmanship.

Materially we must strive to secure a broader economic opportunity for all men, so that each shall have a better chance to show the stuff of which he is made. Spiritually and ethically we must strive to bring about clean living and right thinking. We appreciate that the things of the body are important; but we appreciate also that the things of the soul are immeasurably more important.

The foundation stone of national life is, and ever must be, the high individual character of the average citizen.

# 13

## Man in the Arena

★ ★ ★ ★ ★ ★ ★

Theodore Roosevelt
Sorbonne, Paris, France
23 April 1910

*Theodore Roosevelt had left office in 1909. He toured Europe in 1910, attending events and giving speeches.*

*This speech is also known as 'Citizenship in a Republic' but his audience didn't consist of citizens alone. According to Edmund Morris, Roosevelt delivered the following speech before 'ministers in court dress, army and navy officers in full uniform, nine hundred students, and an audience of two thousand ticket holders.'*

*Criticizing comes easily to people. The key point of the speech is to exalt the man who tries to make an effort for the cause he believes in, even though he might not succeed. For such a man is similar to a man fighting in the arena.*

Strange and impressive associations rise in the mind of a man from the New World who speaks before this august body in this ancient institution of learning. Before his eyes pass the shadows of mighty kings and war-like nobles, of great masters of law and theology; through the shining dust of the dead centuries he sees crowded figures that tell of the power and learning and splendour of times gone by, and he sees also the innumerable host of humble students to whom clerkship meant emancipation, to whom it was well-nigh the only outlet from the dark thraldom of the Middle Ages.

This was the most famous university of mediaeval Europe at a time when no one dreamed that there was a New World to discover. Its services to the cause of human knowledge already stretched far back into the remote past at a time when my forefathers, three centuries ago, were among the sparse bands of traders, ploughmen, wood-choppers, and fisher folk who, in hard struggle with the iron unfriendliness of the Indian-haunted land, were laying the foundations of what has now become the giant republic of the West. To conquer a continent, to tame the shaggy roughness of wild nature, means grim warfare; and the generations engaged in it cannot keep, still less add to, the stores of garnered wisdom which where once theirs, and which are still in the hands of their brethren who dwell in the old land. To conquer the wilderness means to wrest victory from the same hostile forces with which mankind struggled on the immemorial infancy of our race. The primeval conditions must be met by the primeval qualities which are incompatible with the retention of much that has been painfully acquired by humanity as through the ages it has striven upward toward civilization. In conditions so primitive there can be but a primitive culture. At first only the rudest school can be established, for no others would meet the needs of the hard-driven, sinewy folk who thrust forward the frontier in the teeth of savage men and savage nature; and many years elapse before any of these schools can develop into seats of higher learning and broader culture.

The pioneer days pass; the stump-dotted clearings expand into vast stretches of fertile farm land; the stockaded clusters of log cabins change into towns; the hunters of game, the fellers of trees, the rude frontier traders and tillers of the soil, the men who wander all their lives long through the wilderness as the heralds and harbingers of an oncoming civilization, themselves vanish before the civilization for which they have prepared the way. The children of their successors and supplanters, and then their children and their children and children's children, change and develop with extraordinary rapidity. The conditions accentuate vices and virtues, energy and ruthlessness, all the good qualities and all the defects of an intense individualism, self-reliant, self-centred, far more conscious of its rights than of its duties, and blind to its own shortcomings. To the hard materialism of the frontier days succeeds the hard materialism of an industrialism even more intense and absorbing than that of the older nations; although these themselves have likewise already entered on the age of a complex and predominantly industrial civilization.

As the country grows, its people, who have won success in so many lines, turn back to try to recover the possessions of the mind and the spirit, which perforce their fathers threw aside in order better to wage the first rough battles for the continent their children inherit. The leaders of thought and of action grope their way forward to a new life, realizing, sometimes dimly, sometimes clear-sightedly, that the life of material gain, whether for a nation or an individual, is of value only as a foundation, only as there is added to it the uplift that comes from devotion to loftier ideals. The new life thus sought can in part be developed afresh from what is roundabout in the New World; but it can be developed in full only by freely drawing upon the treasure-houses of the Old World, upon the treasures stored in the ancient abodes of wisdom and learning, such as this is where I speak today. It is a mistake for any nation to merely copy another; but it is even a greater mistake, it is a proof of weakness in any nation, not to be anxious to learn from one another and willing and able to adapt that learning to the new national conditions and make it fruitful and productive therein. It is for us of the New World to sit at the feet of Gamaliel of the Old; then, if we have the right stuff in us, we can show that Paul in his turn can become a teacher as well as a scholar.

Today I shall speak to you on the subject of individual citizenship, the one subject of vital importance to you, my hearers, and to me and my countrymen, because you and we a great citizens of great democratic republics. A democratic republic such as ours—an effort to realize its full sense government by, of, and for the people—represents the most gigantic of all possible social experiments, the one fraught with great responsibilities alike for good and evil. The success of republics like yours and like ours means the glory, and our failure of despair, of mankind; and for you and for us the question of the quality of the individual citizen is supreme. Under other forms of government, under the rule of one man or very few men, the quality of the leaders is all-important. If, under such governments, the quality of the rulers is high enough, then the nations for generations lead a brilliant career, and add substantially to the sum of world achievement, no matter how low the quality of average citizen; because the average citizen is an almost negligible quantity in working out the final results of that type of national greatness. But with you and us the case is different. With you here, and with us in my own home, in the long run, success or failure will be conditioned upon the way in which the average man, the average women, does his or her duty, first in the ordinary, everyday affairs of life, and next in those great occasional cries which call for heroic virtues. The average citizen must be a good citizen if our republics are to succeed. The stream will not permanently rise higher than the main source; and the main source of national power and national greatness is found in the average citizenship of the nation. Therefore it behoves us to do our best to see that the standard of the average citizen is kept high; and the average cannot be kept high unless the standard of the leaders is very much higher.

It is well if a large proportion of the leaders in any republic, in any democracy, are, as a matter of course, drawn from the classes represented in this audience today; but only provided that those classes possess the gifts of sympathy with plain people and of devotion to great ideals. You and those like you have received special advantages; you have all of you had the opportunity for mental training; many of you have had leisure; most of you have had a chance for enjoyment of life far greater than comes to the majority of your fellows. To you and your kind much has been given, and from you much should be expected. Yet there are certain failings against which it is especially incumbent that both men of trained and cultivated intellect, and men of inherited wealth and position should especially guard themselves, because to these failings they are especially liable; and if yielded to, their—your—chances of useful service are at an end. Let the man of learning, the man of lettered leisure, beware of that queer and cheap temptation to pose to himself and to others as a cynic, as the man who has outgrown emotions and beliefs, the man to whom good and evil are as one. The poorest way to face life is to face it with a sneer. There are many men who feel a kind of twister pride in cynicism; there are many who confine themselves to criticism of the way others do what they themselves dare not even attempt. There is no more unhealthy being, no man less worthy of respect, than he who either really holds, or feigns to hold, an attitude of sneering disbelief toward all that is great and lofty, whether in achievement or in that noble effort which, even if it fails, comes to second achievement. A cynical habit of thought and speech, a readiness to criticize work which the critic himself never tries to perform, an intellectual aloofness which will not accept contact with life's realities—all these are marks, not as the possessor would fain to think, of superiority but of weakness. They mark the men unfit to bear their part painfully in the stern strife of living, who seek, in the affection of contempt for the achievements of others, to hide from others and from themselves in their own weakness. The role is easy; there is none easier, save only the role of the man who sneers alike at both criticism and performance.

It is not the critic who counts; not the man who points out how the strong man stumbles, or where the doer of deeds could have done them better. The credit belongs to the man who is actually in the arena, whose face is marred by dust and sweat and blood; who strives valiantly; who errs, who comes short again and again, because there is no effort without error and shortcoming; but who does actually strive to do the deeds; who knows great enthusiasms, the great devotions; who spends himself in a worthy cause; who at the best knows in the end the triumph of high achievement, and who at the worst, if he fails, at least fails while daring greatly, so that his place shall never be with those cold and timid souls who neither know victory nor defeat. Shame on the man of cultivated taste who permits refinement to develop into fastidiousness that unfits him for doing the rough work of a workaday world. Among the free peoples who govern themselves there is but a small field of usefulness open for the men of cloistered life who shrink from contact with their fellows. Still less room is there for those who deride of slight what is done by those who actually bear the brunt of the day; nor yet for those others who always profess that they would like to take action, if only the conditions of life were not exactly what they actually are. The man who does nothing cuts the same sordid figure in the pages of history, whether he be a cynic, or fop, or voluptuary. There is little use for the being whose tepid soul knows nothing of great and generous emotion, of the high pride, the stern belief, the lofty enthusiasm, of the men who quell the storm and ride the thunder. Well for these men if they succeed; well also, though not so well, if they fail, given only that they have nobly ventured, and have put forth all their heart and strength. It is war-worn Hotspur, spent with hard fighting, he of the many errors and valiant end, over whose memory we love to linger, not over the memory of the young lord who 'but for the vile guns would have been a valiant soldier.'

France has taught many lessons to other nations: surely one of the most important lesson is the lesson her whole history teaches, that a high artistic and literary development is compatible with notable leadership in arms and statecraft. The brilliant gallantry of the French soldier has for many centuries been proverbial; and during these same centuries at every court in Europe the freemasons of fashion: have treated the French tongue as their common speech; while every artist and man of letters, and every man of science able to appreciate that marvellous instrument of precision, French prose, had turned toward France for aid and inspiration. How long the leadership in arms and letters has lasted is curiously illustrated by the fact that the earliest masterpiece in a modern tongue is the splendid French epic which tells of Roland's doom and the vengeance of Charlemange when the lords of the Frankish hosts where stricken at Roncesvalles. Let those who have, keep, let those who have not, strive to attain, a high standard of cultivation and scholarship. Yet let us remember that these stand second to certain other things. There is need of a sound body, and even more of a sound mind. But above mind and above body stands character—the sum of those qualities which we mean when we speak of a man's force and courage, of his good faith and sense of honour. I believe in exercise for the body, always provided that we keep in mind that physical development is a means and not an end. I believe, of course, in giving to all the people a good education. But the education must contain much besides book-learning in order to be really good. We must ever remember that no keenness and subtleness of intellect, no polish, no cleverness, in any way make up for the lack of the great solid qualities. Self-restraint, self-mastery, common sense, the power of accepting individual responsibility and yet of acting in conjunction with others, courage and resolution—these are the qualities which mark a masterful people. Without them no people can control itself, or save itself from being controlled from the outside. I speak to brilliant assemblage; I speak in a great university which represents the flower of the highest intellectual development; I pay all homage to intellect and to elaborate and specialized training of the intellect; and yet I know I shall have the assent of all of you present when I add that more important still are the commonplace, everyday qualities and virtues.

Such ordinary, everyday qualities include the will and the power to work, to fight at need, and to have plenty of healthy children. The need that the average man shall work is so obvious as hardly to warrant insistence. There are a few people in every country so born that they can lead lives of leisure. These fill a useful function if they make it evident that leisure does not mean idleness; for some of the most valuable work needed by civilization is essentially non-remunerative in its character, and of course the people who do this work should in large part be drawn from those to whom remuneration is an object of indifference. But the average man must earn his own livelihood. He should be trained to do so, and he should be trained to feel that he occupies a contemptible position if he does not do so; that he is not an object of envy if he is idle, at whichever end of the social scale he stands, but an object of contempt, an object of derision. In the next place, the good man should be both a strong and a brave man; that is, he should be able to fight, he should be able to serve his country as a soldier, if the need arises. There are well-meaning philosophers who declaim against the unrighteousness of war. They are right only if they lay all their emphasis upon the unrighteousness. War is a dreadful thing, and unjust war is a crime against humanity. But it is such a crime because it is unjust, not because it is a war. The choice must ever be in favour of righteousness, and this is whether the alternative be peace or whether the alternative be war. The question must not be merely, Is there to be peace or war? The question must be, Is it right to prevail? Are the great laws of righteousness once more to be fulfilled? And the answer from a strong and virile people must be 'Yes,' whatever the cost. Every honourable effort should always be made to avoid war, just as every honourable effort should always be made by the individual in private life to keep out of a brawl, to keep out of trouble; but no self-respecting individual, no self-respecting nation, can or ought to submit to wrong.

Finally, even more important than ability to work, even more important than ability to fight at need, is it to remember that chief of blessings for any nations is that it shall leave its seed to inherit the land. It was the crown of blessings in Biblical times and it is the crown of blessings now. The greatest of all curses is the curse of sterility, and the severest of all condemnations should be that visited upon wilful sterility. The first essential in any civilization is that the man and women shall be father and mother of healthy children, so that the race shall increase and not decrease. If that is not so, if through no fault of the society there is failure to increase, it is a great misfortune. If the failure is due to the deliberate and wilful fault, then it is not merely a misfortune, it is one of those crimes of ease and self-indulgence, of shrinking from pain and effort and risk, which in the long run Nature punishes more heavily than any other. If we of the great republics, if we, the free people who claim to have emancipated ourselves from the thraldom of wrong and error, bring down on our heads the curse that comes upon the wilfully barren, then it will be an idle waste of breath to prattle of our achievements, to boast of all that we have done. No refinement of life, no delicacy of taste, no material progress, no sordid heaping up riches, no sensuous development of art and literature, can in any way compensate for the loss of the great fundamental virtues; and of these great fundamental virtues the greatest is the race's power to perpetuate the race. Character must show itself in the man's performance both of the duty he owes himself and of the duty he owes the state. The man's foremost duty is owed to himself and his family; and he can do this duty only by earning money, by providing what is essential to material well-being; it is only after this has been done that he can hope to build a higher superstructure on the solid material foundation; it is only after this has been done that he can help in movements for the general well-being. He must pull his own weight first, and only after this can his surplus strength be of use to the general public. It is not good to excite that bitter laughter which expresses contempt; and contempt is what we feel for the being whose enthusiasm to benefit mankind is such that he is a burden to those nearest him; who wishes to do great things for humanity in the abstract, but who cannot keep his wife in comfort or educate his children.

Nevertheless, while laying all stress on this point, while not merely acknowledging but insisting upon the fact that there must be a basis of material well-being for the individual as for the nation, let us with equal emphasis insist that this material well-being represents nothing but the foundation, and that the foundation, though indispensable, is worthless unless upon it is raised the superstructure of a higher life. That is why I decline to recognize the mere multimillionaire, the man of mere wealth, as an asset of value to any country; and especially as not an asset to my own country. If he has earned or uses his wealth in a way that makes him a real benefit, of real use—and such is often the case—why, then he does become an asset of real worth. But it is the way in which it has been earned or used, and not the mere fact of wealth, that entitles him to the credit. There is need in business, as in most other forms of human activity, of the great guiding intelligences. Their places cannot be supplied by any number of lesser intelligences. It is a good thing that they should have ample recognition, ample reward. But we must not transfer our admiration to the reward instead of to the deed rewarded; and if what should be the reward exists without the service having been rendered, then admiration will only come from those who are mean of soul. The truth is that, after a certain measure of tangible material success or reward has been achieved, the question of increasing it becomes of constantly less importance compared to the other things that can be done in life. It is a bad thing for a nation to raise and to admire a false standard of success; and there can be no falser standard than that set by the deification of material well-being in and for itself. But the man who, having far surpassed the limits of providing for the wants; both of the body and mind, of himself and of those depending upon him, then piles up a great fortune, for the acquisition or retention of which he returns no corresponding benefit to the nation as a whole, should himself be made to feel that, so far from being desirable, he is an unworthy, citizen of the community: that he is to be neither admired nor envied; that his right-thinking fellow countrymen put him low in the scale of citizenship, and leave him to be consoled by the admiration of those whose level of purpose is even lower than his own.

My position as regards the moneyed interests can be put in a few words. In every civilized society property rights must be carefully safeguarded; ordinarily, and in the great majority of cases, human rights and property rights are fundamentally and in the long run identical; but when it clearly appears that there is a real conflict between them, human rights must have the upper hand, for property belongs to man and not man to property. In fact, it is essential to good citizenship clearly to understand that there are certain qualities which we in a democracy are prone to admire in and of themselves, which ought, by rights, to be judged admirable or the reverse solely from the standpoint of the use made of them. Foremost among these I should include two very distinct gifts—the gift of money-making and the gift of oratory. Money-making, the money touch I have spoken of above. It is a quality which in a moderate degree is essential. It may be useful when developed to a very great degree, but only if accompanied and controlled by other qualities; and without such control the possessor tends to develop into one of the least attractive types produced by a modern industrial democracy. So it is with the orator. It is highly desirable that a leader of opinion in democracy should be able to state his views clearly and convincingly. But all that the oratory can do of value to the community is enable the man thus to explain himself; if it enables the orator to put false values on things, it merely makes him power for mischief. Some excellent public servants have not that gift at all, and must merely rely on their deeds to speak for them; and unless oratory does represent genuine conviction based on good common sense and able to be translated into efficient performance, then the better the oratory the greater the damage to the public it deceives. Indeed, it is a sign of marked political weakness in any commonwealth if the people tend to be carried away by mere oratory, if they tend to value words in and for themselves, as divorced from the deeds for which they are supposed to stand. The phrase-maker, the phrase-monger, the ready talker, however great his power, whose speech does not make for courage, sobriety, and right understanding, is simply a noxious element in the body politic, and it speaks ill for the public if he has influence over them. To admire the gift of oratory without regard to the moral quality behind the gift is to do wrong to the republic.

Of course all that I say of the orator applies with even greater force to the orator's latter-day and more influential brother, the journalist. The power of the journalist is great, but he is entitled neither to respect nor admiration because of that power unless it is used aright. He can do, and often does, great good. He can do, and he often does, infinite mischief. All journalists, all writers, for the very reason that they appreciate the vast possibilities of their profession, should bear testimony against those who deeply discredit it. Offenses against taste and morals, which are bad enough in a private citizen, are infinitely worse if made into instruments for debauching the community through a newspaper. Mendacity, slander, sensationalism, inanity, vapid triviality, all are potent factors for the debauchery of the public mind and conscience. The excuse advanced for vicious writing, that the public demands it and that demand must be supplied, can no more be admitted than if it were advanced by purveyors of food who sell poisonous adulterations. In short, the good citizen in a republic must realize that he ought to possess two sets of qualities, and that neither avails without the other. He must have those qualities which make for efficiency; and that he also must have those qualities which direct the efficiency into channels for the public good. He is useless if he is inefficient. There is nothing to be done with that type of citizen of whom all that can be said is that he is harmless. Virtue which is dependent upon a sluggish circulation is not impressive. There is little place in active life for the timid good man. The man who is saved by weakness from robust wickedness is likewise rendered immune from robuster virtues. The good citizen in a republic must first of all be able to hold his own. He is no good citizen unless he has the ability which will make him work hard and which at need will make him fight hard. The good citizen is not a good citizen unless he is an efficient citizen.

But if a man's efficiency is not guided and regulated by a moral sense, then the more efficient he is the worse he is, the more dangerous to the body politic. Courage, intellect, all the masterful qualities, serve but to make a man more evil if they are merely used for that man's own advancement, with brutal indifference to the rights of others. It speaks ill for the community if the community worships these qualities and treats their possessors as heroes regardless of whether the qualities are used rightly or wrongly. It makes no difference as to the precise way in which this sinister efficiency is shown. It makes no difference whether such a man's force and ability betray themselves in a career of money-maker or politician, soldier or orator, journalist or popular leader. If the man works for evil, then the more successful he is the more he should be despised and condemned by all upright and far-seeing men. To judge a man merely by success is an abhorrent wrong; and if the people at large habitually so judge men, if they grow to condone wickedness because the wicked man triumphs, they show their inability to understand that in the last analysis free institutions rest upon the character of citizenship, and that by such admiration of evil they prove themselves unfit for liberty. The homely virtues of the household, the ordinary workaday virtues which make the woman a good housewife and housemother, which make the man a hard worker, a good husband and father, a good soldier at need, stand at the bottom of character. But of course many other must be added thereto if a state is to be not only free but great. Good citizenship is not good citizenship if only exhibited in the home. There remains the duties of the individual in relation to the State, and these duties are none too easy under the conditions which exist where the effort is made to carry on the free government in a complex industrial civilization. Perhaps the most important thing the ordinary citizen, and, above all, the leader of ordinary citizens, has to remember in political life is that he must not be a sheer doctrinaire. The closet philosopher, the refined and cultured individual who from his library tells how men ought to be governed under ideal conditions, is of no use in actual governmental work; and the one-sided fanatic, and still more the mob-leader, and the insincere man who to achieve power promises what by no possibility can be performed, are not merely useless but noxious.

The citizen must have high ideals, and yet he must be able to achieve them in practical fashion. No permanent good comes from aspirations so lofty that they have grown fantastic and have become impossible and indeed undesirable to realize. The impractical visionary is far less often the guide and precursor than he is the embittered foe of the real reformer, of the man who, with stumblings and shortcoming, yet does in some shape, in practical fashion, give effect to the hopes and desires of those who strive for better things. Woe to the empty phrase-maker, to the empty idealist, who, instead of making ready the ground for the man of action, turns against him when he appears and hampers him when he does work! Moreover, the preacher of ideals must remember how sorry and contemptible is the figure which he will cut, how great the damage that he will do, if he does not himself, in his own life, strive measurably to realize the ideals that he preaches for others. Let him remember also that the worth of the ideal must be largely determined by the success with which it can in practice be realized. We should abhor the so-called 'practical' men whose practicality assumes the shape of that peculiar baseness which finds its expression in disbelief in morality and decency, in disregard of high standards of living and conduct. Such a creature is the worst enemy of the body of politic. But only less desirable as a citizen is his nominal opponent and real ally, the man of fantastic vision who makes the impossible better forever the enemy of the possible good.

We can just as little afford to follow the doctrinaires of an extreme individualism as the doctrinaires of an extreme socialism. Individual initiative, so far from being discouraged, should be stimulated; and yet we should remember that, as society develops and grows more complex, we continually find that things which once it was desirable to leave to individual initiative can, under changed conditions, be performed with better results by common effort. It is quite impossible, and equally undesirable, to draw in theory a hard-and-fast line which shall always divide the two sets of cases. This everyone who is not cursed with the pride of the closest philosopher will see, if he will only take the trouble to think about some of our closet phenomena. For instance, when people live on isolated farms or in little hamlets, each house can be left to attend to its own drainage and water-supply; but the mere multiplication of families in a given area produces new problems which, because they differ in size, are found to differ not only in degree, but in kind from the old; and the questions of drainage and water-supply have to be considered from the common standpoint. It is not a matter for abstract dogmatizing to decide when this point is reached; it is a matter to be tested by practical experiment. Much of the discussion about socialism and individualism is entirely pointless, because of the failure to agree on terminology. It is not good to be a slave of names. I am a strong individualist by personal habit, inheritance, and conviction; but it is a mere matter of common sense to recognize that the State, the community, the citizens acting together, can do a number of things better than if they were left to individual action. The individualism which finds its expression in the abuse of physical force is checked very early in the growth of civilization, and we of today should in our turn strive to shackle or destroy that individualism which triumphs by greed and cunning, which exploits the weak by craft instead of ruling them by brutality. We ought to go with any man in the effort to bring about justice and the equality of opportunity, to turn the tool-user more and more into the tool-owner, to shift burdens so that they can be more equitably borne. The deadening effect on any race of the adoption of a logical and extreme socialistic system could not be overstated; it would spell sheer destruction; it would produce grosser wrong and outrage, fouler immortality, than any existing system. But this does not mean that we may not with great advantage adopt certain of the principles professed by some given set of men who happen to call themselves Socialists; to be afraid to do so would be to make a mark of weakness on our part.

But we should not take part in acting a lie any more than in telling a lie. We should not say that men are equal where they are not equal, nor proceed upon the assumption that there is an equality where it does not exist; but we should strive to bring about a measurable equality, at least to the extent of preventing the inequality which is due to force or fraud. Abraham Lincoln, a man of the plain people, blood of their blood, and bone of their bone, who all his life toiled and wrought and suffered for them, at the end died for them, who always strove to represent them, who would never tell an untruth to or for them, spoke of the doctrine of equality with his usual mixture of idealism and sound common sense. He said (I omit what was of merely local significance):

'I think the authors of the Declaration of Independence intended to include all men, but they did not mean to declare all men equal in all respects. They did not mean to say all men were equal in colour, size, intellect, moral development or social capacity. They defined with tolerable distinctness in what they did consider all men created equal—equal in certain inalienable rights, among which are life, liberty and pursuit of happiness. This they said, and this they meant. They did not mean to assert the obvious untruth that all were actually enjoying that equality, or yet that they were about to confer it immediately upon them. They meant to set up a standard maxim for free society which should be familiar to all—constantly looked to, constantly laboured for, and, even though never perfectly attained, constantly approximated, and thereby constantly spreading and deepening its influence, and augmenting the happiness and value of life to all people, everywhere.'

We are bound in honour to refuse to listen to those men who would make us desist from the effort to do away with the inequality which means injustice; the inequality of right, opportunity, of privilege. We are bound in honour to strive to bring ever nearer the day when, as far is humanly possible, we shall be able to realize the ideal that each man shall have an equal opportunity to show the stuff that is in him by the way in which he renders service. There should, so far as possible, be equal of opportunity to render service; but just so long as there is inequality of service there should and must be inequality of reward. We may be sorry for the general, the painter, the artists, the worker in any profession or of any kind, whose misfortune rather than whose fault it is that he does his work ill. But the reward must go to the man who does his work well; for any other course is to create a new kind of privilege, the privilege of folly and weakness; and special privilege is injustice, whatever form it takes.

To say that the thriftless, the lazy, the vicious, the incapable, ought to have reward given to those who are far-sighted, capable, and upright, is to say what is not true and cannot be true. Let us try to level up, but let us beware of the evil of levelling down. If a man stumbles, it is a good thing to help him to his feet. Every one of us needs a helping hand now and then. But if a man lies down, it is a waste of time to try and carry him; and it is a very bad thing for every one if we make men feel that the same reward will come to those who shirk their work and those who do it. Let us, then, take into account the actual facts of life, and not be misled into following any proposal for achieving the millennium, for recreating the golden age, until we have subjected it to hard-headed examination. On the other hand, it is foolish to reject a proposal merely because it is advanced by visionaries. If a given scheme is proposed, look at it on its merits, and, in considering it, disregard formulas. It does not matter in the least who proposes it, or why. If it seems good, try it. If it proves good, accept it; otherwise reject it. There are plenty of good men calling themselves Socialists with whom, up to a certain point, it is quite possible to work. If the next step is one which both we and they wish to take, why of course take it, without any regard to the fact that our views as to the tenth step may differ. But, on the other hand, keep clearly in mind that, though it has been worthwhile to take one step, this does not in the least mean that it may not be highly disadvantageous to take the next. It is just as foolish to refuse all progress because people demanding it desire at some points to go to absurd extremes, as it would be to go to these absurd extremes simply because some of the measures advocated by the extremists were wise.

The good citizen will demand liberty for himself, and as a matter of pride he will see to it that others receive liberty which he thus claims as his own. Probably the best test of true love of liberty in any country in the way in which minorities are treated in that country. Not only should there be complete liberty in matters of religion and opinion, but complete liberty for each man to lead his life as he desires, provided only that in so he does not wrong his neighbour. Persecution is bad because it is persecution, and without reference to which side happens at the most to be the persecutor and which the persecuted. Class hatred is bad in just the same way, and without regard to the individual who, at a given time, substitutes loyalty to a class for loyalty to a nation, or substitutes hatred of men because they happen to come in a certain social category, for judgement awarded them according to their conduct. Remember always that the same measure of condemnation should be extended to the arrogance which would look down upon or crush any man because he is poor and to envy and hatred which would destroy a man because he is wealthy. The overbearing brutality of the man of wealth or power, and the envious and hateful malice directed against wealth or power, are really at root merely different manifestations of the same quality, merely two sides of the same shield. The man who, if born to wealth and power, exploits and ruins his less fortunate brethren is at heart the same as the greedy and violent demagogue who excites those who have not property to plunder those who have. The gravest wrong upon his country is inflicted by that man, whatever his station, who seeks to make his countrymen divide primarily in the line that separates class from class, occupation from occupation, men of more wealth from men of less wealth, instead of remembering that the only safe standard is that which judges each man on his worth as a man, whether he be rich or whether he be poor, without regard to his profession or to his station in life. Such is the only true democratic test, the only test that can with propriety be applied in a republic. There have been many republics in the past, both in what we call antiquity and in what we call the Middle Ages. They fell, and the prime factor in their fall was the fact that the parties tended to divide along the wealth that separates wealth from poverty. It made no difference which side was successful; it made no difference whether the republic fell under the rule of oligarchy or the rule of a mob. In either case, when once loyalty to a class had been substituted for loyalty to the republic, the end of the republic was at hand. There is no greater need today than the need to keep ever in mind the fact that the cleavage between right and wrong, between good citizenship and bad citizenship, runs at right angles to, and not parallel with, the lines of cleavage between class and class, between occupation and occupation. Ruin looks us in the face if we judge a man by his position instead of judging him by his conduct in that position.

In a republic, to be successful we must learn to combine intensity of conviction with a broad tolerance of difference of conviction. Wide differences of opinion in matters of religious, political, and social belief must exist if conscience and intellect alike are not be stunted, if there is to be room for healthy growth. Bitter internecine hatreds, based on such differences, are signs, not of earnestness of belief, but of that fanaticism which, whether religious or antireligious, democratic or antidemocratic, it itself but a manifestation of the gloomy bigotry which has been the chief factor in the downfall of so many, many nations.

Of one man in especial, beyond anyone else, the citizens of a republic should beware, and that is of the man who appeals to them to support him on the ground that he is hostile to other citizens of the republic, that he will secure for those who elect him, in one shape or another, profit at the expense of other citizens of the republic. It makes no difference whether he appeals to class hatred or class interest, to religious or antireligious prejudice. The man who makes such an appeal should always be presumed to make it for the sake of furthering his own interest. The very last thing an intelligent and self-respecting member of a democratic community should do is to reward any public man because that public man says that he will get the private citizen something to which this private citizen is not entitled, or will gratify some emotion or animosity which this private citizen ought not to possess. Let me illustrate this by one anecdote from my own experience. A number of years ago I was engaged in cattle-ranching on the great plains of the western United States. There were no fences. The cattle wandered free, the ownership of each one was determined by the brand; the calves were branded with the brand of the cows they followed. If on a round-up an animal was passed by, the following year it would appear as an unbranded yearling, and was then called a maverick. By the custom of the country these mavericks were branded with the brand of the man on whose range they were found. One day I was riding the range with a newly hired cowboy, and we came upon a maverick. We roped and threw it;

then we built a fire, took out a cinch-ring, heated it in the fire; and then the cowboy started to put on the brand. I said to him, 'It so-and-so's brand,' naming the man on whose range we happened to be. He answered: 'That's all right, boss; I know my business.' In another moment I said to him: 'Hold on, you are putting on my brand!' To which he answered: 'That's all right; I always put on the boss's brand.' I answered: 'Oh, very well. Now you go straight back to the ranch and get whatever is owing to you; I don't need you any longer.' He jumped up and said: 'Why, what's the matter? I was putting on your brand.' And I answered: 'Yes, my friend, and if you will steal for me then you will steal from me.'

Now, the same principle which applies in private life applies also in public life. If a public man tries to get your vote by saying that he will do something wrong in your interest, you can be absolutely certain that if ever it becomes worth his while he will do something wrong against your interest. So much for the citizenship to the individual in his relations to his family, to his neighbour, to the state. There remain duties of citizenship which the state, the aggregation of all the individuals, owes in connection with other States, with other nations. Let me say at once that I am no advocate of a foolish cosmopolitanism. I believe that a man must be a good patriot before he can be, and as the only possible way of being, a good citizen of the world. Experience teaches us that the average man who protests that his international feeling swamps his national feeling, that he does not care for his country because he cares so much for mankind, in actual practice proves himself the foe of mankind; that the man who says that he does not care to be a citizen of any one country, because he is the citizen of the world, is in fact usually and exceedingly undesirable citizen of whatever corner of the world he happens at the moment to be in. In the dim future all moral needs and moral standards may change; but at present, if a man can view his own country and all others countries from the same level with tepid indifference, it is wise to distrust him, just as it is wise to distrust the man who can take the same dispassionate view of his wife and mother. However broad and deep a man's sympathies, however intense his activities, he need have no fear that they will be cramped by love of his native land.

Now, this does not mean in the least that a man should not wish to good outside of his native land. On the contrary, just as I think that the man who loves his family is more apt to be a good neighbour than the man who does not, so I think that the most useful member of the family of nations is normally a strongly patriotic nation. So far from patriotism being inconsistent with a proper regard for the rights of other nations, I hold that the true patriot, who is as jealous of the national honour as a gentleman of his own honour, will be careful to see that the nations neither inflicts nor suffers wrong, just as a gentleman scorns equally to wrong others or to suffer others to wrong him. I do not for one moment admit that a man should act deceitfully as a public servant in his dealing with other nations, any more than he should act deceitfully in his dealings as a private citizen with other private citizens. I do not for one moment admit that a nation should treat other nations in a different spirit from that in which an honourable man would treat other men.

In practically applying this principle to the two sets of cases there is, of course, a great practical difference to be taken into account. We speak of international law; but international law is something wholly different from private or municipal law, and the capital difference is that there is a sanction for the one and no sanction for the other; that there is an outside force which compels individuals to obey the one, while there is no such outside force to compel obedience as regards to the other. International law will, I believe, as the generations pass, grow stronger and stronger until in some way or other there develops the power to make it respected. But as yet it is only in the first formative period. As yet, as a rule, each nation is of necessity to judge for itself in matters of vital importance between it and its neighbours, and actions must be of necessity, where this is the case, be different from what they are where, as among private citizens, there is an outside force whose action is all-powerful and must be invoked in any crisis of importance. It is the duty of wise statesman, gifted with the power of looking ahead, to try to encourage and build up every movement which will substitute or tend to substitute some other agency for force in the settlement of international disputes. It is the duty of every honest statesman to try to guide the nation so that it shall not wrong any other nation. But as yet the great civilized peoples, if they are to be true to themselves and to the cause of humanity and civilization, must keep in mind that in the last resort they must possess both the will and the power to resent wrong-doings from others. The men who sanely believe in a lofty morality preach righteousness; but they do not preach weakness, whether among private citizens or among nations. We believe that our ideals should be so high, but not so high as to make it impossible measurably to realize them. We sincerely and earnestly believe in peace; but if peace and justice conflict, we scorn the man who would not stand for justice though the whole world came in arms against him.

And now, my hosts, a word in parting. You and I belong to the only two republics among the great powers of the world. The ancient friendship between France and the United States has been, on the whole, a sincere and disinterested friendship. A calamity to you would be a sorrow to us. But it would be more than that. In the seething turmoil of the history of humanity certain nations stand out as possessing a peculiar power or charm, some special gift of beauty or wisdom of strength, which puts them among the immortals, which makes them rank forever with the leaders of mankind. France is one of these nations. For her to sink would be a loss to all the world. There are certain lessons of brilliance and of generous gallantry that she can teach better than any of her sister nations. When the French peasantry sang of Malbrook, it was to tell how the soul of this warrior-foe took flight upward through the laurels he had won. Nearly seven centuries ago, Froisart, writing of the time of dire disaster, said that the realm of France was never so stricken that there were not left men who would valiantly fight for it. You have had a great past. I believe you will have a great future. Long may you carry yourselves proudly as citizens of a nation which bears a leading part in the teaching and uplifting of mankind.

# 14

## War Message

★ ★ ★ ★ ★ ★ ★

Thomas Woodrow Wilson
Washington, D.C., U.S.A.
2 April 1917

*The United States had proclaimed its neutrality from the beginning of World War I. However, in 1915, the Germans sunk 'Lusitania,' a British passenger ship, killing one hundred and twenty-eight Americans. America still maintained its neutrality in war, though Wilson sent a warning to Germany.*

*The year 1917 brought with it fresh offences committed by the Germans. Their unabated submarine warfare, sinking of the American cargo ship 'Housatonic' made Wilson break off his diplomatic ties with them.*

*Realizing that neutrality seemed impossible now, a month after his second inaugural address, Wilson addressed the Congress and asked for a declaration of war against Germany.*

*Two days after this speech, the U.S. Senate voted in favour of war by eighty-two votes to six.*

Gentlemen of the Congress:

I have called the Congress into extraordinary session because there are serious, very serious, choices of policy to be made, and made immediately, which it was neither right nor constitutionally permissible that I should assume the responsibility of making.

On the third of February last I officially laid before you the extraordinary announcement of the Imperial German Government that on and after the first day of February it was its purpose to put aside all restraints of law or of humanity and use its submarines to sink every vessel that sought to approach either the ports of Great Britain and Ireland or the western coasts of Europe or any of the ports controlled by the enemies of Germany within the Mediterranean. That had seemed to be the object of the German submarine warfare earlier in the war, but since April of last year the Imperial Government had somewhat restrained the commanders of its undersea craft in conformity with its promise then given to us that passenger boats should not be sunk and that due warning would be given to all other vessels which its submarines might seek to destroy, when no resistance was offered or escape attempted, and care taken that their crews were given at least a fair chance to save their lives in their open boats. The precautions taken were meagre and haphazard enough, as was proved in distressing instance after instance in the progress of the cruel and unmanly business, but a certain degree of restraint was observed The new policy has swept every restriction aside. Vessels of every kind, whatever their flag, their character, their cargo, their destination, their errand, have been ruthlessly sent to the bottom without warning and without thought of help or mercy for those on board, the vessels of friendly neutrals along with those of belligerents. Even hospital ships and ships carrying relief to the sorely bereaved and stricken people of Belgium, though the latter were provided with safe conduct through the proscribed areas by the German Government itself and were distinguished by unmistakable marks of identity, have been sunk with the same reckless lack of compassion or of principle.

I was for a little while unable to believe that such things would in fact be done by any government that had hitherto subscribed to the humane practices of civilized nations. International law had its origin in the attempt to set up some law which would be respected and observed upon the seas, where no nation had right of dominion and where lay the free highways of the world. By painful stage after stage has that law been built up, with meagre enough results, indeed, after all was accomplished that could be accomplished, but always with a clear view, at least, of what the heart and conscience of mankind demanded. This minimum of right the German Government has swept aside under the plea of retaliation and necessity and because it had no weapons which it could use at sea except these which it is impossible to employ as it is employing them without throwing to the winds all scruples of humanity or of respect for the understandings that were supposed to underlie the intercourse of the world. I am not now thinking of the loss of property involved, immense and serious as that is, but only of the wanton and wholesale destruction of the lives of non-combatants, men, women, and children, engaged in pursuits which have always, even in the darkest periods of modern history, been deemed innocent and legitimate. Property can be paid for; the lives of peaceful and innocent people cannot be. The present German submarine warfare against commerce is a warfare against mankind.

It is a war against all nations. American ships have been sunk, American lives taken, in ways which it has stirred us very deeply to learn of, but the ships and people of other neutral and friendly nations have been sunk and overwhelmed in the waters in the same way. There has been no discrimination. The challenge is to all mankind. Each nation must decide for itself how it will meet it. The choice we make for ourselves must be made with a moderation of counsel and a temperateness of judgment befitting our character and our motives as a nation. We must put excited feeling away. Our motive will not be revenge or the victorious assertion of the physical might of the nation, but only the vindication of right, of human right, of which we are only a single champion.

When I addressed the Congress on the twenty-sixth of February last, I thought that it would suffice to assert our neutral rights with arms, our right to use the seas against unlawful interference, our right to keep our people safe against unlawful violence. But armed neutrality, it now appears, is impracticable. Because submarines are in effect outlaws when used as the German submarines have been used against merchant shipping, it is impossible to defend ships against their attacks as the law of nations has assumed that merchantmen would defend themselves against privateers or cruisers, visible craft giving chase upon the open sea. It is common prudence in such circumstances, grim necessity indeed, to endeavour to destroy them before they have shown their own intention. They must be dealt with upon sight, if dealt with at all. The German Government denies the right of neutrals to use arms at all within the areas of the sea which it has proscribed, even in the defence of rights which no modern publicist has ever before questioned their right to defend. The intimation is conveyed that the armed guards which we have placed on our merchant ships will be treated as beyond the pale of law and subject to be dealt with as pirates would be. Armed neutrality is ineffectual enough at best; in such circumstances and in the face of such pretensions it is worse than ineffectual; it is likely only to produce what it was meant to prevent; it is practically certain to draw us into the war without either the rights or the effectiveness of belligerents. There is one choice we cannot make, we are incapable of making: we will not choose the path of submission and suffer the most sacred rights of our nation and our people to be ignored or violated. The wrongs against which we now array ourselves are no common wrongs; they cut to the very roots of human life.

With a profound sense of the solemn and even tragical character of the step I am taking and of the grave responsibilities which it involves, but in unhesitating obedience to what I deem my constitutional duty, I advise that the Congress declare the recent course of the Imperial German Government to be in fact nothing less than war against the Government and people of the United

States; that it formally accept the status of belligerent which has thus been thrust upon it, and that it take immediate steps not only to put the country in a more thorough state of defence but also to exert all its power and employ all its resources to bring the Government of the German Empire to terms and end the war.

What this will involve is clear. It will involve the utmost practicable cooperation in counsel and action with the governments now at war with Germany, and, as incident to that, the extension to those governments of the most liberal financial credits, in order that our resources may so far as possible be added to theirs. It will involve the organization and mobilization of all the material resources of the country to supply the materials of war and serve the incidental needs of the nation in the most abundant and yet the most economical and efficient way possible. It will involve the immediate full equipment of the Navy in all respects but particularly in supplying it with the best means of dealing with the enemy's submarines. It will involve the immediate addition to the armed forces of the United States already provided for by law in case of war at least 500,000 men, who should, in my opinion, be chosen upon the principle of universal liability to service, and also the authorization of subsequent additional increments of equal force so soon as they may be needed and can be handled in training. It will involve also, of course, the granting of adequate credits to the government, sustained, I hope, so far as they can equitably be sustained by the present generation, by well-conceived taxation.

While we do these things, these deeply momentous things, let us be very clear, and make very clear to all the world what our motives and our objects are. My own thought has not been driven from its habitual and normal course by the unhappy events of the last two months, and I do not believe that the thought of the nation has been altered or clouded by them I have exactly the same things in mind now that I had in mind when I addressed the Senate on the 22nd of January last; the same that I had in mind when I addressed the Congress on the 3rd of February and on the 26th of February.

Our object now, as then, is to vindicate the principles of peace and justice in the life of the world as against selfish and autocratic power and to set up amongst the really free and self-governed peoples of the world such a concert of purpose and of action as will henceforth ensure the observance of those principles. Neutrality is no longer feasible or desirable where the peace of the world is involved and the freedom of its peoples, and the menace to that peace and freedom lies in the existence of autocratic governments backed by organized force which is controlled wholly by their will, not by the will of their people. We have seen the last of neutrality in such circumstances. We are at the beginning of an age in which it will be insisted that the same standards of conduct and of responsibility for wrong done shall be observed among nations and their governments that are observed among the individual citizens of civilized states.

We have no quarrel with the German people. We have no feeling towards them but one of sympathy and friendship. It was not upon their impulse that their government acted in entering this war. It was not with their previous knowledge or approval. It was a war determined upon as wars used to be determined upon in the old, unhappy days when peoples were nowhere consulted by their rulers and wars were provoked and waged in the interest of dynasties or of little groups of ambitious men who were accustomed to use their fellow men as pawns and tools. Self-governed nations do not fill their neighbour states with spies or set the course of intrigue to bring about some critical posture of affairs which will give them an opportunity to strike and make conquest. Such designs can be successfully worked out only under cover and where no one has the right to ask questions. Cunningly contrived plans of deception or aggression, carried, it may be, from generation to generation, can be worked out and kept from the light only within the privacy of courts or behind the carefully guarded confidences of a narrow and privileged class. They are happily impossible where public opinion commands and insists upon full information concerning all the nation's affairs.

A steadfast concert for peace can never be maintained except by a partnership of democratic nations. No autocratic government could be trusted to keep faith within it or observe its covenants. It must be a league of honour, a partnership of opinion. Intrigue would eat its vitals away; the plottings of inner circles who could plan what they would and render account to no one would be a corruption seated at its very heart. Only free peoples can hold their purpose and their honour steady to a common end and prefer the interests of mankind to any narrow interest of their own.

Does not every American feel that assurance has been added to our hope for the future peace of the world by the wonderful and heartening things that have been happening within the last few weeks in Russia? Russia was known by those who knew it best to have been always in fact democratic at heart, in all the vital habits of her thought, in all the intimate relationships of her people that spoke their natural instinct, their habitual attitude towards life. The autocracy that crowned the summit of her political structure, long as it had stood and terrible as was the reality of its power, was not in fact Russian in origin, character, or purpose; and now it has been shaken off and the great, generous Russian people have been added in all their naive majesty and might to the forces that are fighting for freedom in the world, for justice, and for peace. Here is a fit partner for a league of honour.

One of the things that has served to convince us that the Prussian autocracy was not and could never be our friend is that from the very outset of the present war it has filled our unsuspecting communities and even our offices of government with spies and set criminal intrigues everywhere afoot against our national unity of counsel, our peace within and without our industries and our commerce. Indeed it is now evident that its spies were here even before the war began; and it is unhappily not a matter of conjecture but a fact proved in our courts of justice that the intrigues which have more than once come perilously near to disturbing the peace and dislocating the industries of the country have been carried on at the instigation, with the support, and even under the personal direction of official agents of the Imperial Government accredited to the Government of the United States. Even in checking these things and trying to extirpate them we have sought to put the most generous interpretation possible upon them because we knew that their source lay, not in any hostile feeling or purpose of the German people towards us (who were, no doubt, as ignorant of them as we ourselves were), but only in the selfish designs of a government that did what it pleased and told its people nothing. But they have played their part in serving to convince us at last that that government entertains no real friendship for us and means to act against our peace and security at its convenience. That it means to stir up enemies against us at our very doors the intercepted note to the German Minister at Mexico City is eloquent evidence.

We are accepting this challenge of hostile purpose because we know that in such a government, following such methods, we can never have a friend; and that in the presence of its organized power, always lying in wait to accomplish we know not what purpose, there can be no assured security for the democratic governments of the world. We are now about to accept gage of battle with this natural foe to liberty and shall, if necessary, spend the whole force of the nation to check and nullify its pretensions and its power. We are glad, now that we see the facts with no veil of false pretence about them, to fight thus for the ultimate peace of the world and for the liberation of its peoples, the German peoples included: for the rights of nations great and small and the privilege of men everywhere to choose their way of life and of obedience. The world must be made safe for democracy. Its peace must be planted upon the tested foundations of political liberty. We have no selfish ends to serve. We desire no conquest, no dominion. We seek no indemnities for ourselves, no material compensation for the sacrifices we shall freely make. We are but one of the champions of the rights of mankind. We shall be satisfied when those rights have been made as secure as the faith and the freedom of nations can make them.

Just because we fight without rancour and without selfish object, seeking nothing for ourselves but what we shall wish to share with all free peoples, we shall, I feel confident, conduct our operations as belligerents without passion and ourselves observe with proud punctilio the principles of right and of fair play we profess to be fighting for.

I have said nothing of the governments allied with the Imperial Government of Germany because they have not made war upon us or challenged us to defend our right and our honour. The Austro-Hungarian Government has, indeed, avowed its unqualified endorsement and acceptance of the reckless and lawless submarine warfare adopted now without disguise by the Imperial German Government, and it has therefore not been possible for this government to receive Count Tarnowski, the Ambassador recently accredited to this government by the Imperial and Royal Government of Austria-Hungary; but that government has not actually engaged in warfare against citizens of the United States on the seas, and I take the liberty, for the present at least, of postponing a discussion of our relations with the authorities at Vienna. We enter this war only where we are clearly forced into it because there are no other means of defending our rights.

It will be all the easier for us to conduct ourselves as belligerents in a high spirit of right and fairness because we act without animus, not in enmity towards a people or with the desire to bring any injury or disadvantage upon them, but only in armed opposition to an irresponsible government which has thrown aside all considerations of humanity and of right and is running amuck. We are, let me say again, the sincere friends of the German people, and shall desire nothing so much as the early reestablishment of intimate relations of mutual advantage between us—however hard it may be for them, for the time being, to believe that this is spoken from our hearts. We have borne with their present government through all these bitter months because of that friendship—exercising a patience and forbearance which would otherwise have been impossible. We shall, happily, still have an opportunity to prove that friendship in our daily attitude and actions towards the millions of men and women of German birth and native sympathy, who live amongst us and share our life, and we shall be proud to prove it towards all who are in fact loyal to their neighbours and to the government in the hour of test. They are, most of them, as true and loyal Americans as if they had never known any other fealty or allegiance. They will be prompt to stand with us in rebuking and restraining the few who may be of a different mind and purpose. If there should be disloyalty, it will be dealt with, with a firm hand of stern repression; but, if it lifts its head at all, it will lift it only here and there and without countenance except from a lawless and malignant few.

It is a distressing and oppressive duty, gentlemen of the Congress, which I have performed in thus addressing you. There are, it may be, many months of fiery trial and sacrifice ahead of us. It is a fearful thing to lead this great peaceful people into war, into the most terrible and disastrous of all wars, civilization itself seeming to be in the balance. But the right is more precious than peace, and we shall fight for the things which we have always carried nearest our hearts—for democracy, for the right of those who submit to authority to have a voice in their own governments, for the rights and liberties of small nations, for a universal dominion of right by such a concert of free peoples as shall bring peace and safety to all nations and make the world itself at last free. To such a task we can dedicate our lives and our fortunes, everything that we are and everything that we have, with the pride of those who know that the day has come when America is privileged to spend her blood and her might for the principles that gave her birth and happiness and the peace which she has treasured. God helping her, she can do no other.

# 15

## The Fourteen Points

★★★★★★★

Thomas Woodrow Wilson
Washington, D.C., U.S.A.
8 January 1918

*President Wilson, addressing the Congress, lay down a blueprint for peace negotiations after World War I ended. The following speech was translated and distributed to the soldiers and citizens of Germany and Austria-Hungary.*

*Though the ideas presented in the speech were liberal and democratic, many leaders of other Allied nations disagreed with them. Some of them demanded stiff penalties for Germany at the Paris Peace Conference, held a year after this speech was delivered.*

Gentlemen of the Congress:

Once more, as repeatedly before, the spokesmen of the Central Empires have indicated their desire to discuss the objects of the war and the possible basis of a general peace. Parleys have been in progress at Brest-Litovsk between Russian representatives and representatives of the Central Powers to which the attention of all the belligerents has been invited for the purpose of ascertaining whether it may be possible to extend these parleys into a general conference with regard to terms of peace and settlement.

The Russian representatives presented not only a perfectly definite statement of the principles upon which they would be willing to conclude peace, but also an equally definite program of the concrete application of those principles. The representatives of the Central Powers, on their part, presented an outline of settlement which, if much less definite, seemed susceptible of liberal interpretation until their specific program of practical terms was added. That program proposed no concessions at all, either to the sovereignty of Russia or to the preferences of the populations with whose fortunes it dealt, but meant, in a word, that the Central Empires were to keep every foot of territory their armed forces had occupied—every province, every city, every point of vantage as a permanent addition to their territories and their power.

It is a reasonable conjecture that the general principles of settlement which they at first suggested originated with the more liberal statesmen of Germany and Austria, the men who have begun to feel the force of their own peoples' thought and purpose, while the concrete terms of actual settlement came from the military leaders who have no thought but to keep what they have got. The negotiations have been broken off. The Russian representatives were sincere and in earnest. They cannot entertain such proposals of conquest and domination.

The whole incident is full of significance. It is also full of perplexity. With whom are the Russian representatives dealing? For whom are the representatives of the Central Empires speaking? Are they speaking for the majorities of their respective parliaments or for the minority parties, that military and imperialistic minority which has so far dominated their whole policy and controlled the affairs of Turkey and of the Balkan States which have felt obliged to become their associates in this war?

The Russian representatives have insisted, very justly, very wisely, and in the true spirit of modern democracy, that the conferences they have been holding with the Teutonic and Turkish statesmen should be held within open, not closed, doors, and all the world lies been audience, as was desired. To whom have we been listening, then? To those who speak the spirit and intention of the resolutions of the German Reichstag of the 9th of July last, the spirit and intention of the liberal leaders and parties of Germany, or to those who resist and defy that spirit and intention and insist upon conquest and subjugation? Or are we listening, in fact, to both, unreconciled and in open and hopeless contradiction? These are very serious and pregnant questions. Upon the answer to them depends the peace of the world.

But whatever the results of the parleys at Brest-Litovsk, whatever the confusions of counsel and of purpose in the utterances of the spokesmen of the Central Empires, they have again attempted to acquaint the world with their objects in the war and have again challenged their adversaries to say what their objects are and what sort of settlement they would deem just and satisfactory. There is no good reason why that challenge should not be responded to, and responded to with the utmost candour. We did not wait for it. Not once, but again and again we have laid our whole thought and purpose before the world, not in general terms only, but each time with sufficient definition to make it clear what sort of definite terms of settlement must necessarily spring out of them. Within the last week, Mr. Lloyd George has spoken with admirable candour and in admirable spirit for the people and Government of Great Britain.

There is no confusion of counsel among the adversaries of the Central Powers, no uncertainty of principle, no vagueness of detail. The only secrecy of counsel, the only lack of fearless frankness, the only failure to make definite statement of the objects of the war, lies with Germany and her allies. The issues of life and death hang upon these definitions. No statesman who has the least conception of his responsibility ought for a moment to permit himself to continue this tragical and appalling outpouring of blood and treasure unless he is sure beyond a peradventure that the objects of the vital sacrifice are part and parcel of the very life of society and that the people for whom he speaks think them right and imperative as he does.

There is, moreover, a voice calling for these definitions of principle and of purpose which is, it seems to me, more thrilling and more compelling than any of the many moving voices with which the troubled air of the world is filled. It is the voice of the Russian people. They are prostrate and all but helpless, it would seem, before the grim power of Germany, which has hitherto known no relenting and no pity. Their power, apparently, is shattered. And yet their soul is not subservient. They will not yield either in principle or in action. Their conception of what is right, of what is humane and honourable for them to accept, has been stated with a frankness, a largeness of view, a generosity of spirit, and a universal human sympathy which must challenge the admiration of every friend of mankind; and they have refused to compound their ideals or desert others that they themselves may be safe.

They call to us to say what it is that we desire, in what, if in anything, our purpose and our spirit differ from theirs; and I believe that the people of the United States would wish me to respond, with utter simplicity and frankness. Whether their present leaders believe it or not, it is our heartfelt desire and hope that some way may be opened whereby we may be privileged to assist the people of Russia to attain their utmost hope of liberty and ordered peace.

It will be our wish and purpose that the processes of peace, when they are begun, shall be absolutely open and that they shall involve and permit henceforth no secret understandings of any kind. The day of conquest and aggrandizement is gone by; so is also the day of secret covenants entered into in the interest of particular governments and likely at some unlooked-for moment to upset the peace of the world. It is this happy fact, now clear to the view of every public man whose thoughts do not still linger in an age that is dead and gone, which makes it possible for every nation whose purposes are consistent with justice and the peace of the world to avow now or at any other time the objects it has in view.

We entered this war because violations of right had occurred which touched us to the quick and made the life of our own people impossible unless they were corrected and the world secured once for all against their recurrence.

What we demand in this war, therefore, is nothing peculiar to ourselves. It is that the world be made fit and safe to live in; and particularly that it be made safe for every peace-loving nation which, like our own, wishes to live its own life, determine its own institutions, be assured of justice and fair dealing by the other peoples of the world, as against force and selfish aggression.

All the peoples of the world are in effect partners in this interest, and for our own part we see very clearly that unless justice be done to others it will not be done to us.

The program of the world's peace, therefore, is our programme; and that programme, the only possible programme, all we see it, is this:

1. Open covenants of peace must be arrived at, after which there will surely be no private international action or rulings of any kind, but diplomacy shall proceed always frankly and in the public view.
2. Absolute freedom of navigation upon the seas, outside territorial waters, alike in peace and in war, except as the seas may be closed in whole or in part by international action for the enforcement of international covenants.
3. The removal, so far as possible, of all economic barriers and the establishment of an equality of trade conditions among all the nations consenting to the peace and associating themselves for its maintenance.
4. Adequate guarantees given and taken that national armaments will be reduced to the lowest points consistent with domestic safety.
5. A free, open-minded, and absolutely impartial adjustment of all colonial claims, based upon a strict observance of the principle that in determining all such questions of sovereignty

the interests of the population concerned must have equal weight with the equitable claims of the government whose title is to be determined.

6. The evacuation of all Russian territory and such a settlement of all questions affecting Russia as will secure the best and freest cooperation of the other nations of the world in obtaining for her an unhampered and unembarrassed opportunity for the independent determination of her own political development and national policy, and assure her of a sincere welcome into the society of free nations under institutions of her own choosing; and, more than a welcome, assistance also of every kind that she may need and may herself desire. The treatment accorded Russia by her sister nations in the months to come will be the acid test of their good will, of their comprehension of her needs as distinguished from their own interests, and of their intelligent and unselfish sympathy.
7. Belgium, the whole world will agree, must be evacuated and restored, without any attempt to limit the sovereignty which she enjoys in common with all other free nations. No other single act will serve as this will serve to restore confidence among the nations in the laws which they have themselves set and determined for the government of their relations with one another. Without this healing act the whole structure and validity of international law is forever impaired.
8. All French territory should be freed and the invaded portions restored, and the wrong done to France by Prussia in 1871 in the matter of Alsace-Lorraine, which has unsettled the peace of the world for nearly fifty years, should be righted, in order that peace may once more be made secure in the interest of all.
9. A readjustment of the frontiers of Italy should be effected along clearly recognizable lines of nationality.
10. The peoples of Austria-Hungary, whose place among the nations we wish to see safeguarded and assured, should be accorded the freest opportunity of autonomous development.

11. Romania, Serbia, and Montenegro should be evacuated; occupied territories restored; Serbia accorded free and secure access to the sea; and the relations of the several Balkan states to one another determined by friendly counsel along historically established lines of allegiance and nationality; and international guarantees of the political and economic independence and territorial integrity of the several Balkan states should be entered into.
12. The Turkish portion of the present Ottoman Empire should be assured a secure sovereignty, but the other nationalities which are now under Turkish rule should be assured an undoubted security of life and an absolutely unmolested opportunity of autonomous development, and the Dardanelles should be permanently opened as a free passage to the ships and commerce of all nations under international guarantees.
13. An independent Polish state should be erected which should include the territories inhabited by indisputably Polish populations, which should be assured a free and secure access to the sea, and whose political and economic independence and territorial integrity should be guaranteed by international covenant.
14. A general association of nations must be formed under specific covenants for the purpose of affording mutual guarantees of political independence and territorial integrity to great and small states alike.

In regard to these essential rectifications of wrong and assertions of right, we feel ourselves to be intimate partners of all the governments and peoples associated together against the imperialists. We cannot be separated in interest or divided in purpose. We stand together until the end.

For such arrangements and covenants we are willing to fight and to continue to fight until they are achieved; but only because we wish the right to prevail and desire a just and stable peace such as can be secured only by removing the chief provocations to war, which this program does remove.

We have no jealousy of German greatness, and there is nothing in this program that impairs it. We grudge her no achievement or distinction of learning or of pacific enterprise such as have made her record very bright and very enviable. We do not wish to injure her or to block in any way her legitimate influence or power. We do not wish to fight her either with arms or with hostile arrangements of trade, if she is willing to associate herself with us and the other peace-loving nations of the world in covenants of justice and law and fair dealing.

We wish her only to accept a place of equality among the peoples of the world—the new world in which we now live—instead of a place of mastery.

Neither do we presume to suggest to her any alteration or modification of her institutions. But it is necessary, we must frankly say, and necessary as a preliminary to any intelligent dealings with her on our part, that we should know whom her spokesmen speak for when they speak to us, whether for the Reichstag majority or for the military party and the men whose creed is imperial domination.

We have spoken now, surely, in terms too concrete to admit of any further doubt or question. An evident principle runs through the whole program I have outlined. It is the principle of justice to all peoples and nationalities, and their right to live on equal terms of liberty and safety with one another, whether they be strong or weak.

Unless this principle be made its foundation, no part of the structure of international justice can stand. The people of the United States could act upon no other principle, and to the vindication of this principle they are ready to devote their lives, their honour, and everything that they possess. The moral climax of this, the culminating and final war for human liberty has come, and they are ready to put their own strength, their own highest purpose, their own integrity and devotion to the test.

# 16

## League of Nations: Final Address

★ ★ ★ ★ ★ ★ ★

Thomas Woodrow Wilson
Pueblo, Colorado, U.S.A.
25 September 1919

*Wilson, in his 'Fourteen Points' speech called for 'a general association of nations for the purpose of affording mutual guarantees of political independence and territorial integrity to great and small states alike.' Thus, League of Nations was formed. It was an organization made to assure international cooperation in maintaining peace and resolving disputes after World War I ended.*

*Wilson was an enthusiastic proponent of the League of Nations. But it failed to prevent the outbreak of World War II and, eventually, had to cease its operations.*

Mr. Chairman and fellow countrymen:

It is with a great deal of genuine pleasure that I find myself in Pueblo, and I feel it a compliment in this beautiful hall. One of the advantages of this hall, as I look about, is that you are not too far away from me, because there is nothing so reassuring to men who are trying to express the public sentiment as getting into real personal contact with their fellow citizens. I have gained a renewed impression as I have crossed the continent this time of the homogeneity of this great people to whom we belong. They come from many stocks, but they are all of one kind. They come from many origins, but they are all shot through with the same principles and desire the same righteous and honest things. I have received a more inspiring impression this time of the public opinion of the United States than it was ever my privilege to receive before.

The chief pleasure of my trip has been that it has nothing to do with my personal fortunes, that it has nothing to do with my personal reputation, that it has nothing to do with anything except great principles uttered by Americans of all sorts and of all parties which we are now trying to realize at this crisis of the affairs of the world. But there have been unpleasant impressions as well as pleasant impressions, my fellow citizens, as I have crossed the continent. I have perceived more and more that men have been busy creating an absolutely false impression of what the treaty of peace and the Covenant of the League of Nations contain and mean. I find, moreover, that there is an organized propaganda against the League of Nations and against the treaty proceeding from exactly the same sources that the organized propaganda proceeded from which threatened this country here and there with disloyalty, and I want to say—I cannot say too often—any man who carries a hyphen about with him carries a dagger that he is ready to plunge into the vitals of this Republic whenever he gets ready.

If I can catch any man with a hyphen in this great contest I will know that I have got an enemy of the Republic. My fellow citizens, it is only certain bodies of foreign sympathies, certain bodies of sympathy with foreign nations that are organized against this great document which the American representatives have brought back from Paris. Therefore, in order to clear away the mists, in order to remove the impressions, in order to check the falsehoods that have clustered around this great subject, I want to tell you a few very simple things about the treaty and the covenant.

Do not think of this treaty of peace as merely a settlement with Germany. It is that. It is a very severe settlement with Germany, but there is not anything in it that she did not earn. Indeed, she earned more than she can ever be able to pay for, and the punishment exacted of her is not a punishment greater than she can bear, and it is absolutely necessary in order that no other nation may ever plot such a thing against humanity and civilization. But the treaty is so much more than that. It is not merely a settlement with Germany; it is a readjustment of those great injustices which underlie the whole structure of European and Asiatic society. This is only the first of several treaties. They are all constructed upon the same plan. The Austrian treaty follows the same lines. The treaty with Hungary follows the same lines. The treaty with Bulgaria follows the same lines. The treaty with Turkey, when it is formulated, will follow the same lines.

What are those lines? They are based upon the purpose to see that every government dealt with in this great settlement is put in the hands of the people and taken out of the hands of coteries and of sovereigns, who had no right to rule over the people. It is a people's treaty, that accomplishes by a great sweep of practical justice the liberation of men who never could have liberated themselves, and the power of the most powerful nations has been devoted not to their aggrandizement but to the liberation of people whom they could have put under their control if they had chosen to do so. Not one foot of territory is demanded by submission to their authority is demanded by them. The men who sat around the table in Paris knew that the time had come when the people were no longer going to consent to live under masters, but were going to live the lives that they chose themselves, to live under such governments as they chose themselves to erect. That is the fundamental principle of this great settlement.

And we did not stop with that. We added a great international charter for the rights of labour. Reject this treaty, impair it, and this is the consequence of the labouring men of the world, that there is no international tribunal which can bring the moral judgments of the world to bear upon the great labour questions of the day. What we need to do with regard to the labour questions of the day, my fellow countrymen, is to lift them into the light, is to lift them out of the haze and distraction of passion, of hostility, out into the calm spaces where men look at things without passion.

The more men you get into a great discussion the more you exclude passion. Just as soon as the calm judgment of the worlds is directed upon the question of justice to labour, labour is going to have to forum such as it never was supplied with before, and men everywhere are going to see that the problem of labour is nothing more not less than the problem of the elevation of humanity. We must see that all the questions which have disturbed the world, all the questions which have disturbed the processes of industry, shall be brought out where men of all points of view, Men of all attitudes of mind, men of all kinds of experience, may contribute their part of the settlement of the great questions which we must settle and cannot ignore.

At the front of this great treaty is put the Covenant of the League of Nations. It will also be at the front of the Austrian treaty and the Hungarian treaty and the Bulgarian treaty and the treaty with Turkey. Every one of them will contain the Covenant of the League of Nations, because you cannot work any of them without the Covenant of the League of Nations. Unless you get the united, concerted purpose and power of the great governments of the world behind this settlement, it will fall down like a house of cards. There is only one power to put behinds the liberation of mankind, and that is the power of mankind. It is the power of the united moral forces of the world, and in the Covenant of the League of Nations the moral forces of the world are mobilized.

For what purpose? Reflect, my fellow citizens, that the membership of this great League is going to include all the great fighting nations of the world, as well as the weak ones. It is not for the present going to include Germany, but for the time being Germany is not a great fighting country. All the nations that have power that can be mobilized are going to be members of this League, including the United States.

And what do they unite for? They enter into a solemn promise to one another they will never use their power against one another for aggression; that they never will impair the territorial integrity of a neighbour; that they never will interfere with the political independence of a neighbour; that they will abide by the principle that great populations are entitled to determine their own destiny and that they will not interfere with that destiny; and that no matter what differences arise amongst them they will never resort to war without first having done one or other of two things—either submitted the matter of controversy to arbitration, in which case they agree to abide by the result without question, or submitted it to the consideration of the council of the League of Nations, laying before that council all the documents, all the facts, agreeing that the council can publish the documents, all the facts, agreeing that the council can publish the documents and the facts to the whole world, agreeing that there shall be six months allowed for the mature consideration of those facts by the council, and agreeing that at the expiration of the six months, even if they are not then ready to accept the advice of the council with regard to the settlement of the dispute, they will still not go to war for another three months.

In other words, they consent, no matter what happens, to submit every matter of difference between them to the judgment of mankind, and just so certainly as they do that, my fellow citizens, war will be in the far background, war will be pushed out of that foreground of terror in which it has kept the world for generation after generation, and men will know that there will be a calm time of deliberate counsel. The most dangerous thing for a bad cause is to expose it to the opinion of the world. The most certain way that you can prove that a man is mistaken is by letting all his neighbours know what he thinks, by letting all his neighbours know what he thinks, by letting all his neighbours discuss what he thinks, and if he is in the wrong you will notice that he will stay at home, he will not walk on the street. He will be afraid of the eyes of his neighbours. He will be afraid of their judgment of his character. He will know that his cause is lost unless he can sustain it by the arguments of right and of justice. The same law that applies to individuals applies to nations.

But, you say, 'We have heard that we might be at a disadvantage in the League of Nations.' Well, whoever told you that either was deliberately falsifying or he had not read the Covenant of the League of Nations. I leave him the choice. I want to give you a very simple account of the organization of the League of Nations and let you judge for yourselves. It is a very simple organization. The power of the League, or rather the activities of the league, lie in two bodies. There is the council, which consists of one representative from each of the principal allied and associated powers—that is to say, the United States, Great Britain, France, Italy, and Japan, along with four other representatives of smaller powers chosen out of the general body of the membership of the League.

The council is the source of very active policy of the League, and no active policy of the League can be adopted without a unanimous vote of the council. That is explicitly stated in the Covenant itself. Does it not evidently follow that the League of Nations can adopt no policy whatever without the consent of the United States? The affirmative vote of the representative of the United States is necessary in every case. Now, you have heard of six votes belonging to the British Empire. Those six votes are not in the council. They are in the assembly, and the interesting thing is that the assembly does not vote. I must qualify that statement a little, but essentially it is absolutely true. In every matter in which the assembly is given a voice, and there are only four or five, its vote does not count unless concurred in by the representatives of all the nations represented on the council, so the at there is no validity to any vote of the assembly unless in that vote also the representative of the United States concurs. That one vote of the United States is as big as the six votes of the British Empire. I am not jealous for advantage, my fellow citizens, but I think that is a perfectly safe situation. There is no validity in a vote, either by the council or the assembly, in which we do not concur. So much for the statements about the six votes for the British Empire.

Look at it in another aspect. The assembly is the talking body. The assembly was created in order that anybody that purposed anything wrong should be subjected to the awkward circumstance that everybody could talk about it. This is the great assembly in which all the things that are likely to disturb the peace of the world or the good understanding between nations are to be exposed to the general view, and I want to ask you if you think it was unjust, unjust to the United States, that speaking parts should be assigned to the several portions of the British Empire? Do you think it unjust that there should be some spokesman in debate for that fine little stout Republic down in the Pacific, New Zealand? Do you think it was unjust that Australia should be allowed to stand up and take part in the debate—Australia, from which we have learned some of the most useful progressive policies of modern time, a little nation only five million in a great continent, but counting for several times five in its activities and in its interest in liberal reform? Do you think it unjust that that little Republic down in South Africa, whose gallant resistance to being subjected to any outside authority at all we admired for so many months and whose fortunes we followed with such interest, should have a speaking part? Great Britain obliged South Africa to submit to her sovereignty, but she immediately after that felt that it was convenient and right to hand the whole self-government of that colony over to the very men whom she had beaten.

The representatives of South Africa in Paris were two of the most distinguished generals of the Boer Army, two of the realest men I ever met, two men that could talk sober counsel and wise advice, along with the best statesmen in Europe. To exclude Gen. Botha and Gen. Smuts from the right to stand up in the parliament of the world and say something concerning the affairs of mankind would be absurd. And what about Canada? Is not Canada a good neighbour? I ask you is not Canada more likely to agree with the United States than with Great Britain? Canada has a speaking part. And then, for the first time in the history of the world, that great voiceless multitude, that throng hundreds of millions strong in India, has a voice, and I want to testify that some of the wisest and most dignified figures in the peace conference at Paris came from India, men who seemed to carry in their minds an older wisdom than the rest of us had, whose traditions ran back into so many of the unhappy fortunes of mankind that they seemed very useful counsellors as to how some ray of hope and some prospect of happiness could be opened to its people. I for my part have no jealousy whatever of those five speaking parts in the assembly. Those speaking parts cannot translate themselves into five votes that can in any matter override the voice and purpose of the United States.

Let us sweep aside all this language of jealousy. Let us be big enough to know the facts and to welcome the facts, because the facts are based upon the principle that America has always fought for, namely, the equality of self-governing peoples, whether they were big or little—not counting men, but counting rights, not counting representation, but counting the purpose of that representation. When you hear an opinion quoted you do not count the number of persons who hold it; you ask, 'Who said that?' You weigh opinions, you do not count them, and the beauty of all democracies is that every voice can be heard, every voice can have its effect, every voice can contribute to the general judgment that is finally arrived at. That is the object of democracy. Let us accept what America has always fought for, and accept it with pride that America showed the way and made the proposal. I do not mean that America made the proposal in this particular instance; I mean that the principle was an American principle, proposed by America.

When you come to the heart of the Covenant, my fellow citizens, you will find it in article ten, and I am very much interested to know that the other things have been blown away like bubbles. There is nothing in the other contentions with regard to the league of nations, but there is something in article ten that you ought to realize and ought to accept or reject. Article ten is the heart of the whole matter. What is article ten? I never am certain that I can from memory give a literal repetition of its language, but I am sure that I can give an exact interpretation of its meaning. Article ten provides that every member of the league covenants to respect and preserve the territorial integrity and existing political independence of every other member of the league as against external aggression. Not against internal disturbance. There was not a man at that table who did not admit the sacredness of the right of self-determination, the sacredness of the right of any body of people to say that they would not continue to live under the government they were then living under, and under article eleven of the Covenant they are given a place to say whether they will live under it or not. For following article ten is article eleven, which makes it the right of any member of the League at any time to call attention to anything, anywhere, that is likely to disturb the peace of the world or the good understanding between nations upon which the peace of the world depends. I want to give you an illustration of what that would mean.

You have heard a great deal—something that was true and a great deal that was false—about the provision of the treaty which hands over to Japan the rights which Germany enjoyed in the Province of Shantung in China. In the first place, Germany did not enjoy any rights there that other nations had not already claimed. For my part, my judgment, my moral judgment, is against the whole set of concessions. They were all of them unjust to China, they ought never to have been exacted, they were all exacted by duress, from a great body of thoughtful and ancient and helpless people. There never was any right in any of them. Thank God, America never asked for any, never dreamed of asking for any.

But when Germany got this concession in 1898, the Government of the United States made no protest whatever. That was not because the Government of the United States was not in the hands of thigh-minded and conscientious men. It was. William McKinley was president and John Hay was secretary of state—as safe hands to leave the honour of the United States in as any that you can cite. They made no protest because the state of international law at that time was that it was none of their business unless they could show that the interests of the United States were affected, and the only think that they could show with regard to the interests of the United States was that Germany might close the doors of Shantung Province against the trade of the United States.

They, therefore, demanded and obtained promises that we could continue to sell merchandise in Shantung. Immediately following that concession to Germany there was a concession to Russia of the same sort, of Port Arthur, and Port Arthur was handed over subsequently to Japan on the very territory of the United States. Don't you remember that when Russia and Japan got into war with one another the war was brought to a confusion by a treaty written at Portsmouth, N.H., and in that treaty without the slightest intimation from any authoritative sources in America that the Government of the United States had any objection, Port Arthur, Chinese territory, was turned over to Japan? I want you distinctly to understand that there is no thought of criticism in my mind. I am expounding to you a state of international law.

Now, read articles ten and eleven. You will see that international law is revolutionized by putting morals into it. Article ten says that no member of the League, and that includes all these nations that have demanded these things unjustly of China, shall impair the territorial integrity or the political independence of any other member of the League. China is going to be a member of the League. Article eleven says that nay member of the League can call attention to anything that is likely to disturb the peace of the world or the good understanding between nations, and China is for the first time in the history of mankind afforded a standing before the jury of the world. I, for my part, have a profound sympathy for China, and I am proud to have taken part in an arrangement which promises the protection of the world to the rights of China. The whole atmosphere of the world is changed by a thing like that, my fellow citizens. The whole international practice of the world is revolutionized.

But, you will say, 'What is the second sentence of article ten? That is what gives very disturbing thoughts.' The second sentence is that the council of the League shall advise what steps, if any, are necessary to carry out the guaranty of the first sentence, namely, that the members will respect and preserve the territorial integrity and political independence of the other members. I do not know any other meaning for the word 'advise' except 'advise.' The council advises, and it cannot advise without the vote of the United States. Why gentlemen should fear that the Congress of the United States would be advised to do something that it did not want to do I frankly cannot imagine, because they cannot even be advised to do anything unless their own representative has participated in the advice.

It may be that that will impair somewhat the vigour of the League, but, nevertheless, the fact is so, that we are not obliged to take any advice except our own, which to any man who wants to go his own course is a very satisfactory state of affairs. Every man regards his own advice as best, and I dare say every man mixes his own advice with some thought of his own interest. Whether we use it wisely or unwisely, we can use the vote of the United States to make impossible drawing the United States into any enterprise that she does not care to be drawn into.

Yet article ten strikes at the taproot of war. Article ten is a statement that the very things that have always been sought in imperialistic wars are henceforth foregone by every ambitious nation in the world. I would have felt very much disturbed if, sitting at the peace table in Paris, I had supposed that I was expounding my own ideas. Whether you believe it or not, I know the relative size of my own ideas; I know how they stand related in bulk and proportion to the moral judgments of my fellow countrymen, and I proposed nothing whatever at the peace table at Paris that I had not sufficiently certain knowledge embodied the moral judgment of the citizens of the United States. I had gone over there with, so to say, explicit instruction. Don't you remember that we laid down fourteen points which should contain the principles of the settlement? They were not my points. In every one of them I was conscientiously trying to read the thought of the people of the United States, and after I uttered those points I had every assurance given me that could be given me that they did speak the moral judgment of the United States and not my single judgment.

Then when it came to that critical period just a little less than a year ago, when it was evident that the war was coming to its critical end, all the nations engaged in the war accepted those fourteen principles explicitly as the basis of the armistice and the basis of the peace. In those circumstances I crossed the ocean under bond to my own people and to the other governments with which I was dealing. The whole specification of the method of settlement was written down and accepted beforehand, and we were architects building on those specifications. It reassures me and fortifies my position to find how before I went over men whose judgment the United States has often trusted were of exactly the same opinion that I went abroad to express. Here is something I want to read from Theodore Roosevelt:

'The one effective move for obtaining peace is by an agreement among all the great powers in which each should pledge itself no only to abide by the decisions of a common tribunal but to back its decisions by force. The great civilized nations should combine by solemn agreement in a great would league for the peace of righteousness; a court should be established. A changed and amplified Hague court would meet the requirements, composed of representatives from each nation, whose representatives are sworn to act as judges in each case and not in a representative capacity.'

Now there is article ten. He goes on and says this: 'The nations should agree on certain rights that should not be questioned, such as territorial integrity, their right to deal with their domestic affairs, and with such matters as whom they should admit to citizenship. All such guarantee each of their number in possession of these rights.'

Now, the other specification is the Covenant. The Covenant in another portion guarantees to the members the independent control of their domestic questions. There is not a leg of these gentlemen to stand on when they say that the interests of the United States are not safeguarded in the very points where we are most sensitive. You do not need to be told again that the Covenant expressly says that nothing in this covenant shall be construed as affecting the validity of the Monroe doctrine for example. You could not be more explicit than that. And every point of interest is covered, partly for one very interesting reason. This is not the first time that the Foreign Relations Committee of the Senate of the United States has read and considered this covenant. I bought it to this country in March last in a tentative, provisional form, in practically the form that it now has, with the exception of certain additions which I shall mention immediately. I asked the Foreign Relations Committees of both Houses to come to the White House and we spent a long evening in the frankest discussion of every portion that they wished to discuss. They made certain specific suggestions as to what should be contained in this document when it was to be revised. I carried those suggestions to Paris, and every one of them was adopted. What more could I have done? What more could have been obtained? The very matters upon which these gentlemen were most concerned were, the right of withdrawal, which is now expressly stated; the safeguarding of the Monroe doctrine, which is now accomplished; the exclusion from action by the League of domestic questions, which is now accomplished. All along the line, every suggestion of the United States was adopted after the Covenant had been drawn up in its first form and had been published of the criticism of the world. There is a very true sense in which I can say this is a tested American document.

I am dwelling upon these points, my fellow citizens, in spite of the fact that I dare say to most of you they are perfectly well know, because in order to meet the present situation we have go to know what we are dealing with. We are not dealing with the kind of document which this is represented by some gentlemen to be; and inasmuch as we are dealing with a document simon-pure in respect of the very principles we have professed and lived up to, we have got to do one or other of two things—we have go to adopt it or reject it. There is no middle course. You cannot go in on a special-privilege basis of your own.

I take it that you are too proud to ask to be exempted from responsibilities which the other members of the League will carry. We go in upon equal terms or we do not go in at all; and if we do not go in, my fellow citizens, think of the tragedy of that result—the only sufficient guaranty to the peace of the world withheld! Ourselves drawn apart with that dangerous pride which means that we shall be ready to take care of ourselves, and that means that we shall maintain great standing armies and an irresistible envy; that means we shall have the organization of a military nation; that means we shall have a general staff, with the kind of power that the general staff of Germany had; to mobilize this great manhood of the Nation when it pleases, all the energy of our young men drawn into the thought and preparation for war. What of our pledges to the men that lie dead in France? We said that they went over there not to prove the prowess of America or her readiness for another war but to see to tit hat there never was such a war again. It always seems to make it difficult for me to say anything my fellow citizens, when I think of my clients in this case. My clients are the children; my clients are the next generation. They do not know what promises and bonds I undertook when I ordered the armies of the United States to the soil of France, but I know, and I intend to redeem my pledges to the children; they shall not be sent upon a similar errand.

Again and again, my fellow citizens, mothers who lost their sons in France have come to me and, taking my hand, have shed tears upon it not only, but they added, 'God bless you, Mr. President!' Why, my fellow citizens, should they pray God to bless me? I advised the Congress of the United States to create the situation that led to the death of their sons. I ordered their sons overseas. I consented to their sons being put in the most difficult parts of the battle line, where death was certain, as in the impenetrable difficulties of the forest of Argonne. Why should they weep upon my hand and call down the blessings of God upon me? Because they believe that their boys died for something that vastly transcends any of the immediate and palpable objects of the war. They believe, and they rightly believe, that their sons saved the liberty of the world. They believe that wrapped up with the liberty of the world is the continuous protection of that liberty by the concerted powers of all civilized people. They believe that this sacrifice was made in order that other sons should not be called upon for a similar gift—the gift of life, the gift of all that died—and if we did not see this thing through, if we fulfilled the dearest present wish of Germany and now dissociated ourselves from those alongside whom we fought in the world, would not something of the halo go away from the gun over the mantelpiece, or the sword? Would not the old uniform lose something of its significance? These men were crusaders. They were not going forth to prove the might of the United States. They were going forth to prove the might of justice and right, and all the world accepted them as crusaders, and their transcendent achievement has made all the world believe in America as it believes in no other nation organized in the modern world. There seem to me to stand between us and the rejection or qualification of this treaty the serried ranks of those boys in khaki, not only these boys who came home, but those dear ghosts that still deploy upon the fields of France.

My friends, on last Decoration day I went on a beautiful hillside near Paris, where was located the cemetery of Suresnes, a cemetery given over to the burial of the American dead. Behind me on the slopes was rank upon rank of living American soldiers, and lying before me upon the levels of the plain was rank upon rank of departed American soldiers. Right by the side of the stand where I spoke there was a little group of French women who had adopted those graves, had made themselves mothers of those dear ghosts by putting flowers every day upon those graves, taking them as their own sons, their own beloved, because they had died in the same cause—France was free and the world was free because America had come! I wish some men in public life who are now opposing the settlement for which these men died could visit such a spot as that. I wish that the thought that comes out of those graves could penetrate their consciousness. I wish that they could feel the moral obligation that rests upon us not to go back on those boys, but to see the thing through, to see it through to the end and make good their redemption of the world. For nothing less depends upon this decision, nothing less than liberation and salvation of the world.

You will say, 'Is the League an absolute guaranty against war?' No; I do not know any absolute guaranty against the errors of human judgment or the violence of human passion, but I tell you this: With a cooling space of nine months for human passion, not much of it will keep hot. I had a couple of friends who were in the habit of losing their tempers, and when they lost their tempers they were in the habit of using very unparliamentary language. Some of their friends induced them to make a promise that they never would swear inside the town limits. When the impulse next came upon them, they took a streetcar to go out of town to swear, and by the time they got out of town they did not want to swear. They came back convinced that they were just what they were, a couple of unspeakable fools, and the habit of getting angry and of swearing suffered great inroads upon it by that experience. Now, illustrating the great by the small, that is true of the passion s of nations. It is true of the passions of men however you combine them. Give them space to cool off. I ask you this: If it is not an absolute insurance against war, do you want no insurance at all? Do you want nothing? Do you want not only no probability that war will not recur, but the probability that it will recur? The arrangements of justice do not stand of themselves, my fellow citizens. The arrangements of this treat are just, but they need the support of the combined power of the great nations of the world. And they will have that support.

Now that the mists of this great question have cleared away, I believe that men will see the truth, eye to eye and face to face.

There is one thing that the American people always rise to and extend their hand to, and that is the truth of justice and of liberty and of peace. We have accepted the truth and we are going to be led by it, and it is going to lead us, and through us the world, out into pastures of quietness and peace such as the world never dreamed of before.

*Note: The ineffective League of Nations was replaced by the United Nations, founded at the end of World War II.*

# 17

## The Only Thing We Have to Fear Is Fear Itself

★ ★ ★ ★ ★ ★ ★

Franklin Roosevelt
Washington, D.C., U.S.A.
4 March 1933

*Franklin Delano Roosevelt led America through two of the greatest crisis of the twentieth century—the Great Depression and World War II. Between 1929 and 1933, the G.D.P. had declined by thirty per cent, farm prices went down by fifty-one per cent, and stocks had lost eighty-five per cent of their value.*

*At a time when the American economy was spiralling down, Roosevelt delivered his first inaugural address. He declared a 'war' against depression and appeased an anxious nation by reminding it that though the economy had fallen and the people were being plagued by unemployment, 'the only thing we have to fear is fear itself.'*

President Hoover, Mr. Chief Justice, my friends: This is a day of national consecration, and I am certain that my fellow Americans expect that on my induction into the Presidency I will address them with a candour and a decision which the present situation of our Nation impels. This is pre-eminently the time to speak the truth, the whole truth, frankly and boldly. Nor need we shrink from honestly facing conditions in our country today. This great Nation will endure as it has endured, will revive and will prosper. So, first of all, let me assert my firm belief that the only thing we have to fear is fear itself—nameless, unreasoning, unjustified terror which paralyzes needed efforts to convert retreat into advance. In every dark hour of our national life a leadership of frankness and vigour has met with that understanding and support of the people themselves which is essential to victory. I am convinced that you will again give that support to leadership in these critical days.

In such a spirit on my part and on yours we face our common difficulties. They concern, thank God, only material things. Values have shrunken to fantastic levels; taxes have risen; our ability to pay has fallen; government of all kinds is faced by serious curtailment of income; the means of exchange are frozen in the currents of trade; the withered leaves of industrial enterprise lie on every side; farmers find no markets for their produce; the savings of many years in thousands of families are gone.

More important, a host of unemployed citizens face the grim problem of existence, and an equally great number toil with little return. Only a foolish optimist can deny the dark realities of the moment.

Yet our distress comes from no failure of substance. We are stricken by no plague of locusts. Compared with the perils which our forefathers conquered because they believed and were not afraid, we have still much to be thankful for. Nature still offers her bounty and human efforts have multiplied it. Plenty is at our doorstep, but a generous use of it languishes in the very sight of the supply. Primarily this is because the rulers of the exchange of mankind's goods have failed, through their own stubbornness and their own incompetence, have admitted their failure, and abdicated. Practices of the unscrupulous money changers stand indicted in the court of public opinion, rejected by the hearts and minds of men.

True they have tried, but their efforts have been cast in the pattern of an outworn tradition. Faced by failure of credit they have proposed only the lending of more money. Stripped of the lure of profit by which to induce our people to follow their false leadership, they have resorted to exhortations, pleading tearfully for restored confidence. They know only the rules of a generation of self-seekers. They have no vision, and when there is no vision the people perish.

The money changers have fled from their high seats in the temple of our civilization. We may now restore that temple to the ancient truths. The measure of the restoration lies in the extent to which we apply social values more noble than mere monetary profit.

Happiness lies not in the mere possession of money; it lies in the joy of achievement, in the thrill of creative effort. The joy and moral stimulation of work no longer must be forgotten in the mad chase of evanescent profits. These dark days will be worth all they cost us if they teach us that our true destiny is not to be ministered unto but to minister to ourselves and to our fellow men.

Recognition of the falsity of material wealth as the standard of success goes hand in hand with the abandonment of the false belief that public office and high political position are to be valued only by the standards of pride of place and personal profit; and there must be an end to a conduct in banking and in business which too often has given to a sacred trust the likeness of callous and selfish wrongdoing. Small wonder that confidence languishes, for it thrives only on honesty, on honour, on the sacredness of obligations, on faithful protection, on unselfish performance; without them it cannot live.

Restoration calls, however, not for changes in ethics alone. This Nation asks for action, and action now.

Our greatest primary task is to put people to work. This is no unsolvable problem if we face it wisely and courageously. It can be accomplished in part by direct recruiting by the government itself, treating the task as we would treat the emergency of a war, but at the same time, through this employment, accomplishing greatly needed projects to stimulate and reorganize the use of our natural resources.

Hand in hand with this we must frankly recognize the overbalance of population in our industrial centres and, by engaging on a national scale in a redistribution, endeavour to provide a better use of the land for those best fitted for the land. The task can be helped by definite efforts to raise the values of agricultural products and with this the power to purchase the output of our cities. It can be helped by preventing realistically the tragedy of the growing loss through foreclosure of our small homes and our farms. It can be helped by insistence that the Federal, State, and local governments act forthwith on the demand that their cost be drastically reduced. It can be helped by the unifying of relief activities which today are often scattered, uneconomical, and unequal. It can be helped by national planning for and supervision of all forms of transportation and of communications and other utilities which have a definitely public character. There are many ways in which it can be helped, but it can never be helped merely by talking about it. We must act and act quickly.

Finally, in our progress toward a resumption of work we require two safeguards against a return of the evils of the old order; there must be a strict supervision of all banking and credits and investments; there must be an end to speculation with other people's money, and there must be provision for an adequate but sound currency.

There are the lines of attack. I shall presently urge upon a new Congress in special session detailed measures for their fulfilment, and I shall seek the immediate assistance of the several states.

Through this program of action we address ourselves to putting our own national house in order and making income balance outgo. Our international trade relations, though vastly important, are in point of time and necessity secondary to the establishment of a sound national economy. I favour as a practical policy the putting of first things first. I shall spare no effort to restore world trade by international economic readjustment, but the emergency at home cannot wait on that accomplishment.

The basic thought that guides these specific means of national recovery is not narrowly nationalistic. It is the insistence, as a first consideration, upon the interdependence of the various elements in all parts of the United States—a recognition of the old and permanently important manifestation of the American spirit of the pioneer. It is the way to recovery. It is the immediate way. It is the strongest assurance that the recovery will endure.

In the field of world policy I would dedicate this Nation to the policy of the good neighbour—the neighbour who resolutely respects himself and, because he does so, respects the rights of others—the neighbour who respects his obligations and respects the sanctity of his agreements in and with a world of neighbours.

If I read the temper of our people correctly, we now realize as we have never realized before our interdependence on each other; that we cannot merely take but we must give as well; that if we are to go forward, we must move as a trained and loyal army willing to sacrifice for the good of a common discipline, because without such discipline no progress is made, no leadership becomes effective. We are, I know, ready and willing to submit our lives and property to such discipline, because it makes possible a leadership which aims at a larger good. This I propose to offer, pledging that the larger purposes will bind upon us all as a sacred obligation with a unity of duty hitherto evoked only in time of armed strife.

With this pledge taken, I assume unhesitatingly the leadership of this great army of our people dedicated to a disciplined attack upon our common problems.

Action in this image and to this end is feasible under the form of government which we have inherited from our ancestors. Our Constitution is so simple and practical that it is possible always to meet extraordinary needs by changes in emphasis and arrangement without loss of essential form. That is why our constitutional system has proved itself the most superbly enduring political mechanism the modern world has produced. It has met every stress of vast expansion of territory, of foreign wars, of bitter internal strife, of world relations.

It is to be hoped that the normal balance of executive and legislative authority may be wholly adequate to meet the unprecedented task before us. But it may be that an unprecedented demand and need for undelayed action may call for temporary departure from that normal balance of public procedure.

I am prepared under my constitutional duty to recommend the measures that a stricken nation in the midst of a stricken world may require. These measures, or such other measures as the Congress may build out of its experience and wisdom, I shall seek, within my constitutional authority, to bring to speedy adoption.

But in the event that the Congress shall fail to take one of these two courses, and in the event that the national emergency is still critical, I shall not evade the clear course of duty that will then confront me. I shall ask the Congress for the one remaining instrument to meet the crisis—broad executive power to wage a war against the emergency, as great as the power that would be given to me if we were in fact invaded by a foreign foe.

For the trust reposed in me I will return the courage and the devotion that befit the time. I can do no less.

We face the arduous days that lie before us in the warm courage of the national unity; with the clear consciousness of seeking old and precious moral values; with the clean satisfaction that comes from the stern performance of duty by old and young alike. We aim at the assurance of a rounded and permanent national life.

We do not distrust the future of essential democracy. The people of the United States have not failed. In their need they have registered a mandate that they want direct, vigorous action. They have asked for discipline and direction under leadership. They have made me the present instrument of their wishes. In the spirit of the gift I take it.

In this dedication of a Nation we humbly ask the blessing of God. May He protect each and every one of us. May He guide me in the days to come.

*Note: Roosevelt added the famous line 'the only thing we have to fear it fear itself' a day before giving his inaugural address.*

# 18

## First Fireside Chat

★ ★ ★ ★ ★ ★ ★

Franklin Roosevelt
Washington, D.C., U.S.A.
12 March 1933

*Roosevelt addressed the Americans in as many as twenty-eight speeches. Broadcasted over the radio between 1933 to 1944, they came to be known as fireside chats. He discussed varied things in these chats—from economic policies to fascism.*

*The country was reeling from the Great Depression which had started in 1929. Roosevelt, in this speech, explained his decision to close all banks. After the stock market crashed, bank investors worried about an impending financial disaster. The situation was panic-inducing to the public, which would then rush to cash out the deposits. Roosevelt, thus, closed the banks till the situation had stabilized.*

My friends:

I want to talk for a few minutes with the people of the United States about banking—with the comparatively few who understand the mechanics of banking but more particularly with the overwhelming majority who use banks for the making of deposits and the drawing of checks. I want to tell you what has been done in the last few days, why it was done, and what the next steps are going to be. I recognize that the many proclamations from State capitols and from Washington, the legislation, the Treasury regulations, etc., couched for the most part in banking and legal terms, should be explained for the benefit of the average citizen. I owe this in particular because of the fortitude and good temper with which everybody has accepted the inconvenience and hardships of the banking holiday. I know that when you understand what we in Washington have been about I shall continue to have your cooperation as fully as I have had your sympathy and help during the past week.

First of all, let me state the simple fact that when you deposit money in a bank the bank does not put the money into a safe deposit vault. It invests your money in many different forms of credit—bonds, commercial paper, mortgages and many other kinds of loans. In other words, the bank puts your money to work to keep the wheels of industry and of agriculture turning around. A comparatively small part of the money you put into the bank is kept in currency—an amount which in normal times is wholly sufficient to cover the cash needs of the average citizen. In other words, the total amount of all the currency in the country is only a small fraction of the total deposits in all of the banks.

What, then, happened during the last few days of February and the first few days of March? Because of undermined confidence on the part of the public, there was a general rush by a large portion of our population to turn bank deposits into currency or gold—a rush so great that the soundest banks could not get enough currency to meet the demand. The reason for this was that on the spur of the moment it was, of course, impossible to sell perfectly sound assets of a bank and convert them into cash except at panic prices far below their real value.

By the afternoon of March 3rd—a week ago last Friday—scarcely a bank in the country was open to do business. Proclamations temporarily closing them in whole or in part had been issued by the Governors in almost all the States.

It was then that I issued the proclamation providing for the nationwide bank holiday, and this was the first step in the government's reconstruction of our financial and economic fabric.

The second step was the legislation promptly and patriotically passed by the Congress confirming my proclamation and broadening my powers so that it became possible in view of the requirement of time to extend the holiday and lift the ban of that holiday gradually. This law also gave authority to develop a program of rehabilitation of our banking facilities. I want to tell our citizens in every part of the Nation that the national Congress—Republicans and Democrats alike—showed by this action a devotion to public welfare and a realization of the emergency and the necessity for speed that it is difficult to match in our history.

The third stage has been the series of regulations permitting the banks to continue their functions to take care of the distribution of food and household necessities and the payment of payrolls.

This bank holiday, while resulting in many cases in great inconvenience, is affording us the opportunity to supply the currency necessary to meet the situation. No sound bank is a dollar worse off than it was when it closed its doors last Monday. Neither is any bank which may turn out not to be in a position for immediate opening. The new law allows the twelve Federal Reserve Banks to issue additional currency on good assets and thus the banks which reopen will be able to meet every legitimate call. The new currency is being sent out by the Bureau of Engraving and Printing in large volume to every part of the country. It is sound currency because it is backed by actual, good assets.

A question you will ask is this: why are all the banks not to be reopened at the same time? The answer is simple. Your government does not intend that the history of the past few years shall be repeated. We do not want and will not have another epidemic of bank failures.

As a result, we start tomorrow, Monday, with the opening of banks in the twelve Federal Reserve Bank cities—those banks which on first examination by the Treasury have already been found to be all right. This will be followed on Tuesday by the resumption of all their functions by banks already found to be sound in cities where there are recognized clearing houses. That means about two hundred and fifty cities of the United States.

On Wednesday and succeeding days banks in smaller places all through the country will resume business, subject, of course, to the government's physical ability to complete its survey. It is necessary that the reopening of banks be extended over a period in order to permit the banks to make applications for necessary loans, to obtain currency needed to meet their requirements and to enable the government to make common sense check-ups.

Let me make it clear to you that if your bank does not open the first day you are by no means justified in believing that it will not open. A bank that opens on one of the subsequent days is in exactly the same status as the bank that opens tomorrow. I know that many people are worrying about State banks not members of the Federal Reserve System. These banks can and will receive assistance from member banks and from the Reconstruction Finance Corporation. These State banks are following the same course as the National banks except that they get their licenses to resume business from the State authorities, and these authorities have been asked by the Secretary of the Treasury to permit their good banks to open up on the same schedule as the national banks. I am confident that the State Banking Departments will be as careful as the national government in the policy relating to the opening of banks and will follow the same broad policy.

It is possible that when the banks resume a very few people who have not recovered from their fear may again begin withdrawals. Let me make it clear that the banks will take care of all needs—and it is my belief that hoarding during the past week has become an exceedingly unfashionable pastime. It needs no prophet to tell you that when the people find that they can get their money—that they can get it when they want it for all legitimate purposes—the phantom of fear will soon be laid. People will again be glad to have their money where it will be safely taken care of and where they can use it conveniently at any time. I can assure you that it is safer to keep your money in a reopened bank than under the mattress.

The success of our whole great national program depends, of course, upon the cooperation of the public—on its intelligent support and use of a reliable system.

Remember that the essential accomplishment of the new legislation is that it makes it possible for banks more readily to convert their assets into cash than was the case before. More liberal provision has been made for banks to borrow on these assets at the Reserve Banks and more liberal provision has also been made for issuing currency on the security of these good assets. This currency is not fiat currency. It is issued only on adequate security, and every good bank has an abundance of such security.

One more point before I close. There will be, of course, some banks unable to reopen without being reorganized. The new law allows the government to assist in making these reorganizations quickly and effectively and even allows the government to subscribe to at least a part of new capital which may be required. I hope you can see from this elemental recital of what your government is doing that there is nothing complex, or radical, in the process.

We had a bad banking situation. Some of our bankers had shown themselves either incompetent or dishonest in their handling of the people's funds. They had used the money entrusted to them in speculations and unwise loans. This was, of course, not true in the vast majority of our banks, but it was true in enough of them to shock the people for a time into a sense of insecurity and to put them into a frame of mind where they did not differentiate, but seemed to assume that the acts of a comparative few had tainted them all. It was the government's job to straighten out this situation and do it as quickly as possible. And the job is being performed.

I do not promise you that every bank will be reopened or that individual losses will not be suffered, but there will be no losses that possibly could be avoided; and there would have been more and greater losses had we continued to drift. I can even promise you salvation for some at least of the sorely pressed banks. We shall be engaged not merely in reopening sound banks but in the creation of sound banks through reorganization.

It has been wonderful to me to catch the note of confidence from all over the country. I can never be sufficiently grateful to the people for the loyal support they have given me in their acceptance of the judgment that has dictated our course, even though all our processes may not have seemed clear to them.

After all, there is an element in the readjustment of our financial system more important than currency, more important than gold, and that is the confidence of the people. Confidence and courage are the essentials of success in carrying out our plan. You people must have faith; you must not be stampeded by rumours or guesses. Let us unite in banishing fear. We have provided the machinery to restore our financial system; it is up to you to support and make it work.

It is your problem no less than it is mine. Together we cannot fail.

# 19

## The Arsenal of Democracy

★ ★ ★ ★ ★ ★ ★

Franklin Roosevelt
Washington, D.C., U.S.A.
29 December 1940

*Roosevelt had declared that America would not go to war on the Axis powers unless it was attacked. During World War II, Britain struggled to fight off Germany and turned to the U.S. for the provision of weapons. Roosevelt offered to help them fight by giving them military supplies while America stayed out of the actual fighting. In this speech given on a radio broadcast, Roosevelt implored the American public to become an 'arsenal of democracy' as though their own country was at war.*

My friends:

This is not a fireside chat on war. It is a talk on national security; because the nub of the whole purpose of your president is to keep you now, and your children later, and your grandchildren much later, out of a last-ditch war for the preservation of American independence and all the things that American independence means to you and to me and to ours.

Tonight, in the presence of a world crisis, my mind goes back eight years to a night in the midst of a domestic crisis. It was a time when the wheels of American industry were grinding to a full stop, when the whole banking system of our country had ceased to function. I well remember that while I sat in my study in the White House, preparing to talk with the people of the United States, I had before my eyes the picture of all those Americans with whom I was talking. I saw the workmen in the mills, the mines, the factories; the girl behind the counter; the small shopkeeper; the farmer doing his spring ploughing; the widows and the old men wondering about their life's savings. I tried to convey to the great mass of American people what the banking crisis meant to them in their daily lives.

Tonight, I want to do the same thing, with the same people, in this new crisis which faces America. We met the issue of 1933 with courage and realism. We face this new crisis—this new threat to the security of our nation—with the same courage and realism. Never before since Jamestown and Plymouth Rock has our American civilization been in such danger as now. For, on 27th September 1940—this year—by an agreement signed in Berlin, three powerful nations, two in Europe and one in Asia, joined themselves together in the threat that if the United States of America interfered with or blocked the expansion program of these three nations—a program aimed at world control—they would unite in ultimate action against the United States.

The Nazi masters of Germany have made it clear that they intend not only to dominate all life and thought in their own country, but also to enslave the whole of Europe, and then to use the resources of Europe to dominate the rest of the world. It was only three weeks ago that their leader stated this: 'There are two worlds that stand opposed to each other.' And then in defiant reply to his opponents, he said this: 'Others are correct when they say: 'With this world we cannot ever reconcile ourselves' I can beat any other power in the world.' So said the leader of the Nazis.

In other words, the Axis not merely admits but the Axis proclaims that there can be no ultimate peace between their philosophy—their philosophy of government—and our philosophy of government. In view of the nature of this undeniable threat, it can be asserted, properly and categorically, that the United States has no right or reason to encourage talk of peace, until the day shall come when there is a clear intention on the part of the aggressor nations to abandon all thought of dominating or conquering the world.

At this moment, the forces of the States that are leagued against all peoples who live in freedom, are being held away from our shores. The Germans and the Italians are being blocked on the other side of the Atlantic by the British, and by the Greeks, and by thousands of soldiers and sailors who were able to escape from subjugated countries. In Asia, the Japanese are being engaged by the Chinese nation in another great defence. In the Pacific Ocean is our fleet.

Some of our people like to believe that wars in Europe and in Asia are of no concern to us. But it is a matter of most vital concern to us that European and Asiatic war-makers should not gain control of the oceans which lead to this hemisphere. One hundred and seventeen years ago, the Monroe Doctrine was conceived by our government as a measure of defence in the face of a threat against this hemisphere by an alliance in Continental Europe. Thereafter, we stood guard in the Atlantic, with the British as neighbours. There was no treaty. There was no 'unwritten agreement.' And yet, there was the feeling, proven correct by history, that we as neighbours could settle any disputes in peaceful fashion. And the fact is that during the whole of this time the Western Hemisphere has remained free from aggression from Europe or from Asia.

Does anyone seriously believe that we need to fear attack anywhere in the Americas while a free Britain remains our most powerful naval neighbour in the Atlantic? Does anyone seriously believe, on the other hand, that we could rest easy if the Axis powers were our neighbours there? If Great Britain goes down, the Axis powers will control the continents of Europe, Asia, Africa, Austral-Asia, and the high seas. And they will be in a position to bring enormous military and naval resources against this hemisphere. It is no exaggeration to say that all of us, in all the Americas, would be living at the point of a gun—a gun loaded with explosive bullets, economic as well as military. We should enter upon a new and terrible era in which the whole world, our hemisphere included, would be run by threats of brute force. And to survive in such a world, we would have to convert ourselves permanently into a militaristic power on the basis of war economy.

Some of us like to believe that even if Britain falls, we are still safe, because of the broad expanse of the Atlantic and of the Pacific. But the width of those oceans is not what it was in the days of clipper ships. At one point between Africa and Brazil, the distance is less from Washington than it is from Washington to Denver, Colorado—five hours for the latest type of bomber. And at the north end of the Pacific Ocean, America and Asia almost touch each other. Why, even today we have planes that could fly from the British Isles to New England and back again without refuelling. And remember that the range of the modern bomber is ever being increased.

During the past week many people in all parts of the nation have told me what they wanted me to say tonight. Almost all of them expressed a courageous desire to hear the plain truth about the gravity of the situation. One telegram, however, expressed the attitude of the small minority who want to see no evil and hear no evil, even though they know in their hearts that evil exists. That telegram begged me not to tell again of the ease with which our American cities could be bombed by any hostile power which had gained bases in this Western Hemisphere. The gist of that telegram was: 'Please, Mr. President, don't frighten us by telling us the facts.' Frankly and definitely there is danger ahead—danger against which we must prepare. But we well know that we cannot escape danger, or the fear of danger, by crawling into bed and pulling the covers over our heads.

Some nations of Europe were bound by solemn non-intervention pacts with Germany. Other nations were assured by Germany that they need never fear invasion. Non-intervention pact or not, the fact remains that they were attacked, overrun and thrown into modern slavery at an hour's notice, or even without any notice at all. As an exiled leader of one of these nations said to me the other day—'The notice was a minus quantity. It was given to my government two hours after German troops had poured into my country in a hundred places.' The fate of these nations tells us what it means to live at the point of a Nazi gun.

The Nazis have justified such actions by various pious frauds. One of these frauds is the claim that they are occupying a nation for the purpose of 'restoring order.' Another is that they are occupying or controlling a nation on the excuse that they are 'protecting it' against the aggression of somebody else.

For example, Germany has said that she was occupying Belgium to save the Belgians from the British. Would she then hesitate to say to any South American country, 'We are occupying you to protect you from aggression by the United States?' Belgium today is being used as an invasion base against Britain, now fighting for its life. Any South American country, in Nazi hands, would always constitute a jumping-off place for German attack on any one of the other Republics of this hemisphere.

Analyse for yourselves the future of two other places even nearer to Germany if the Nazis won. Could Ireland hold out? Would Irish freedom be permitted as an amazing pet exception in an unfree world? Or the islands of the Azores which still fly the flag of Portugal after five centuries? You and I think of Hawaii as an outpost of defence in the Pacific. And yet, the Azores are closer to our shores in the Atlantic than Hawaii is on the other side.

There are those who say that the Axis powers would never have any desire to attack the Western Hemisphere. That is the same dangerous form of wishful thinking which has destroyed the powers of resistance of so many conquered peoples. The plain facts are that the Nazis have proclaimed, time and again, that all other races are their inferiors and therefore subject to their orders. And most important of all, the vast resources and wealth of this American Hemisphere constitute the most tempting loot in all the round world.

Let us no longer blind ourselves to the undeniable fact that the evil forces which have crushed and undermined and corrupted so many others are already within our own gates. Your government knows much about them and every day is ferreting them out. Their secret emissaries are active in our own and in neighbouring countries. They seek to stir up suspicion and dissension, to cause internal strife. They try to turn capital against labour, and vice versa. They try to reawaken long slumbering racial and religious enmities which should have no place in this country. They are active in every group that promotes intolerance. They exploit for their own ends our natural abhorrence of war. These trouble-breeders have but one purpose. It is to divide our people—to divide them into hostile groups and to destroy our unity and shatter our will to defend ourselves.

There are also American citizens, many of them in high places, who, unwittingly in most cases, are aiding and abetting the work of these agents. I do not charge these American citizens with being foreign agents. But I do charge them with doing exactly the kind of work that the dictators want done in the United States. These people not only believe that we can save our own skins by shutting our eyes to the fate of other nations. Some of them go much further than that. They say that we can and should become the friends and even the partners of the Axis powers. Some of them even suggest that we should imitate the methods of the dictatorships. Americans never can and never will do that.

The experience of the past two years has proven beyond doubt that no nation can appease the Nazis. No man can tame a tiger into a kitten by stroking it. There can be no appeasement with ruthlessness. There can be no reasoning with an incendiary bomb. We know now that a nation can have peace with the Nazis only at the price of total surrender. Even the people of Italy have been forced to become accomplices of the Nazis; but at this moment they do not know how soon they will be embraced to death by their allies.

The American appeasers ignore the warning to be found in the fate of Austria, Czechoslovakia, Poland, Norway, Belgium, the Netherlands, Denmark, and France. They tell you that the Axis powers are going to win anyway; that all of this bloodshed in the world could be saved; that the United States might just as well throw its influence into the scale of a dictated peace, and get the best out of it that we can. They call it a 'negotiated peace.' Nonsense! Is it a negotiated peace if a gang of outlaws surrounds your community and on threat of extermination makes you pay tribute to save your own skins? Such a dictated peace would be no peace at all. It would be only another armistice, leading to the most gigantic armament race and the most devastating trade wars in all history. And in these contests the Americas would offer the only real resistance to the Axis powers. With all their vaunted efficiency, with all their parade of pious purpose in this war, there are still in their background the concentration camp and the servants of God in chains.

The history of recent years proves that the shootings and the chains and the concentration camps are not simply the transient tools but the very altars of modern dictatorships. They may talk of a 'new order' in the world, but what they have in mind is only a revival of the oldest and the worst tyranny. In that there is no liberty, no religion, no hope. The proposed 'new order' is the very opposite of a United States of Europe or a United States of Asia. It is not a government based upon the consent of the governed. It is not a union of ordinary, self-respecting men and women to protect themselves and their freedom and their dignity from oppression. It is an unholy alliance of power and pelf to dominate and to enslave the human race.

The British people and their allies today are conducting an active war against this unholy alliance. Our own future security is greatly dependent on the outcome of that fight. Our ability to 'keep out of war' is going to be affected by that outcome. Thinking in terms of today and tomorrow, I make the direct statement to the American people that there is far less chance of the United States getting into war, if we do all we can now to support the nations defending themselves against attack by the Axis than if we acquiesce in their defeat, submit tamely to an Axis victory, and wait our turn to be the object of attack in another war later on.

If we are to be completely honest with ourselves, we must admit that there is risk in any course we may take. But I deeply believe that the great majority of our people agree that the course that I advocate involves the least risk now and the greatest hope for world peace in the future.

The people of Europe who are defending themselves do not ask us to do their fighting. They ask us for the implements of war, the planes, the tanks, the guns, the freighters which will enable them to fight for their liberty and for our security. Emphatically we must get these weapons to them, get them to them in sufficient volume and quickly enough, so that we and our children will be saved the agony and suffering of war which others have had to endure.

Let not the defeatists tell us that it is too late. It will never be earlier. Tomorrow will be later than today.

Certain facts are self-evident. In a military sense, Great Britain and the British Empire are today the spearhead of resistance to world conquest. And they are putting up a fight which will live forever in the story of human gallantry. There is no demand for sending an American Expeditionary Force outside our own borders. There is no intention by any member of your government to send such a force. You can, therefore, nail—nail any talk about sending armies to Europe as deliberate untruth.

Our national policy is not directed toward war. Its sole purpose is to keep war away from our country and our people. Democracy's fight against world conquest is being greatly aided, and must be more greatly aided, by the rearmament of the United States and by sending every ounce and every ton of munitions and supplies that we can possibly spare to help the defenders who are in the front lines. It is no more unneutral for us to do that than it is for Sweden, Russia and other nations near Germany, to send steel and ore and oil and other war materials into Germany every day in the week.

We are planning our own defence with the utmost urgency; and in its vast scale we must integrate the war needs of Britain and the other free nations which are resisting aggression. This is not a matter of sentiment or of controversial personal opinion. It is a matter of realistic, practical military policy, based on the advice of our military experts who are in close touch with existing warfare. These military and naval experts and the members of the Congress and the Administration have a single-minded purpose—the defence of the United States.

This nation is making a great effort to produce everything that is necessary in this emergency—and with all possible speed. This great effort requires great sacrifice. I would ask no one to defend a democracy which in turn would not defend everyone in the nation against want and privation. The strength of this nation shall not be diluted by the failure of the government to protect the economic well-being of its citizens. If our capacity to produce is limited by machines, it must ever be remembered that these machines are operated by the skill and the stamina of the workers.

As the government is determined to protect the rights of the workers, so the nation has a right to expect that the men who man the machines will discharge their full responsibilities to the urgent needs of defence. The worker possesses the same human dignity and is entitled to the same security of position as the engineer or the manager or the owner. For the workers provide the human power that turns out the destroyers, the airplanes and the tanks. The nation expects our defence industries to continue operation without interruption by strikes or lock-outs. It expects and insists that management and workers will reconcile their differences by voluntary or legal means, to continue to produce the supplies that are so sorely needed. And on the economic side of our great defence program, we are, as you know, bending every effort to maintain stability of prices and with that the stability of the cost of living.

Nine days ago I announced the setting up of a more effective organization to direct our gigantic efforts to increase the production of munitions. The appropriation of vast sums of money and a well-coordinated executive direction of our defence efforts are not in themselves enough. Guns, planes, ships and many other things have to be built in the factories and arsenals of America. They have to be produced by workers and managers and engineers with the aid of machines which in turn have to be built by hundreds of thousands of workers throughout the land. In this great work there has been splendid cooperation between the government and industry and labour; and I am very thankful.

American industrial genius, unmatched throughout the world in the solution of production problems, has been called upon to bring its resources and its talents into action. Manufacturers of watches, farm implements, linotypes, cash registers, automobiles, sewing machines, lawn mowers and locomotives are now making fuses, bomb packing crates, telescope mounts, shells, pistols, and tanks.

But all our present efforts are not enough. We must have more ships, more guns, more planes—more of everything. This can only be accomplished if we discard the notion of 'business as usual.' This job cannot be done merely by superimposing on the existing productive facilities the added requirements of the nation for defence. Our defence efforts must not be blocked by those who fear the future consequences of surplus plant capacity. The possible consequences of failure of our defence efforts now are much more to be feared. After the present needs of our defences are past, a proper handling of the country's peace-time needs will require all the new productive capacity—if not more. No pessimistic policy about the future of America shall delay the immediate expansion of those industries essential to defence. We need them.

I want to make it clear that it is the purpose of the nation to build now with all possible speed every machine, every arsenal, every factory that we need to manufacture our defence material. We have the men, the skill, the wealth, and above all, the will. I am confident that if and when production of consumer or luxury goods in certain industries requires the use of machines and raw materials that are essential for defence purposes, then such production must yield, and will gladly yield, to our primary and compelling purpose.

I appeal to the owners of plants, to the managers, to the workers, to our own government employees to put every ounce of effort into producing these munitions swiftly and without stint. With this appeal I give you the pledge that all of us who are officers of your government will devote ourselves to the same whole-hearted extent to the great task that lies ahead.

As planes and ships and guns and shells are produced, your government, with its defence experts, can then determine how best to use them to defend this hemisphere. The decision as to how much shall be sent abroad and how much shall remain at home must be made on the basis of our over-all military necessities.

We must be the great arsenal of democracy.

For us this is an emergency as serious as war itself. We must apply ourselves to our task with the same resolution, the same sense of urgency, the same spirit of patriotism and sacrifice as we would show were we at war.

We have furnished the British great material support and we will furnish far more in the future. There will be no 'bottlenecks' in our determination to aid Great Britain. No dictator, no combination of dictators, will weaken that determination by threats of how they will construe that determination. The British have received invaluable military support from the heroic Greek army, and from the forces of all the governments in exile. Their strength is growing. It is the strength of men and women who value their freedom more highly than they value their lives.

I believe that the Axis powers are not going to win this war. I base that belief on the latest and best information.

We have no excuse for defeatism. We have every good reason for hope—hope for peace, hope for the defence of our civilization and for the building of a better civilization in the future. I have the profound conviction that the American people are now determined to put forth a mightier effort than they have ever yet made to increase our production of all the implements of defence, to meet the threat to our democratic faith.

As President of the United States, I call for that national effort. I call for it in the name of this nation which we love and honour and which we are privileged and proud to serve. I call upon our people with absolute confidence that our common cause will greatly succeed.

*Note: Roosevelt tried to keep America out of the war. But the country entered World War II less than a year after this speech was delivered, a day after the Pearl Harbor attack.*

# 20

## The Four Freedoms

★ ★ ★ ★ ★ ★ ★

Franklin Roosevelt
Washington, D.C., U.S.A.
6 January 1941

*Franklin Roosevelt addressed the Congress members and his countrymen in his effort to rally the public support to intervene and fight against Germany in the Second World War. The United States was not involved in the war yet, but Roosevelt warned that isolationism does not guarantee safety.*

*Every citizen in every nation has a right to freedom—freedom of speech and worship, and freedom from want and fear. The president conveyed in the following speech that he envisioned a world where every nation would be built on these essential four freedoms.*

Mr. President, Mr. Speaker, Members of the Seventy-seventh Congress:

I address you, the Members of the members of this new Congress, at a moment unprecedented in the history of the Union. I use the word 'unprecedented,' because at no previous time has American security been as seriously threatened from without as it is today.

Since the permanent formation of our government under the Constitution, in 1789, most of the periods of crisis in our history have related to our domestic affairs. And fortunately, only one of these—the four-year War Between the States—ever threatened our national unity. Today, thank God, one hundred and thirty million Americans, in forty-eight States, have forgotten points of the compass in our national unity.

It is true that prior to 1914 the United States often had been disturbed by events in other Continents. We had even engaged in two wars with European nations and in a number of undeclared wars in the West Indies, in the Mediterranean and in the Pacific for the maintenance of American rights and for the principles of peaceful commerce. But in no case had a serious threat been raised against our national safety or our continued independence.

What I seek to convey is the historic truth that the United States as a nation has at all times maintained opposition, clear, definite opposition, to any attempt to lock us in behind an ancient Chinese wall while the procession of civilization went past. Today, thinking of our children and of their children, we oppose enforced isolation for ourselves or for any other part of the Americas.

That determination of ours, extending over all these years, was proved, for example, in the early days during the quarter century of wars following the French Revolution.

While the Napoleonic struggles did threaten interests of the United States because of the French foothold in the West Indies and in Louisiana, and while we engaged in the War of 1812 to vindicate our right to peaceful trade, it is nevertheless clear that neither France nor Great Britain, nor any other nation, was aiming at domination of the whole world.

And in like fashion from 1815 to 1914—ninety-nine years—no single war in Europe or in Asia constituted a real threat against our future or against the future of any other American nation.

Except in the Maximilian interlude in Mexico, no foreign power sought to establish itself in this Hemisphere; and the strength of the British fleet in the Atlantic has been a friendly strength. It is still a friendly strength.

Even when the World War broke out in 1914, it seemed to contain only small threat of danger to our own American future. But, as time went on, as we remember, the American people began to visualize what the downfall of democratic nations might mean to our own democracy.

We need not overemphasize imperfections in the Peace of Versailles. We need not harp on failure of the democracies to deal with problems of world reconstruction. We should remember that the Peace of 1919 was far less unjust than the kind of 'pacification' which began even before Munich, and which is being carried on under the new order of tyranny that seeks to spread over every continent today. The American people have unalterably set their faces against that tyranny.

I suppose that every realist knows that the democratic way of life is at this moment being directly assailed in every part of the world—assailed either by arms, or by secret spreading of poisonous propaganda by those who seek to destroy unity and promote discord in nations that are still at peace.

During sixteen long months this assault has blotted out the whole pattern of democratic life in an appalling number of independent nations, great and small. And the assailants are still on the march, threatening other nations, great and small.

Therefore, as your president, performing my constitutional duty to 'give to the Congress information of the state of the Union,' I find it, unhappily, necessary to report that the future and the safety of our country and of our democracy are overwhelmingly involved in events far beyond our borders.

Armed defence of democratic existence is now being gallantly waged in four continents. If that defence fails, all the population and all the resources of Europe, and Asia, and Africa and Australasia will be dominated by conquerors. And let us remember that the total of those populations in those four continents, the total of those populations and their resources greatly exceeds the sum total of the population and the resources of the whole of the Western Hemisphere—yes, many times over.

In times like these it is immature—and incidentally, untrue—for anybody to brag that an unprepared America, single-handed, and with one hand tied behind its back, can hold off the whole world.

No realistic American can expect from a dictator's peace international generosity, or return of true independence, or world disarmament, or freedom of expression, or freedom of religion—or even good business.

Such a peace would bring no security for us or for our neighbours. 'Those, who would give up essential liberty to purchase a little temporary safety, deserve neither liberty nor safety.'

As a nation, we may take pride in the fact that we are soft-hearted; but we cannot afford to be soft-headed.

We must always be wary of those who with sounding brass and a tinkling cymbal preach the 'ism' of appeasement.

We must especially beware of that small group of selfish men who would clip the wings of the American eagle in order to feather their own nests.

I have recently pointed out how quickly the tempo of modern warfare could bring into our very midst the physical attack which we must eventually expect if the dictator nations win this war.

There is much loose talk of our immunity from immediate and direct invasion from across the seas. Obviously, as long as the British Navy retains its power, no such danger exists. Even if there were no British Navy, it is not probable that any enemy would be stupid enough to attack us by landing troops in the United States from across thousands of miles of ocean, until it had acquired strategic bases from which to operate.

But we learn much from the lessons of the past years in Europe—particularly the lesson of Norway, whose essential seaports were captured by treachery and surprise built up over a series of years.

The first phase of the invasion of this Hemisphere would not be the landing of regular troops. The necessary strategic points would be occupied by secret agents and by their dupes—and great numbers of them are already here, and in Latin America.

As long as the aggressor nations maintain the offensive, they—not we—will choose the time and the place and the method of their attack.

And that is why the future of all the American Republics is today in serious danger.

That is why this Annual Message to the Congress is unique in our history.

That is why every member of the Executive Branch of the government and every member of the Congress face great responsibility and great accountability.

The need of the moment is that our actions and our policy should be devoted primarily—almost exclusively—to meeting this foreign peril. For all our domestic problems are now a part of the great emergency.

Just as our national policy in internal affairs has been based upon a decent respect for the rights and the dignity of all of our fellow men within our gates, so our national policy in foreign affairs has been based on a decent respect for the rights and the dignity of all nations, large and small. And the justice of morality must and will win in the end.

Our national policy is this:

First, by an impressive expression of the public will and without regard to partisanship, we are committed to all-inclusive national defence.

Second, by an impressive expression of the public will and without regard to partisanship, we are committed to full support of all those resolute people everywhere who are resisting aggression and are thereby keeping war away from our Hemisphere. By this support, we express our determination that the democratic cause shall prevail; and we strengthen the defence and the security of our own nation.

Third, by an impressive expression of the public will and without regard to partisanship, we are committed to the proposition that principles of morality and considerations for our own security will never permit us to acquiesce in a peace dictated by aggressors and sponsored by appeasers. We know that enduring peace cannot be bought at the cost of other people's freedom.

In the recent national election there was no substantial difference between the two great parties in respect to that national policy. No issue was fought out on this line before the American electorate. And today it is abundantly evident that American citizens everywhere are demanding and supporting speedy and complete action in recognition of obvious danger.

Therefore, the immediate need is a swift and driving increase in our armament production.

Leaders of industry and labour have responded to our summons. Goals of speed have been set. In some cases these goals are being reached ahead of time; in some cases we are on schedule; in other cases there are slight but not serious delays; and in some cases—and I am sorry to say very important cases—we are all concerned by the slowness of the accomplishment of our plans.

The Army and Navy, however, have made substantial progress during the past year. Actual experience is improving and speeding up our methods of production with every passing day. And today's best is not good enough for tomorrow.

I am not satisfied with the progress thus far made. The men in charge of the program represent the best in training, in ability, and in patriotism. They are not satisfied with the progress thus far made. None of us will be satisfied until the job is done.

No matter whether the original goal was set too high or too low, our objective is quicker and better results.

We are behind schedule in turning out finished airplanes; we are working day and night to solve the innumerable problems and to catch up.

We are ahead of schedule in building warships but we are working to get even further ahead of that schedule.

To change a whole nation from a basis of peacetime production of implements of peace to a basis of wartime production of implements of war is no small task. And the greatest difficulty comes at the beginning of the program, when new tools, new plant facilities, new assembly lines, and new ship ways must first be constructed before the actual materiel begins to flow steadily and speedily from them.

The Congress, of course, must rightly keep itself informed at all times of the progress of the program. However, there is certain information, as the Congress itself will readily recognize, which, in the interests of our own security and those of the nations that we are supporting, must of needs be kept in confidence.

New circumstances are constantly begetting new needs for our safety. I shall ask this Congress for greatly increased new appropriations and authorizations to carry on what we have begun.

I also ask this Congress for authority and for funds sufficient to manufacture additional munitions and war supplies of many kinds, to be turned over to those nations which are now in actual war with aggressor nations.

Our most useful and immediate role is to act as an arsenal for them as well as for ourselves. They do not need man power, but they do need billions of dollars worth of the weapons of defence.

The time is near when they will not be able to pay for them all in ready cash. We cannot, and we will not, tell them that they must surrender, merely because of present inability to pay for the weapons which we know they must have.

I do not recommend that we make them a loan of dollars with which to pay for these weapons—a loan to be repaid in dollars.

I recommend that we make it possible for those nations to continue to obtain war materials in the United States, fitting their orders into our own program. And nearly all of their materiel would, if the time ever came, be useful in our own defence.

Taking counsel of expert military and naval authorities, considering what is best for our own security, we are free to decide how much should be kept here and how much should be sent abroad to our friends who by their determined and heroic resistance are giving us time in which to make ready our own defence.

For what we send abroad, we shall be repaid, repaid within a reasonable time following the close of hostilities, repaid in similar materials, or, at our option, in other goods of many kinds, which they can produce and which we need.

Let us say to the democracies: 'We Americans are vitally concerned in your defence of freedom. We are putting forth our energies, our resources and our organizing powers to give you the strength to regain and maintain a free world. We shall send you, in ever-increasing numbers, ships, planes, tanks, guns. This is our purpose and our pledge.'

In fulfilment of this purpose we will not be intimidated by the threats of dictators that they will regard as a breach of international law or as an act of war our aid to the democracies which dare to resist their aggression. Such aid . . . Such aid is not an act of war, even if a dictator should unilaterally proclaim it so to be.

And when the dictators, if the dictators, are ready to make war upon us, they will not wait for an act of war on our part. They did not wait for Norway or Belgium or the Netherlands to commit an act of war.

Their only interest is in a new one-way international law, which lacks mutuality in its observance, and, therefore, becomes an instrument of oppression.

The happiness of future generations of Americans may well depend upon how effective and how immediate we can make our aid felt. No one can tell the exact character of the emergency situations that we may be called upon to meet. The Nation's hands must not be tied when the Nation's life is in danger.

Yes, and we must all prepare—all of us prepare—to make the sacrifices that the emergency—almost as serious as war itself—demands. Whatever stands in the way of speed and efficiency in defence—in defence preparations of any kind—must give way to the national need.

A free nation has the right to expect full cooperation from all groups. A free nation has the right to look to the leaders of business, of labour, and of agriculture to take the lead in stimulating effort, not among other groups but within their own groups.

The best way of dealing with the few slackers or trouble makers in our midst is, first, to shame them by patriotic example, and, if that fails, to use the sovereignty of government to save government.

As men do not live by bread alone, they do not fight by armaments alone. Those who man our defences, and those behind them who build our defences, must have the stamina and the courage which come from unshakable belief in the manner of life which they are defending. The mighty action that we are calling for cannot be based on a disregard of all things the worth fighting for.

The Nation takes great satisfaction and much strength from the things which have been done to make its people conscious of their individual stake in the preservation of democratic life in America. Those things have toughened the fibre of our people, have renewed their faith and strengthened their devotion to the institutions we make ready to protect.

Certainly this is no time for any of us to stop thinking about the social and economic problems which are the root cause of the social revolution which is today a supreme factor in the world.

For there is nothing mysterious about the foundations of a healthy and strong democracy. The basic things expected by our people of their political and economic systems are simple. They are:

Equality of opportunity for youth and for others.

Jobs for those who can work.

Security for those who need it.

The ending of special privilege for the few.

The preservation of civil liberties for all.

The enjoyment... The enjoyment of the fruits of scientific progress in a wider and constantly rising standard of living.

These are the simple, the basic things that must never be lost sight of in the turmoil and unbelievable complexity of our modern world.

The inner and abiding strength of our economic and political systems is dependent upon the degree to which they fulfil these expectations.

Many subjects connected with our social economy call for immediate improvement.

As examples:

We should bring more citizens under the coverage of old-age pensions and unemployment insurance.

We should widen the opportunities for adequate medical care.

We should plan a better system by which persons deserving or needing gainful employment may obtain it.

I have called for personal sacrifice. And I am assured of the willingness of almost all Americans to respond to that call.

A part of the sacrifice means the payment of more money in taxes. In my Budget Message I will recommend that a greater portion of this great defence program be paid for from taxation than we are paying for today. No person should try, or be allowed, to get rich out of the program; and the principle of tax payments in accordance with ability to pay should be constantly before our eyes to guide our legislation.

If the Congress maintains these principles, the voters, putting patriotism ahead of pocketbooks, will give you their applause.

In the future days, which we seek to make secure, we look forward to a world founded upon four essential human freedoms.

The first is freedom of speech and expression—everywhere in the world.

The second is freedom of every person to worship God in his own way—everywhere in the world.

The third is freedom from want—which, translated into world terms, means economic understandings which will secure to every nation a healthy peacetime life for its inhabitants—everywhere in the world.

The fourth is freedom from fear—which, translated into world terms, means a world-wide reduction of armaments to such a point and in such a thorough fashion that no nation will be in a position to commit an act of physical aggression against any neighbor—anywhere in the world.

That is no vision of a distant millennium. It is a definite basis for a kind of world attainable in our own time and generation. That kind of world is the very antithesis of the so-called new order of tyranny which the dictators seek to create with the crash of a bomb.

To that new order we oppose the greater conception—the moral order. A good society is able to face schemes of world domination and foreign revolutions alike without fear.

Since the beginning of our American history, we have been engaged in change—in a perpetual peaceful revolution—a revolution which goes on steadily, quietly adjusting itself to changing conditions—without the concentration camp or the quick-lime in the ditch. The world order which we seek is the cooperation of free countries, working together in a friendly, civilized society.

This nation has placed its destiny in the hands and heads and hearts of its millions of free men and women; and its faith in freedom under the guidance of God. Freedom means the supremacy of human rights everywhere. Our support goes to those who struggle to gain those rights and keep them. Our strength is our unity of purpose.

To that high concept there can be no end save victory.

# 21

## What Is an American

★★★★★★★

Harold Ickes
New York, U.S.A.
18 May 1941

*Harold Ickes was President Franklin Roosevelt's secretary of the interior. In this speech, he addressed the public and talked about what an American stands for and why America should participate in the war.*

*At the time Ickes gave this speech, the Second World War was going on and the scales were tipping towards Hitler. Germany seemed inches away from world domination. Consequently, many Americans were becoming pacifists and did not want America to enter in the war.*

I want to ask a few simple questions. And then I shall answer them.

What has happened to our vaunted idealism? Why have some of us been behaving like scared chickens? Where is the million-throated, democratic voice of America?

For years it has been dinned into us that we are a weak nation; that we are an inefficient people; that we are simple-minded. For years we have been told that we are beaten, decayed, and that no part of the world belongs to us any longer.

Some amongst us have fallen for this carefully pickled tripe. Some amongst us have fallen for this calculated poison. Some amongst us have begun to preach that the 'wave of the future' has passed over us and left us a wet, dead fish.

They shout—from public platforms in printed pages, through the microphones—that it is futile to oppose the 'wave of the future.' They cry that we Americans, we free Americans nourished on Magna Carta and the Declaration of Independence, hold moth-eaten ideas. They exclaim that there is no room for free men in the world anymore and that only the slaves will inherit the earth. America—the America of Washington and Jefferson and Lincoln and Walt Whitman—they say, is waiting for the undertaker and all the hopes and aspirations that have gone into the making of America are dead too.

However, my fellow citizens, this is not the real point of the story. The real point—the shameful point—is that many of us are listening to them and some of us almost believe them.

I say that it is time for the great American people to raise its voice and cry out in mighty triumph what it is to be an American. And why it is that only Americans, with the aid of our brave allies—yes, let's call them 'allies'—the British, can and will build the only future worth having. I mean a future, not of concentration camps, not of physical torture and mental straitjackets, not of sawdust bread or of sawdust Caesars—I mean a future when free men will live free lives in dignity and in security.

This tide of the future, the democratic future, is ours. It is ours if we show ourselves worthy of our culture and of our heritage.

But make no mistake about it; the tide of the democratic future is not like the ocean tide—regular, relentless, and inevitable. Nothing in human affairs is mechanical or inevitable. Nor are Americans mechanical. They are very human indeed. What constitutes an

American? Not colour nor race nor religion. Not the pedigree of his family nor the place of his birth. Not the coincidence of his citizenship. Not his social status nor his bank account. Not his trade nor his profession. An American is one who loves justice and believes in the dignity of man. An American is one who will fight for his freedom and that of his neighbour. An American is one who will sacrifice property, ease and security in order that he and his children may retain the rights of free men. An American is one in whose heart is engraved the immortal second sentence of the Declaration of Independence.

Americans have always known how to fight for their rights and their way of life. Americans are not afraid to fight. They fight joyously in a just cause.

We Americans know that freedom, like peace, is indivisible. We cannot retain our liberty if three-fourths of the world is enslaved. Brutality, injustice and slavery, if practiced as dictators would have them, universally and systematically, in the long run would destroy us as surely as a fire raging in our nearby neighbour's house would burn ours if we didn't help to put out his.

If we are to retain our own freedom, we must do everything within our power to aid Britain. We must also do everything to restore to the conquered peoples their freedom. This means the Germans too.

Such a program, if you stop to think, is selfishness on our part. It is the sort of enlightened selfishness that makes the wheels of history go around. It is the sort of enlightened selfishness that wins victories.

Do you know why? Because we cannot live in the world alone, without friends and without allies. If Britain should be defeated, then the totalitarian undertaker will prepare to hang crepe on the door of our own independence.

Perhaps you wonder how this could come about? Perhaps you have heard 'them'—the wavers of the future—cry, with calculated malice, that even if Britain were defeated we could live alone and defend ourselves single handed, even against the whole world.

I tell you that this is a cold blooded lie.

We would be alone in the world, facing an unscrupulous military-economic bloc that would dominate all of Europe, all of Africa, most of Asia, and perhaps even Russia and South America. Even to do that, we would have to spend most of our national income on tanks and guns and planes and ships. Nor would this be all. We would have to live perpetually as an armed camp, maintaining a huge standing army, a gigantic air force, two vast navies. And we could not do this without endangering our freedom, our democracy, our way of life.

Perhaps such is the America 'they'—the wavers of the future—foresee. Perhaps such is the America that a certain aviator, with his contempt for democracy, would prefer. Perhaps such is the America that a certain Senator desires. Perhaps such is the America that a certain mail order executive longs for.

But a perpetually militarized, isolated and impoverished America is not the America that our fathers came here to build.

It is not the America that has been the dream and the hope of countless generations in all parts of the world.

It is not the America that one hundred and thirty million of us would care to live in.

The continued security of our country demands that we aid the enslaved millions of Europe—yes, even of Germany—to win back their liberty and independence. I am convinced that if we do not embark upon such a program we will lose our own freedom.

We should be clear on this point. What is convulsing the world today is not merely another old-fashioned war. It is a counter revolution against our ideas and ideals, against our sense of justice and our human values.

Three systems today compete for world domination. Communism, fascism, and democracy are struggling for social-economic-political world control. As the conflict sharpens, it becomes clear that the other two, fascism and communism, are merging into one. They have one common enemy, democracy. They have one common goal, the destruction of democracy.

This is why this war is not an ordinary war. It is not a conflict for markets or territories. It is a desperate struggle for the possession of the souls of men.

This is why the British are not fighting for themselves alone. They are fighting to preserve freedom for mankind. For the moment, the battleground is the British Isles. But they are fighting our war; they are the first soldiers in trenches that are also our front-line trenches.

In this world war of ideas and of loyalties we believers in democracy must do two things. We must unite our forces to form one great democratic international. We must offer a clear program to freedom-loving peoples throughout the world.

Freedom-loving men and women in every land must organize and tighten their ranks. The masses everywhere must be helped to fight their oppressors and conquerors. We, free, democratic Americans are in a position to help. We know that the spirit of freedom never dies. We know that men have fought and bled for freedom since time immemorial. We realize that the liberty-loving German people are only temporarily enslaved. We do not doubt that the Italian people are looking forward to the appearance of another Garibaldi. We know how the Poles have for centuries maintained a heroic resistance against tyranny. We remember the brave struggle of the Hungarians under Kossuth and other leaders. We recall the heroic figure of Masaryk and the gallant fight for freedom of the Czech people. The story of the Yugoslavs', especially the Serbs' blows for liberty and independence is a saga of extraordinary heroism. The Greeks will stand again at Thermopylae, as they have in the past. The annals of our American sister-republics, too, are glorious with freedom-inspiring exploits. The noble figure of Simon Bolivar, the great South American liberator, has naturally been compared with that of George Washington.

No, liberty never dies. The Genghis Khans come and go. The Attilas come and go. The Hitlers flash and sputter out. But freedom endures.

Destroy a whole generation of those who have known how to walk with heads erect in God's free air, and the next generation will rise against the oppressors and restore freedom. Today in Europe, the Nazi Attila may gloat that he has destroyed democracy. He is wrong. In small farmhouses all over Central Europe, in the shops of Germany and Italy, on the docks of Holland and Belgium, freedom still lives in the hearts of men. It will endure like a hardy tree gone into the wintertime, awaiting the spring.

And, like spring, spreading from the South into Scandinavia, the democratic revolution will come. And men with democratic hearts will experience comradeship across artificial boundaries.

These men and women, hundreds of millions of them, now in bondage or threatened with slavery, are our comrades and our allies. They are only waiting for our leadership and our encouragement, for the spark that we can supply.

These hundreds of millions, of liberty-loving people, now oppressed, constitute the greatest sixth column in history. They have the will to destroy the Nazi gangsters.

We have always helped in struggles for human freedom. And we will help again. But our hundreds of millions of liberty-loving allies would despair if we did not provide aid and encouragement. The quicker we help them the sooner this dreadful revolution will be over. We cannot, we must not, we dare not delay much longer.

The fight for Britain is in its crucial stages. We must give the British everything we have. And by everything, I mean everything needed to beat the life out of our common enemy.

The second step must be to aid and encourage our friends and allies everywhere. And by everywhere I mean Europe and Asia and Africa and America.

And finally, the most important of all, we Americans must gird spiritually for the battle. We must dispel the fog of uncertainty and vacillation. We must greet with raucous laughter the corroding arguments of our appeasers and fascists. They doubt democracy. We affirm it triumphantly so that all the world may hear:

Here in America we have something so worth living for that it is worth dying for! The so-called 'wave of the future' is but the slimy backwash of the past. We have not heaved from our necks the tyrant's crushing heel, only to stretch our necks out again for its weight. Not only will we fight for democracy, we will make it more worth fighting for. Under our free institutions, we will work for the good of mankind, including Hitler's victims in Germany, so that all may have plenty and security.

We American democrats know that when good will prevails among men there will be a world of plenty and a world of security.

In the words of Winston Churchill, 'Are we downhearted? No, we are not! But someone is downhearted!' Witness the terrified flight of Hess, Hitler's Number Three Man. And listen to this—listen carefully:

'The British nation can be counted upon to carry through to victory any struggle that it once enters upon no matter how long such a struggle may last or however great the sacrifices that may be necessary or whatever the means that have to be employed; and all this even though the actual military equipment at hand may be utterly inadequate when compared with that of other nations.'

Do you know who wrote that? Adolf Hitler in *Mein Kampf.* And do you know who took down that dictation? Rudolf Hess.

We will help to make Hitler's prophecy come true. We will help brave England drive back the hordes from Hell who besiege her and then we will join for the destruction of savage and bloodthirsty dictators everywhere. But we must be firm and decisive. We must know our will and make it felt. And we must hurry.

# 22

## A Date Which Will Live in Infamy

★ ★ ★ ★ ★ ★ ★

Franklin Roosevelt
Washington, D.C., U.S.A.
8 December 1941

*Roosevelt delivered the following speech to the joint session of the U.S. Congress the day after the naval and air forces of Japan attacked Pearl Harbor. The speech urged the Congress to formally declare war on Japan.*

*It was noted by Paul M. Sparrow, one of the president's confidante, that Roosevelt delivered this speech with a solemn and determined tone, showing a fierce determination that justice would be served. Less than an hour after the speech, the Senate and the House voted for war.*

Mr. Vice President, Mr. Speaker, members of the Senate and the House of Representatives:

Yesterday, December 7th, 1941—a date which will live in infamy—the United States of America was suddenly and deliberately attacked by naval and air forces of the Empire of Japan.

The United States was at peace with that nation, and, at the solicitation of Japan, was still in conversation with its government and its Emperor looking toward the maintenance of peace in the Pacific.

Indeed, one hour after Japanese air squadrons had commenced bombing in the American island of Oahu, the Japanese Ambassador to the United States and his colleague delivered to our Secretary of State a formal reply to a recent American message. And, while this reply stated that it seemed useless to continue the existing diplomatic negotiations, it contained no threat or hint of war or of armed attack.

It will be recorded that the distance of Hawaii from Japan makes it obvious that the attack was deliberately planned many days or even weeks ago. During the intervening time the Japanese Government has deliberately sought to deceive the United States by false statements and expressions of hope for continued peace.

The attack yesterday on the Hawaiian Islands has caused severe damage to American naval and military forces. I regret to tell you that very many American lives have been lost. In addition, American ships have been reported torpedoed on the high seas between San Francisco and Honolulu.

Yesterday the Japanese Government also launched an attack against Malaya.

Last night Japanese forces attacked Hong Kong.

Last night Japanese forces attacked Guam.

Last night Japanese forces attacked the Philippine Islands.

Last night the Japanese attacked Wake Island.

And this morning the Japanese attacked Midway Island.

Japan has, therefore, undertaken a surprise offensive extending throughout the Pacific area. The facts of yesterday and today speak for themselves. The people of the United States have already formed their opinions and well understand the implications to the very life and safety of our nation.

As Commander-in-Chief of the Army and Navy, I have directed that all measures be taken for our defence, that always will our whole nation remember the character of the onslaught against us.

No matter how long it may take us to overcome this premeditated invasion, the American people, in their righteous might, will win through to absolute victory.

I believe that I interpret the will of the Congress and of the people when I assert that we will not only defend ourselves to the uttermost but will make it very certain that this form of treachery shall never again endanger us.

Hostilities exist. There is no blinking at the fact that our people, our territory and our interests are in grave danger.

With confidence in our armed forces, with the unbounding determination of our people, we will gain the inevitable triumph—so help us God.

I ask that the Congress declare that since the unprovoked and dastardly attack by Japan on Sunday, December 7th, 1941, a state of war has existed between the United States and the Japanese Empire.

*Note: In the first draft of this speech, Roosevelt wrote the famous first line as 'a date that will live in world history' but later changed it to 'a date which will live in infamy.'*

# 23

## D-Day Prayer

★ ★ ★ ★ ★ ★ ★

Franklin Roosevelt
Washington, D.C.
6 June 1944

*The night before this speech, Roosevelt had announced that Allied troops had entered Rome. The good news of Rome's liberation had been shadowed by the D-Day invasion which had started at 6:30 a.m. on 6th June. That evening, the Allied troops stormed the beaches of Normandy. Many of their men were killed and wounded.*

*As Roosevelt addressed his countrymen that day, his speech took the form of a prayer.*

My fellow Americans:

Last night, when I spoke with you about the fall of Rome, I knew at that moment that troops of the United States and our Allies were crossing the Channel in another and greater operation. It has come to pass with success thus far.

And so, in this poignant hour, I ask you to join with me in prayer:

Almighty God: Our sons, pride of our nation, this day have set upon a mighty endeavour, a struggle to preserve our Republic, our religion, and our civilization, and to set free a suffering humanity.

Lead them straight and true; give strength to their arms, stoutness to their hearts, steadfastness in their faith.

They will need Thy blessings. Their road will be long and hard. For the enemy is strong. He may hurl back our forces. Success may not come with rushing speed, but we shall return again and again; and we know that by Thy grace, and by the righteousness of our cause, our sons will triumph.

They will be sore tried, by night and by day, without rest—until the victory is won. The darkness will be rent by noise and flame. Men's souls will be shaken with the violences of war.

For these men are lately drawn from the ways of peace. They fight not for the lust of conquest. They fight to end conquest. They fight to liberate. They fight to let justice arise, and tolerance and goodwill among all Thy people. They yearn but for the end of battle, for their return to the haven of home.

Some will never return. Embrace these, Father, and receive them, Thy heroic servants, into Thy kingdom.

And for us at home—fathers, mothers, children, wives, sisters, and brothers of brave men overseas, whose thoughts and prayers are ever with them—help us, Almighty God, to rededicate ourselves in renewed faith in Thee in this hour of great sacrifice.

Many people have urged that I call the nation into a single day of special prayer. But because the road is long and the desire is great, I ask that our people devote themselves in a continuance of prayer. As we rise to each new day, and again when each day is spent, let words of prayer be on our lips, invoking Thy help to our efforts.

Give us strength, too—strength in our daily tasks, to redouble the contributions we make in the physical and the material support of our armed forces.

And let our hearts be stout, to wait out the long travail, to bear sorrows that may come, to impart our courage unto our sons wheresoever they may be.

And, O Lord, give us faith. Give us faith in Thee; faith in our sons; faith in each other; faith in our united crusade. Let not the keenness of our spirit ever be dulled. Let not the impacts of temporary events, of temporal matters of but fleeting moment—let not these deter us in our unconquerable purpose.

With Thy blessing, we shall prevail over the unholy forces of our enemy. Help us to conquer the apostles of greed and racial arrogances. Lead us to the saving of our country, and with our sister nations into a world unity that will spell a sure peace—a peace invulnerable to the schemings of unworthy men. And a peace that will let all of men live in freedom, reaping the just rewards of their honest toil.

Thy will be done, Almighty God.

Amen.

# 24

## Farewell Address

★ ★ ★ ★ ★ ★ ★

George Washington
Philadelphia, U.S.A.
17 September 1796

*George Washington was the first President of the United States. In 1796, nearing the end of his second term, he chose to step down from his post. He addressed the American masses for the last time, most of which wanted him to run for another term as president.*

*The following speech was not spoken but published in Philadelphia's newspaper American Daily Advertiser. Washington advised his people to be wary of geographical sectionalism, political factionalism, and interference by foreign powers.*

Friends and Citizens:

The period for a new election of a citizen to administer the executive Government of the United States being not far distant, and the time actually arrived when your thoughts must be employed in designating the person who is to be clothed with that important trust, it appears to me proper, especially as it may conduce to a more distinct expression of the public voice, that I should now apprise you of the resolution I have formed to decline being considered among the number of those out of whom a choice is to be made.

I beg you, at the same time, to do me the justice to be assured that this resolution has not been taken without a strict regard to all the considerations appertaining to the relation which binds a dutiful citizen to his country; and that, in withdrawing the tender of service, which silence in my situation might imply, I am influenced by no diminution of zeal for your future interest, no deficiency of grateful respect for your past kindness, but am supported by a full conviction that the step is compatible with both.

The acceptance of, and continuance hitherto in, the office to which your suffrages have twice called me, have been a uniform sacrifice of inclination to the opinion of duty, and to a deference for what appeared to be your desire. I constantly hoped that it would have been much earlier in my power, consistently with motives which I was not at liberty to disregard, to return to that retirement from which I had been reluctantly drawn. The strength of my inclination to do this, previous to the last election, had even led to the preparation of an address to declare it to you; but mature reflection on the then perplexed and critical posture of our affairs with foreign nation, and the unanimous advice of persons entitled to my confidence, impelled me to abandon the idea.

I rejoice that the state of your concerns, external as well as internal, no longer renders the pursuit of inclination incompatible with the sentiment of duty or propriety; and am persuaded, whatever partiality may be retained for my services, that, in the present circumstances of our country, you will not disapprove my determination to retire.

The impressions with which I first undertook the arduous trust were explained on the proper occasion. In the discharge of this trust, I will only say that I have, with good intentions, contributed towards the organization and administration of the government the best exertions of which a very fallible judgement was capable. Not unconscious in the outset of the inferiority of my qualifications, experience in my own eyes, perhaps still more in the eyes of others, has strengthened the motives to diffidence of myself; and every day the increasing weight of years admonishes me more and more that the shade of retirement is as necessary to me as it will be welcome. Satisfied that if any circumstances have given peculiar value to my services, they were temporary, I have the consolation to believe that, while choice and prudence invite me to quit the political scene, patriotism does not forbid it.

In looking forward to the moment which is intended to terminate the career of my public life, my feelings do not permit me to suspend the deep acknowledgment of that debt of gratitude which I owe to my beloved country for the many honours it has conferred upon me; still more for the steadfast confidence with which it has supported me, and for the opportunities I have thence enjoyed of manifesting my inviolable attachment by services faithful and persevering, though in usefulness unequal to my zeal. If benefits have resulted to our country from these services let it always be remembered to your praise, and as an instructive example in our annals, that, under circumstances in which the passions, agitated in every direction, were liable to mislead, amid appearances sometimes dubious, vicissitudes of fortune often discouraging, in situations in which not unfrequently want of success has countenanced the spirit of criticism, the constancy of your support was the essential prop of the efforts and a guaranty of the plans by which they were effected. Profoundly penetrated with this idea, I shall carry it with me to my grave as a strong incitement to unceasing vows that heaven may continue to you the choicest tokens of its beneficence; that your union and brotherly affection may be perpetual; that the free Constitution, which is the work of your hands, may be sacredly maintained; that its administration in every department may be stamped with wisdom and virtue; that, in fine, the happiness of the people of these States, under the auspices of liberty, may be made complete by so careful a preservation and so prudent a use of this blessing as will acquire to them the glory of recommending it to the applause, the affection, and adoption of every nation which is yet a stranger to it.

Here, perhaps, I ought to stop. But a solicitude for your welfare which cannot end but with my life, and the apprehension of danger natural to that solicitude, urge me, on an occasion like the present, to offer to your solemn contemplation and to recommend to your frequent review some sentiments which are the result of much reflection of no inconsiderable observation, and which appear to me all-important to the permanency of your felicity as a people. These will be offered to you with the more freedom as you can only see in them the disinterested warnings of a parting friend who can possibly have no personal motive to bias his counsel. Nor can I forget, as an encouragement to it, your indulgent reception of my sentiments on a former and not dissimilar occasion.

Interwoven as is the love of liberty with every ligament of your hearts, no recommendation of mine is necessary to fortify or confirm the attachment.

The unity of government which constitutes you one people is also now dear to you. It is justly so, for it is a main pillar in the edifice of your real independence; the support of your tranquillity at home, your peace abroad; of your safety; of your prosperity; of that very liberty which you so highly prize. But as it is easy to foresee that from different causes and from different quarters much pains will be taken, many artifices employed, to weaken in your minds the conviction of this truth; as this is the point in your political fortress against which the batteries of internal and external enemies will be most constantly and actively (though often covertly and insidiously) directed, it is of infinite moment that you should properly estimate the immense value of your national Union to your collective and individual happiness; that you should cherish a cordial, habitual, and immovable attachment to it; accustoming yourselves to think and speak of it as the palladium of your political safety and prosperity; watching for its preservation with jealous anxiety; discountenancing whatever may suggest even a suspicion that it can in any event be abandoned; and indignantly frowning upon the first dawning of every attempt to alienate any portion of our country from the rest, or to enfeeble the sacred ties which now link together the various parts.

For this you have every inducement of sympathy and of interest. Citizens, either by birth or choice, of a common country, that country has a right to concentrate your affections. The name of American which belongs to you in your national capacity must always exalt the just pride of patriotism more than any appellation derived from local discriminations. With slight shades of difference you have the same religion, manners, habits, and political principles. You have in a common cause fought and triumphed together; the independence and liberty you possess are the work of joint counsels and joint efforts, of common dangers, sufferings, and successes.

But these considerations, however powerfully they address themselves to your sensibility, are greatly outweighed by those which apply more immediately to your interest. Here every portion of our country finds the most commanding motives for carefully guarding and preserving the union of the whole.

The North, in an unrestrained intercourse with the South, protected by the equal laws of a common government, finds in the productions of the latter great additional resources of maritime and commercial enterprise and precious materials of manufacturing industry. The South, in the same intercourse, benefiting by the agency of the North, sees its agriculture grow and its commerce expand. Turning partly into its own channels the seamen of the North, it finds its particular navigation invigorated, and while it contributes, in different ways, to nourish and increase the general mass of the national navigation, it looks forward to the protection of a maritime strength, to which itself is unequally adapted. The East, in a like intercourse with the West, already finds—and in a progressive improvement of interior communications by land and water will more and more find—a valuable vent for the commodities which it brings from abroad or manufactures at home. The West derives from the East supplies requisite to its growth and comfort, and what is perhaps of still greater consequence, it must of necessity owe the secure enjoyment of indispensable outlets for its own productions to the weight, influence, and the future maritime strength of the Atlantic side of the Union, directed by an indissoluble community of interest as one nation. Any other tenure by which the West can hold this essential advantage, whether derived from its own separate strength or from an apostate and unnatural connection with any foreign power, must be intrinsically precarious.

While, then, every part of our country thus feels an immediate and particular interest in union, all the parts combined cannot fail to find in the united mass of means and efforts greater strength, greater resource, proportionably greater security from external danger, a less frequent interruption of their peace by foreign nations; and, what is of inestimable value, they must derive from union an exemption from those broils and wars between themselves which so frequently afflict neighbouring countries not tied together by the same governments, which their own rivalships alone would be sufficient to produce, but which opposite foreign alliances, attachments, and intrigues would stimulate and embitter. Hence, likewise, they will avoid the necessity of those overgrown military establishments, which, under any form of government, are inauspicious to liberty, and which are to be regarded as particularly hostile to republican liberty. In this sense it is that your union ought to be considered as a main prop of your liberty, and that the love of the one ought to endear to you the preservation of the other.

These considerations speak a persuasive language to every reflecting and virtuous mind, and exhibit the continuance of the Union as a primary object of patriotic desire. Is there a doubt whether a common government can embrace so large a sphere? Let experience solve it. To listen to mere speculation in such a case were criminal. We are authorized to hope that a proper organization of the whole, with the auxiliary agency of governments for the respective subdivisions, will afford a happy issue to the experiment. It is well worth a fair and full experiment. With such powerful and obvious motives to union affecting all parts of our country, while experience shall not have demonstrated its impracticability, there will always be reason to distrust the patriotism of those who in any quarter may endeavour to weaken its bands.

In contemplating the causes which may disturb our Union it occurs as a matter of serious concern that any ground should have been furnished for characterizing parties by geographical discriminations, Northern and Southern, Atlantic and Western; whence designing men may endeavour to excite a belief that there is a real difference of local interests and views. One of the expedients of party to acquire influence within particular districts is to misrepresent the opinions and aims of other districts. You cannot shield yourselves too much against the jealousies and heartburnings which spring from these misrepresentations; they tend to render alien to each other those who ought to be bound together by fraternal affection. The inhabitants of our Western country have lately had a useful lesson on this head; they have seen, in the negotiation by the executive, and in the unanimous ratification by the Senate, of the treaty with Spain, and in the universal satisfaction at that event throughout the United States, a decisive proof how unfounded were the suspicions propagated among them of a policy in the general government and in the Atlantic States unfriendly to their interests in regard to the Mississippi; they have been witnesses to the formation of two treaties, that with Great Britain and that with Spain, which secure to them everything they could desire, in respect to our foreign relations, toward confirming their prosperity. Will it not be their wisdom to rely for the preservation of these advantages on the Union by which they were procured? Will they not henceforth be deaf to those advisers, if such there are, who would sever them from their brethren, and connect them with aliens?

To the efficacy and permanency of your Union a government for the whole is indispensable. No alliances, however strict, between the parts can be an adequate substitute; they must inevitably experience the infractions and interruptions which all alliances in all times have experienced. Sensible of this momentous truth, you have improved upon your first essay by the adoption of a constitution of government better calculated than your former for an intimate union and for the efficacious management of your common concerns. This government, the offspring of your own choice, uninfluenced and unawed, adopted upon full investigation and mature deliberation, completely free in its principles, in the distribution of its powers, uniting security with energy, and containing within itself a provision for its own amendment, has a just claim to your confidence and your support. Respect for its authority, compliance with its laws, acquiescence in its measures, are duties enjoined by the fundamental maxims of true liberty. The basis of our political systems is the right of the people to make and to alter their constitutions of government. But the constitution which at any time exists till changed by an explicit and authentic act of the whole people is sacredly obligatory upon all. The very idea of the power and the right of the people to establish government presupposes the duty of every individual to obey the established government.

All obstructions to the execution of the laws, all combinations and associations, under whatever plausible character, with the real design to direct, control, counteract, or awe the regular deliberation and action of the constituted authorities, are destructive of this fundamental principle, and of fatal tendency. They serve to organize faction, to give it an artificial and extraordinary force; to put, in the place of the delegated will of the nation, the will of a party, often a small but artful and enterprising minority of the community; and, according to the alternate triumphs of different parties, to make the public administration the mirror of the ill-concerted and incongruous projects of fashion, rather than the organs of consistent and wholesome plans digested by common councils, and modified by mutual interests.

However, combinations or associations of the above description may now and then answer popular ends, they are likely, in the course of time and things, to become potent engines, by which cunning, ambitious, and unprincipled men will be enabled to subvert the power of the people, and to usurp for themselves the reins of government, destroying afterward the very engines which have lifted them to unjust dominion.

Towards the preservation of your government, and the permanency of your present happy state, it is requisite, not only that you steadily discountenance irregular oppositions to its acknowledged authority, but also that you resist with care the spirit of innovation upon its principles, however specious the pretexts. One method of assault may be to affect, in the forms of the Constitution, alterations which will impair the energy of the system, and thus to undermine what cannot be directly overthrown. In all the changes to which you may be invited, remember that time and habit are at least as necessary to fix the true character of governments as of other human institutions; that experience is the surest standard by which to test the real tendency of the existing constitution of a country; that facility in changes, upon the credit of mere hypothesis and opinion, exposes to perpetual change, from the endless variety of hypothesis and opinion; and remember especially that for the efficient management of your common interests, in a country so extensive as ours, a government of as much vigour as is consistent with the perfect security of liberty is indispensable. Liberty itself will find in such a government, with powers properly distributed and adjusted, its surest guardian. It is, indeed, little else than a name where the government is too feeble to withstand the enterprises of faction, to confine each member of the society within the limits prescribed by the laws, and to maintain all in the secure and tranquil enjoyment of the rights of person and property.

I have already intimated to you the danger of parties in the State, with particular reference to the founding of them on geographical discrimination. Let me now take a more comprehensive view, and warn you in the most solemn manner against the baneful effects of the spirit of party generally.

This spirit, unfortunately, is inseparable from our nature, having its root in the strongest passions of the human mind. It exists under different shapes in all governments, more or less stifled, controlled, or repressed; but in those of the popular form it is seen in its greatest rankness, and is truly their worst enemy.

The alternate domination of one faction over another, sharpened by the spirit of revenge, natural to party dissension, which in different ages and countries has perpetrated the most horrid enormities, is itself a frightful despotism. But this leads at length to a more formal and permanent despotism. The disorders and miseries which result gradually incline the minds of men to seek security and repose in the absolute power of an individual, and sooner or later the chief of some prevailing faction, more able or more fortunate than his competitors, turns this disposition to the purposes of his own elevation, on the ruins of public liberty.

Without looking forward to an extremity of this kind (which nevertheless ought not to be entirely out of sight), the common and continued mischiefs of the spirit of party are sufficient to make it the interest and duty of a wise people to discourage and restrain it. It serves always to distract the public councils and enfeeble the public administration. It agitates the community with ill-founded jealousies and false alarms; kindles the animosity of one part against another; foments, occasionally, riot and insurrection. It opens the doors to foreign influence and corruption, which find a facilitated access to the government itself through the channels of party passions. Thus the policy and the will of one country are subjected to the policy and will of another.

There is an opinion that parties in free countries are useful checks upon the administration of the government and serve to keep alive the spirit of liberty. This within certain limits is probably true, and in governments of a monarchical cast, patriotism may look with indulgence, if not with favour, upon the spirit of party. But in those of the popular character, in governments purely elective, it is a spirit not to be encouraged. From their natural tendency it is certain there will always be enough of that spirit for every salutary purpose. And there being constant danger of excess, the effort ought to be by force of public opinion to mitigate and assuage it. A fire not to be quenched, it demands a uniform vigilance to prevent its bursting into a flame, lest, instead of warming, it should consume.

It is important, likewise, that the habits of thinking in a free country should inspire caution, in those entrusted with its administration, to confine themselves within their respective constitutional spheres, avoiding in the exercise of the powers of one department to encroach upon another. The spirit of encroachment tends to consolidate the powers of all the departments in one, and thus to create, whatever the form of government, a real despotism. A just estimate of that love of power and proneness to abuse it which predominates in the human heart is sufficient to satisfy us of the truth of this position. The necessity of reciprocal checks in the exercise of political power by dividing and distributing it into different depositories, and constituting each the guardian of the public weal against invasions by the others, has been evinced by experiments, ancient and modern, some of them in our country and under our own eyes. To preserve them must be as necessary as to institute them. If, in the opinion of the people, the distribution or modification of the constitutional powers be in any particular wrong, let it be corrected by an amendment in the way which the Constitution designates. But let there be no change by usurpation; for though this, in one instance, may be the instrument of good, it is the customary weapon by which free governments are destroyed. The precedent must always greatly overbalance in permanent evil any partial or transient benefit which the use can at any time yield.

Of all the dispositions and habits which lead to political prosperity, religion and morality are indispensable supports. In vain would that man claim the tribute of patriotism who should labour to subvert these great pillars of human happiness, these firmest props of the duties of men and citizens. The mere politician, equally with the pious man, ought to respect and to cherish them. A volume could not trace all their connections with private and public felicity. Let it simply be asked, Where is the security for property, for reputation, for life, if the sense of religious obligation desert the oaths, which are the instruments of investigation in courts of justice? And let us with caution indulge the supposition that morality can be maintained without religion. Whatever may be conceded to the influence of refined education on minds of peculiar structure, reason and experience both forbid us to expect that national morality can prevail in exclusion of religious principle.

It is substantially true that virtue or morality is a necessary spring of popular government. The rule, indeed, extends with more or less force to every species of free government. Who that is a sincere friend to it can look with indifference upon attempts to shake the foundation of the fabric?

Promote, then, as an object of primary importance, institutions for the general diffusion of knowledge. In proportion as the structure of a government gives force to public opinion it is essential that public opinion should be enlightened.

As a very important source of strength and security, cherish public credit. One method of preserving it is to use it as sparingly as possible; avoiding occasions of expense by cultivating peace, but remembering also that timely disbursements to prepare for danger frequently prevent much greater disbursements to repel it; avoiding likewise the accumulation of debt, not only by shunning occasions of expense, but by vigorous exertion in time of peace to discharge the debts, which unavoidable wars may have occasioned, not ungenerously throwing upon posterity the burden which we ourselves ought to bear. The execution of these maxims belongs to your representatives, but it is necessary that public opinion should cooperate. To facilitate to them the performance of their duty it is essential that you should practically bear in mind that toward the payment of debts there must be revenue; that to have revenue there must be taxes; that no taxes can be devised which are not more or less inconvenient and unpleasant; that the intrinsic embarrassment, inseparable from the selection of the proper objects (which is always a choice of difficulties), ought to be a decisive motive for a candid construction of the conduct of the government in making it, and for a spirit of acquiescence in the measures for obtaining revenue which the public exigencies may at any time dictate.

Observe good faith and justice toward all nations; cultivate peace and harmony with all. Religion and morality enjoin this conduct, and can it be that good policy does not equally enjoin it? It will be worthy of a free, enlightened, and, at no distant period, a great nation, to give to mankind the magnanimous and novel example of a people always guided by an exalted justice and benevolence. Who can doubt that, in the course of time and things, the fruits of such a plan would richly repay any temporary advantages which might be lost by a steady adherence to it? Can it be that providence has not connected the permanent felicity of a nation with its virtue? The experiment, at least, is recommended by every sentiment which ennobles human nature. Alas! Is it rendered impossible by its vices?

In the execution of such a plan nothing is more essential than that permanent, inveterate antipathies against particular nations and passionate attachments for others should be excluded, and that, in place of them, just and amicable feelings toward all should be cultivated. The nation which indulges toward another an habitual hatred or an habitual fondness is in some degree a slave. It is a slave to its animosity or to its affection, either of which is sufficient to lead it astray from its duty and its interest. Antipathy in one nation against another disposes each more readily to offer insult and injury, to lay hold of slight causes of umbrage, and to be haughty and intractable, when accidental or trifling occasions of dispute occur. Hence, frequent collisions; obstinate, envenomed, and bloody contests. The nation, prompted by ill will and resentment, sometimes impels to war the government, contrary to the best calculations of policy. The government sometimes participates in the national propensity, and adopts through passion what reason would reject; at other times it makes the animosity of the nation subservient to projects of hostility instigated by pride, ambition, and other sinister and pernicious motives. The peace often, sometimes perhaps the liberty, of nations has been the victim.

So, likewise, a passionate attachment of one nation for another produces a variety of evils. Sympathy for the favourite nation, facilitating the illusion of an imaginary common interest in cases where no real common interest exists, and infusing into one the enmities of the other, betrays the former into a participation in the quarrels and wars of the latter, without adequate inducement or justification. It leads also to concessions to the favourite nation of privileges denied to others, which is apt doubly to injure the nation making the concessions by unnecessarily parting with what ought to have been retained, and by exciting jealousy, ill will, and a disposition to retaliate, in the parties from whom equal privileges are withheld. And it gives to ambitious, corrupted, or deluded citizens (who devote themselves to the favourite nation), facility to betray or sacrifice the interests of their own country without odium, sometimes even with popularity; gilding with the appearances of a virtuous sense of obligation, a commendable deference for public opinion, or a laudable zeal for public good, the base or foolish compliances of ambition, corruption, or infatuation.

As avenues to foreign influence in innumerable ways, such attachments are particularly alarming to the truly enlightened and independent patriot. How many opportunities do they afford to tamper with domestic factions, to practise the arts of seduction, to mislead public opinion, to influence or awe the public councils! Such an attachment of a small or weak toward a great and powerful nation dooms the former to be the satellite of the latter.

Against the insidious wiles of foreign influence (I conjure you to believe me, fellow citizens), the jealousy of a free people ought to be constantly awake, since history and experience prove that foreign influence is one of the most baneful foes of republican government. But that jealousy, to be useful, must be impartial, else it becomes the instrument of the very influence to be avoided, instead of a defence against it. Excessive partiality for one foreign nation and excessive dislike of another cause those whom they actuate to see danger only on one side, and serve to veil and even second the arts of influence on the other. Real patriots, who may resist the intrigues of the favourite, are liable to become suspected and odious; while its tools and dupes usurp the applause and confidence of the people, to surrender their interests.

The great rule of conduct for us, in regard to foreign nations, is, in extending our commercial relations, to have with them as little political connection as possible. So far as we have already formed engagements, let them be fulfilled with perfect good faith. Here let us stop. Europe has a set of primary interests which to us have none, or a very remote, relation. Hence she must be engaged in frequent controversies, the causes of which are essentially foreign to our concerns. Hence, therefore, it must be unwise in us to implicate ourselves, by artificial ties, in the ordinary vicissitudes of her politics or the ordinary combinations and collisions of her friendships or enmities.

Our detached and distant situation invites and enables us to pursue a different course. If we remain one people, under an efficient government the period is not far off when we may defy material injury from external annoyance; when we may take such an attitude as will cause the neutrality we may at any time resolve upon to be scrupulously respected; when belligerent nations, under the impossibility of making acquisitions upon us, will not lightly hazard the giving us provocation; when we may choose peace or war, as our interest, guided by justice, shall counsel.

Why forego the advantages of so peculiar a situation? Why quit our own to stand upon foreign ground? Why, by interweaving our destiny with that of any part of Europe, entangle our peace and prosperity in the toils of European ambition, rivalship, interest, humour, or caprice?

It is our true policy to steer clear of permanent alliances with any portion of the foreign world—so far, I mean, as we are now at liberty to do it; for let me not be understood as capable of patronizing infidelity to existing engagements. I hold the maxim no less applicable to public than to private affairs, that honesty is always the best policy. I repeat it, therefore, let those engagements be observed in their genuine sense. But, in my opinion, it is unnecessary and would be unwise to extend them.

Taking care always to keep ourselves, by suitable establishments, on a respectable defensive posture, we may safely trust to temporary alliances for extraordinary emergencies.

Harmony, liberal intercourse with all nations, are recommended by policy, humanity, and interest. But even our commercial policy should hold an equal and impartial hand; neither seeking nor granting exclusive favours or preferences; consulting the natural course of things; diffusing and diversifying by gentle means the streams of commerce, but forcing nothing; establishing, with powers so disposed, in order to give trade a stable course, to define the rights of our merchants, and to enable the government to support them, conventional rules of intercourse, the best that present circumstances and mutual opinion will permit, but temporary, and liable to be from time to time abandoned or varied, as experience and circumstances shall dictate; constantly keeping in view that it is folly in one nation to look for disinterested favours from another; that it must pay with a portion of its independence for whatever it may accept under that character; that, by such acceptance, it may place itself in the condition of having given equivalents for nominal favours, and yet of being reproached with ingratitude for not giving more. There can be no greater error than to expect or calculate upon real favours from nation to nation. It is an illusion which experience must cure, which a just pride ought to discard.

In offering to you, my countrymen, these counsels of an old and affectionate friend, I dare not hope they will make the strong and lasting impression I could wish; that they will control the usual current of the passions, or prevent our nation from running the course which has hitherto marked the destiny of nations. But if I may even flatter myself that they may be productive of some partial benefit, some occasional good; that they may now and then recur to moderate the fury of party spirit, to warn against the mischiefs of foreign intrigue, to guard against the impostures of pretended patriotism: this hope will be a full recompense for the solicitude for your welfare by which they have been dictated.

How far in the discharge of my official duties I have been guided by the principles which have been delineated, the public records and other evidences of my conduct must witness to you and to the world. To myself, the assurance of my own conscience is, that I have at least believed myself to be guided by them.

In relation to the still subsisting war in Europe, my proclamation of the twenty-second of April 1793, is the index of my plan. Sanctioned by your approving voice, and by that of your representatives in both houses of Congress, the spirit of that measure has continually governed me, uninfluenced by any attempts to deter or divert me from it.

After deliberate examination, with the aid of the best lights I could obtain, I was well satisfied that our country, under all the circumstances of the case, had a right to take, and was bound in duty and interest to take, a neutral position. Having taken it, I determined, as far as should depend upon me, to maintain it, with moderation, perseverance, and firmness.

The considerations which respect the right to hold this conduct, it is not necessary on this occasion to detail. I will only observe that, according to my understanding of the matter, that right, so far from being denied by any of the belligerent powers, has been virtually admitted by all.

The duty of holding a neutral conduct may be inferred, without anything more, from the obligation which justice and humanity impose on every nation, in cases in which it is free to act, to maintain inviolate the relations of peace and amity towards other nations.

The inducements of interest for observing that conduct will best be referred to your own reflections and experience. With me a predominant motive has been to endeavour to gain time to our country to settle and mature its yet recent institutions, and to progress without interruption to that degree of strength and consistency which is necessary to give it, humanly speaking, the command of its own fortunes.

Though in reviewing the incidents of my administration I am unconscious of intentional error, I am nevertheless too sensible of my defects not to think it probable that I may have committed many errors. Whatever they may be, I fervently beseech the Almighty to avert or mitigate the evils to which they may tend. I shall also carry with me the hope that my country will never cease to view them with indulgence; and that, after forty-five years of my life dedicated to its service with an upright zeal, the faults of incompetent abilities will be consigned to oblivion, as myself must soon be to the mansions of rest.

Relying on its kindness in this as in other things, and actuated by that fervent love toward it which is so natural to a man who views in it the native soil of himself and his progenitors for several generations, I anticipate with pleasing expectation that retreat in which I promise myself to realize, without alloy, the sweet enjoyment of partaking in the midst of my fellow citizens the benign influence of good laws under a free government, the ever favourite object of my heart, and the happy reward, as I trust, of our mutual cares, labours, and dangers.

*Note: The handwritten draft of this speech was thirty-two pages long.*

# 25

## Inaugural Address

★ ★ ★ ★ ★ ★ ★

John F. Kennedy
Washington, D.C., U.S.A.
20 January 1961

*Shadowed by the Cold War and the U.S. Civil Rights Movement, Kennedy delivered his brief inaugural address, inspiring the nation. He appealed to the people to contribute something to the public good and service their country and hoped that the new generation will bring a better, brighter future with it.*

*Theodore O. Windt Jr. called this speech 'one of the few truly memorable inaugural addresses in U.S. history.'*

Vice President Johnson, Mr. Speaker, Mr. Chief Justice, President Eisenhower, Vice President Nixon, President Truman, reverend clergy, fellow citizens:

We observe today not a victory of party, but a celebration of freedom—symbolizing an end, as well as a beginning—signifying renewal, as well as change. For I have sworn before you and Almighty God the same solemn oath our forebears prescribed nearly a century and three quarters ago.

The world is very different now. For man holds in his mortal hands the power to abolish all forms of human poverty and all forms of human life. And yet the same revolutionary beliefs for which our forebears fought are still at issue around the globe—the belief that the rights of man come not from the generosity of the state, but from the hand of God.

We dare not forget today that we are the heirs of that first revolution. Let the word go forth from this time and place, to friend and foe alike, that the torch has been passed to a new generation of Americans, born in this century, tempered by war, disciplined by a hard and bitter peace, proud of our ancient heritage and unwilling to witness or permit the slow undoing of those human rights to which this Nation has always been committed, and to which we are committed today at home and around the world.

Let every nation know, whether it wishes us well or ill, that we shall pay any price, bear any burden, meet any hardship, support any friend, oppose any foe, to assure the survival and the success of liberty.

This much we pledge—and more.

To those old allies whose cultural and spiritual origins we share, we pledge the loyalty of faithful friends. United, there is little we cannot do in a host of cooperative ventures. Divided, there is little we can do—for we dare not meet a powerful challenge at odds and split asunder.

To those new states whom we welcome to the ranks of the free, we pledge our word that one form of colonial control shall not have passed away merely to be replaced by a far more iron tyranny. We shall not always expect to find them supporting our view. But we shall always hope to find them strongly supporting their own freedom—and to remember that, in the past, those who foolishly sought power by riding the back of the tiger ended up inside.

To those peoples in the huts and villages across the globe struggling to break the bonds of mass misery, we pledge our best efforts to help them help themselves, for whatever period is required—not because the Communists may be doing it, not because we seek their votes, but because it is right. If a free society cannot help the many who are poor, it cannot save the few who are rich.

To our sister republics south of our border, we offer a special pledge—to convert our good words into good deeds in a new alliance for progress—to assist free men and free governments in casting off the chains of poverty. But this peaceful revolution of hope cannot become the prey of hostile powers. Let all our neighbours know that we shall join with them to oppose aggression or subversion anywhere in the Americas. And let every other power know that this Hemisphere intends to remain the master of its own house.

To that world assembly of sovereign states, the United Nations, our last best hope in an age where the instruments of war have far outpaced the instruments of peace, we renew our pledge of support—to prevent it from becoming merely a forum for invective—to strengthen its shield of the new and the weak and to enlarge the area in which its writ may run.

Finally, to those nations who would make themselves our adversary, we offer not a pledge but a request: that both sides begin anew the quest for peace, before the dark powers of destruction unleashed by science engulf all humanity in planned or accidental self-destruction.

We dare not tempt them with weakness. For only when our arms are sufficient beyond doubt can we be certain beyond doubt that they will never be employed.

But neither can two great and powerful groups of nations take comfort from our present course—both sides overburdened by the cost of modern weapons, both rightly alarmed by the steady spread of the deadly atom, yet both racing to alter that uncertain balance of terror that stays the hand of mankind's final war.

So let us begin anew, remembering on both sides that civility is not a sign of weakness, and sincerity is always subject to proof. Let us never negotiate out of fear. But let us never fear to negotiate.

Let both sides explore what problems unite us instead of belabouring those problems which divide us.

Let both sides, for the first time, formulate serious and precise proposals for the inspection and control of arms and bring the absolute power to destroy other nations under the absolute control of all nations.

Let both sides seek to invoke the wonders of science instead of its terrors. Together let us explore the stars, conquer the deserts, eradicate disease, tap the ocean depths, and encourage the arts and commerce.

Let both sides unite to heed in all corners of the earth the command of Isaiah—to 'undo the heavy burdens . . . and let the oppressed go free.'

And if a beachhead of cooperation may push back the jungle of suspicion, let both sides join in creating a new endeavour, not a new balance of power, but a new world of law, where the strong are just and the weak secure and the peace preserved.

All this will not be finished in the first hundred days. Nor will it be finished in the first thousand days, nor in the life of this administration, nor even perhaps in our lifetime on this planet. But let us begin.

In your hands, my fellow citizens, more than mine, will rest the final success or failure of our course. Since this country was founded, each generation of Americans has been summoned to give testimony to its national loyalty. The graves of young Americans who answered the call to service surround the globe.

Now the trumpet summons us again—not as a call to bear arms, though arms we need—not as a call to battle, though embattled we are—but a call to bear the burden of a long twilight struggle, year in and year out, 'rejoicing in hope, patient in tribulation'—a struggle against the common enemies of man: tyranny, poverty, disease, and war itself.

Can we forge against these enemies a grand and global alliance, North and South, East and West, that can assure a more fruitful life for all mankind? Will you join in that historic effort?

In the long history of the world, only a few generations have been granted the role of defending freedom in its hour of maximum danger. I do not shrink from this responsibility—I welcome it. I do not believe that any of us would exchange places with any other people or any other generation. The energy, the faith, the devotion which we bring to this endeavour will light our country and all who serve it—and the glow from that fire can truly light the world.

And so, my fellow Americans: ask not what your country can do for you—ask what you can do for your country.

My fellow citizens of the world: ask not what America will do for you, but what together we can do for the freedom of man.

Finally, whether you are citizens of America or citizens of the world, ask of us here the same high standards of strength and sacrifice which we ask of you. With a good conscience our only sure reward, with history the final judge of our deeds, let us go forth to lead the land we love, asking His blessing and His help, but knowing that here on earth God's work must truly be our own.

*Note: Before writing this speech, Kennedy had asked his speechwriter to study Lincoln's speech 'The Gettysburg Address.'*

# 26

## We Choose to Go to the Moon

★ ★ ★ ★ ★ ★ ★

John F. Kennedy
Houston, Texas, U.S.A.
12 September 1962

*The space race was on between the Cold War rivals, United States of America and the Soviet Union.*

*A year before Kennedy gave the following speech, Soviet cosmonaut, Yuri Gagarin became the first person to ever go into space.*

*In the following speech, the president dramatically announced his ambitious goal to land a person on the moon within a decade. This goal was realized seven years later, when Apollo 11's commander, Neil Armstrong, became the first man to go to the moon.*

President Pitzer, Mr. Vice President, Governor, Congressman Thomas, Senator Wiley, and Congressman Miller, Mr. Webb, Mr. Bell, scientists, distinguished guests, and ladies and gentlemen:

I appreciate your president having made me an

honorary visiting professor, and I will assure you that my first lecture will be very brief.

I am delighted to be here and I'm particularly delighted to be here on this occasion.

We meet at a college noted for knowledge, in a city noted for progress, in a state noted for strength, and we stand in need of all three, for we meet in an hour of change and challenge, in a decade of hope and fear, in an age of both knowledge and ignorance. The greater our knowledge increases, the greater our ignorance unfolds.

Despite the striking fact that most of the scientists that the world has ever known are alive and working today, despite the fact that this Nation's own scientific manpower is doubling every twelve years in a rate of growth more than three times that of our population as a whole, despite that, the vast stretches of the unknown and the unanswered and the unfinished still far outstrip our collective comprehension.

No man can fully grasp how far and how fast we have come, but condense, if you will, the fifty thousand years of man's recorded history in a time span of but a half-century. Stated in these terms, we know very little about the first forty years, except at the end of them advanced man had learned to use the skins of animals to cover them. Then about ten years ago, under this standard, man emerged from his caves to construct other kinds of shelter. Only five years ago man learned to write and use a cart with wheels. Christianity began less than two years ago. The printing press came this year, and then less than two months ago, during this whole fifty-year span of human history, the steam engine provided a new source of power. Newton explored the meaning of gravity. Last month electric lights and telephones and automobiles and airplanes became available. Only last week did we develop penicillin and television and nuclear power, and now if America's new spacecraft succeeds in reaching Venus, we will have literally reached the stars before midnight tonight.

This is a breathtaking pace, and such a pace cannot help but create new ills as it dispels old, new ignorance, new problems, new dangers.

Surely the opening vistas of space promise high costs and hardships, as well as high reward.

So it is not surprising that some would have us stay where we are a little longer to rest, to wait. But this city of Houston, this state of Texas, this country of the United States was not built by those who waited and rested and wished to look behind them. This country was conquered by those who moved forward—and so will space.

William Bradford, speaking in 1630 of the founding of the Plymouth Bay Colony, said that all great and honourable actions are accompanied with great difficulties, and both must be enterprised and overcome with answerable courage.

If this capsule history of our progress teaches us anything, it is that man, in his quest for knowledge and progress, is determined and cannot be deterred. The exploration of space will go ahead, whether we join in it or not, and it is one of the great adventures of all time, and no nation which expects to be the leader of other nations can expect to stay behind in this race for space.

Those who came before us made certain that this country rode the first waves of the industrial revolution, the first waves of modern invention, and the first wave of nuclear power, and this generation does not intend to founder in the backwash of the coming age of space. We mean to be a part of it—we mean to lead it. For the eyes of the world now look into space, to the moon and to the planets beyond, and we have vowed that we shall not see it governed by a hostile flag of conquest, but by a banner of freedom and peace. We have vowed that we shall not see space filled with weapons of mass destruction, but with instruments of knowledge and understanding.

Yet the vows of this Nation can only be fulfilled if we in this Nation are first, and, therefore, we intend to be first. In short, our leadership in science and industry, our hopes for peace and security, our obligations to ourselves as well as others, all require us to make this effort, to solve these mysteries, to solve them for the good of all men, and to become the world's leading space-faring nation.

We set sail on this new sea because there is new knowledge to be gained, and new rights to be won, and they must be won and used for the progress of all people. For space science, like nuclear science and all technology, has no conscience of its own. Whether it will become a force for good or ill depends on man, and only if the United States occupies a position of pre-eminence can we help decide whether this new ocean will be a sea of peace or a new terrifying theatre of war. I do not say that we should or will go unprotected against the hostile misuse of space any more than we go unprotected against the hostile use of land or sea, but I do say that space can be explored and mastered without feeding the fires of war, without repeating the mistakes that man has made in extending his writ around this globe of ours.

There is no strife, no prejudice, no national conflict in outer space as yet. Its hazards are hostile to us all. Its conquest deserves the best of all mankind, and its opportunity for peaceful cooperation many never come again. But why, some say, the moon? Why choose this as our goal? And they may well ask why climb the highest mountain? Why, thirty-five years ago, fly the Atlantic? Why does Rice play Texas?

We choose to go to the moon. We choose to go to the moon in this decade and do the other things, not because they are easy, but because they are hard, because that goal will serve to organize and measure the best of our energies and skills, because that challenge is one that we are willing to accept, one we are unwilling to postpone, and one which we intend to win, and the others, too.

It is for these reasons that I regard the decision last year to shift our efforts in space from low to high gear as among the most important decisions that will be made during my incumbency in the office of the Presidency.

In the last twenty-four hours we have seen facilities now being created for the greatest and most complex exploration in man's history. We have felt the ground shake and the air shattered by the testing of a Saturn C-1 booster rocket, many times as powerful as the Atlas which launched John Glenn, generating power equivalent to ten thousand automobiles with their accelerators on the floor. We have seen the site where five F-1 rocket engines, each one as powerful as all eight engines of the Saturn combined, will be clustered together to make the advanced Saturn missile, assembled in a new building to be built at Cape Canaveral as tall as a forty-eight story structure, as wide as a city block, and as long as two lengths of this field.

Within these last nineteen months at least forty-five satellites have circled the earth. Some forty of them were made in the United States of America and they were far more sophisticated and supplied far more knowledge to the people of the world than those of the Soviet Union.

The Mariner spacecraft now on its way to Venus is the most intricate instrument in the history of space science. The accuracy of that shot is comparable to firing a missile from Cape Canaveral and dropping it in this stadium between the forty-yard lines.

Transit satellites are helping our ships at sea to steer a safer course. Tiros satellites have given us unprecedented warnings of hurricanes and storms, and will do the same for forest fires and icebergs.

We have had our failures, but so have others, even if they do not admit them. And they may be less public.

To be sure, we are behind, and will be behind for some time in manned flight. But we do not intend to stay behind, and in this decade, we shall make up and move ahead.

The growth of our science and education will be enriched by new knowledge of our universe and environment, by new techniques of learning and mapping and observation, by new tools and computers for industry, medicine, the home as well as the school. Technical institutions, such as Rice, will reap the harvest of these gains.

And finally, the space effort itself, while still in its infancy, has already created a great number of new companies, and tens of thousands of new jobs. Space and related industries are generating new demands in investment and skilled personnel, and this city and this state, and this region, will share greatly in this growth. What was once the furthest outpost on the old frontier of the West will be the furthest outpost on the new frontier of science and space. Houston, your city of Houston, with its Manned Spacecraft Centre, will become the heart of a large scientific and engineering community. During the next five years the National Aeronautics and Space Administration expects to double the number of scientists and engineers in this area, to increase its outlays for salaries and expenses to $60 million a year; to invest some $200 million in plant and laboratory facilities; and to direct or contract for new space efforts over $1 billion from this centre in this city.

To be sure, all this costs us all a good deal of money. This year's space budget is three times what it was in January 1961, and it is greater than the space budget of the previous eight years combined. That budget now stands at $5,400 million a year—a staggering sum, though somewhat less than we pay for cigarettes and cigars every year. Space expenditures will soon rise some more, from forty cents per person per week to more than fifty cents a week for every man, woman and child in the United States, for we have given this program a high national priority—even though I realize that this is in some measure an act of faith and vision, for we do not now know what benefits await us. But if I were to say, my fellow citizens, that we shall send to the moon, 240,000 miles away from the control station in Houston, a giant rocket more than three hundred feet tall, the length of this football field, made of new metal alloys, some of which have not yet been invented, capable of standing heat and stresses several times more than have ever been experienced, fitted together with a precision better than the finest watch, carrying all the equipment needed for propulsion, guidance, control, communications, food and survival, on an untried mission, to an unknown celestial body, and then return it safely to earth, re-entering the atmosphere at speeds of over twenty-five thousand miles per hour, causing heat about half that of the temperature of the sun—almost as hot as it is here today—and do all this, and do it right, and do it first before this decade is out—then we must be bold.

I'm the one who is doing all the work, so we just want you to stay cool for a minute.

However, I think we're going to do it, and I think that we must pay what needs to be paid. I don't think we ought to waste any money, but I think we ought to do the job. And this will be done in the decade of the Sixties. It may be done while some of you are still here at school at this college and university. It will be done during the terms of office of some of the people who sit here on this platform. But it will be done. And it will be done before the end of this decade.

And I am delighted that this university is playing a part in putting a man on the moon as part of a great national effort of the United States of America.

Many years ago the great British explorer George Mallory, who was to die on Mount Everest, was asked why did he want to climb it. He said, 'Because it is there.'

Well, space is there, and we're going to climb it, and the moon and the planets are there, and new hopes for knowledge and peace are there. And, therefore, as we set sail we ask God's blessing on the most hazardous and dangerous and greatest adventure on which man has ever embarked.

Thank you.

# 27

## On the Cuban Crisis

★ ★ ★ ★ ★ ★ ★

John F. Kennedy
Washington, D.C., U.S.A.
22 October 1962

*Kennedy's address to his countrymen was broadcasted on the radio and television, informing them that the Soviet Union had placed nuclear missiles in Cuba, at a distance of ninety miles from the U.S. shores. The United States had responded by constructing a blockade around the area and issuing a warning—if any missiles were fired, it would be taken as a declaration of war and U.S. would respond in kind.*

Good evening my fellow citizens:

This government, as promised, has maintained the closest surveillance of the Soviet Military build-up on the island of Cuba. Within the past week, unmistakable evidence has established the fact that a series of offensive missile sites is now in preparation on that imprisoned island. The purpose of these bases can be none other than to provide a nuclear strike capability against the Western Hemisphere.

Upon receiving the first preliminary hard information of this nature last Tuesday morning at 9 a.m., I directed that our surveillance be stepped up. And having now confirmed and completed our evaluation of the evidence and our decision on a course of action, this government feels obliged to report this new crisis to you in fullest detail.

The characteristics of these new missile sites indicate two distinct types of installations. Several of them include medium range ballistic missiles capable of carrying a nuclear warhead for a distance of more than a thousand nautical miles. Each of these missiles, in short, is capable of striking Washington, D.C., the Panama Canal, Cape Canaveral, Mexico City, or any other city in the south eastern part of the United States, in Central America, or in the Caribbean area.

Additional sites not yet completed appear to be designed for intermediate range ballistic missiles—capable of traveling more than twice as far—and thus capable of striking most of the major cities in the Western Hemisphere, ranging as far north as Hudson Bay, Canada, and as far south as Lima, Peru. In addition, jet bombers, capable of carrying nuclear weapons, are now being uncrated and assembled in Cuba, while the necessary air bases are being prepared.

This urgent transformation of Cuba into an important strategic base—by the presence of these large, long range, and clearly offensive weapons of sudden mass destruction—constitutes an explicit threat to the peace and security of all the Americas, in flagrant and deliberate defiance of the Rio Pact of 1947, the traditions of this Nation and hemisphere, the joint resolution of the eighty-seventh Congress, the Charter of the United Nations, and my own public warnings to the Soviets on September 4th and 13th. This action also contradicts the repeated assurances of Soviet spokesmen, both publicly and privately delivered, that the arms build-up in Cuba would retain its original defensive character, and that the Soviet Union had no need or desire to station strategic missiles on the territory of any other nation.

The size of this undertaking makes clear that it has been planned for some months. Yet only last month, after I had made clear the distinction between any introduction of ground-to-ground missiles and the existence of defensive antiaircraft missiles, the Soviet Government publicly stated on September 11th, and I quote, 'the armaments and military equipment sent to Cuba are designed exclusively for defensive purposes,' that, and I quote the Soviet Government, 'there is no need for the Soviet Government to shift its weapons . . . for a retaliatory blow to any other country, for instance Cuba,' and that, and I quote their government, 'the Soviet Union has so powerful rockets to carry these nuclear warheads that there is no need to search for sites for them beyond the boundaries of the Soviet Union.' That statement was false.

Only last Thursday, as evidence of this rapid offensive build-up was already in my hand, Soviet Foreign Minister Gromyko told me in my office that he was instructed to make it clear once again, as he said his government had already done, that Soviet assistance to Cuba, and I quote, 'pursued solely the purpose of contributing to the defence capabilities of Cuba,' that, and I quote him, 'training by Soviet specialists of Cuban nationals in handling defensive armaments was by no means offensive, and if it were otherwise,' Mr. Gromyko went on, 'the Soviet Government would never become involved in rendering such assistance.' That statement also was false.

Neither the United States of America nor the world community of nations can tolerate deliberate deception and offensive threats on the part of any nation, large or small. We no longer live in a world where only the actual firing of weapons represents a sufficient challenge to a nation's security to constitute maximum peril. Nuclear weapons are so destructive and ballistic missiles are so swift, that any substantially increased possibility of their use or any sudden change in their deployment may well be regarded as a definite threat to peace.

For many years both the Soviet Union and the United States, recognizing this fact, have deployed strategic nuclear weapons with great care, never upsetting the precarious status quo which insured that these weapons would not be used in the absence of some vital challenge. Our own strategic missiles have never been transferred to the territory of any other nation under a cloak of secrecy and deception; and our history—unlike that of the Soviets since the end of World War II—demonstrates that we have no desire to dominate or conquer any other nation or impose our system upon its people. Nevertheless, American citizens have become adjusted to living daily on the bullseye of Soviet missiles located inside the U.S.S.R. or in submarines.

In that sense, missiles in Cuba add to an already clear and present danger—although it should be noted the nations of Latin America have never previously been subjected to a potential nuclear threat.

But this secret, swift, and extraordinary build-up of Communist missiles—in an area well known to have a special and historical relationship to the United States and the nations of the Western Hemisphere, in violation of Soviet assurances, and in defiance of American and hemispheric policy—this sudden, clandestine decision to station strategic weapons for the first time outside of Soviet soil—is a deliberately provocative and unjustified change in the status quo which cannot be accepted by this country, if our courage and our commitments are ever to be trusted again by either friend or foe.

The 1930s taught us a clear lesson: aggressive conduct, if allowed to go unchecked and unchallenged ultimately leads to war. This nation is opposed to war. We are also true to our word. Our unswerving objective, therefore, must be to prevent the use of these missiles against this or any other country, and to secure their withdrawal or elimination from the Western Hemisphere.

Our policy has been one of patience and restraint, as befits a peaceful and powerful nation, which leads a worldwide alliance. We have been determined not to be diverted from our central concerns by mere irritants and fanatics. But now further action is required—and it is under way; and these actions may only be the beginning. We will not prematurely or unnecessarily risk the costs of worldwide nuclear war in which even the fruits of victory would be ashes in our mouth—but neither will we shrink from that risk at any time it must be faced.

Acting, therefore, in the defence of our own security and of the entire Western Hemisphere, and under the authority entrusted to me by the Constitution as endorsed by the resolution of the Congress, I have directed that the following initial steps be taken immediately:

First: To halt this offensive build-up, a strict quarantine on all offensive military equipment under shipment to Cuba is being initiated. All ships of any kind bound for Cuba from whatever nation or port will, if found to contain cargoes of offensive weapons, be turned back. This quarantine will be extended, if needed, to other types of cargo and carriers. We are not at this time, however, denying the necessities of life as the Soviets attempted to do in their Berlin blockade of 1948.

Second: I have directed the continued and increased close surveillance of Cuba and its military build-up. The foreign ministers of the OAS, in their communique of October 6th, rejected secrecy in such matters in this hemisphere. Should these offensive military preparations continue, thus increasing the threat to the hemisphere, further action will be justified. I have directed the Armed Forces to prepare for any eventualities; and I trust that in the interest of both the Cuban people and the Soviet technicians at the sites, the hazards to all concerned in continuing this threat will be recognized.

Third: It shall be the policy of this Nation to regard any nuclear missile launched from Cuba against any nation in the Western Hemisphere as an attack by the Soviet Union on the United States, requiring a full retaliatory response upon the Soviet Union.

Fourth: As a necessary military precaution, I have reinforced our base at Guantanamo, evacuated today the dependents of our personnel there, and ordered additional military units to be on a standby alert basis.

Fifth: We are calling tonight for an immediate meeting of the Organ of Consultation under the Organization of American States, to consider this threat to hemispheric security and to invoke articles 6 and 8 of the Rio Treaty in support of all necessary action. The United Nations Charter allows for regional security arrangements—and the nations of this hemisphere decided long ago against the military presence of outside powers. Our other allies around the world have also been alerted.

Sixth: Under the Charter of the United Nations, we are asking tonight that an emergency meeting of the Security Council be convoked without delay to take action against this latest Soviet threat to world peace. Our resolution will call for the prompt dismantling and withdrawal of all offensive weapons in Cuba, under the supervision of U.N. observers, before the quarantine can be lifted.

Seventh and finally: I call upon Chairman Khrushchev to halt and eliminate this clandestine, reckless and provocative threat to world peace and to stable relations between our two nations. I call upon him further to abandon this course of world domination, and to join in an historic effort to end the perilous arms race and to transform the history of man. He has an opportunity now to move the world back from the abyss of destruction—by returning to his government's own words that it had no need to station missiles outside its own territory, and withdrawing these weapons from Cuba—by refraining from any action which will widen or deepen the present crisis—and then by participating in a search for peaceful and permanent solutions.

This nation is prepared to present its case against the Soviet threat to peace, and our own proposals for a peaceful world, at any time and in any forum—in the OAS, in the United Nations, or in any other meeting that could be useful—without limiting our freedom of action. We have in the past made strenuous efforts to limit the spread of nuclear weapons. We have proposed the elimination of all arms and military bases in a fair and effective disarmament treaty. We are prepared to discuss new proposals for the removal of tensions on both sides—including the possibility of a genuinely independent Cuba, free to determine its own destiny. We have no wish to war with the Soviet Union—for we are a peaceful people who desire to live in peace with all other peoples.

But it is difficult to settle or even discuss these problems in an atmosphere of intimidation. That is why this latest Soviet threat—or any other threat which is made independently or in response to our actions this week—must and will be met with determination. Any hostile move anywhere in the world against the safety and freedom of peoples to whom we are committed—including in particular the brave people of West Berlin—will be met by whatever action is needed.

Finally, I want to say a few words to the captive people of Cuba, to whom this speech is being directly carried by special radio facilities. I speak to you as a friend, as one who knows of your deep attachment to your fatherland, as one who shares your aspirations for liberty and justice for all. And I have watched and the American people have watched with deep sorrow how your nationalist revolution was betrayed—and how your fatherland fell under foreign domination. Now your leaders are no longer Cuban leaders inspired by Cuban ideals. They are puppets and agents of an international conspiracy which has turned Cuba against your friends and neighbours in the Americas—and turned it into the first Latin American country to become a target for nuclear war—the first Latin American country to have these weapons on its soil.

These new weapons are not in your interest. They contribute nothing to your peace and well-being. They can only undermine it. But this country has no wish to cause you to suffer or to impose any system upon you. We know that your lives and land are being used as pawns by those who deny your freedom.

Many times in the past, the Cuban people have risen to throw out tyrants who destroyed their liberty. And I have no doubt that most Cubans today look forward to the time when they will be truly free—free from foreign domination, free to choose their own leaders, free to select their own system, free to own their own land, free to speak and write and worship without fear or degradation. And then shall Cuba be welcomed back to the society of free nations and to the associations of this hemisphere.

My fellow citizens: let no one doubt that this is a difficult and dangerous effort on which we have set out. No one can see precisely what course it will take or what costs or casualties will be incurred. Many months of sacrifice and self-discipline lie ahead—months in which our patience and our will will be tested—months in which many threats and denunciations will keep us aware of our dangers. But the greatest danger of all would be to do nothing.

The path we have chosen for the present is full of hazards, as all paths are—but it is the one most consistent with our character and courage as a nation and our commitments around the world. The cost of freedom is always high—and Americans have always paid it. And one path we shall never choose, and that is the path of surrender or submission.

Our goal is not the victory of might, but the vindication of right—not peace at the expense of freedom, but both peace and freedom, here in this hemisphere, and, we hope, around the world. God willing, that goal will be achieved.

Thank you and good night.

# 28

## A Strategy of Peace

★ ★ ★ ★ ★ ★ ★

John F. Kennedy
Washington, D.C., U.S.A.
10 June 1963

*In October 1962, the leaders of the United States and Soviet Union had a military tussle over the installation of Soviet missiles in Cuba, which was ninety miles from the U.S. shores. People feared that the stand-off would result in a nuclear war. Kennedy had declared that he would use military force to enter Cuba and dissolve this threat to national security.*

*In this speech, Kennedy addressed the graduates at the American University, quelling the rumours of an all-out nuclear war saying that there was 'no more urgent task' than the pursuit of peace.*

President Anderson, members of the faculty, board of trustees, distinguished guests, my old colleague, Senator Bob Byrd, who has earned his degree through many years of attending night law school, while I am earning mine in the next thirty minutes, distinguished guests, ladies, and gentlemen:

It is with great pride that I participate in this ceremony of the American University, sponsored by the Methodist Church, founded by Bishop John Fletcher Hurst, and first opened by President Woodrow Wilson in 1914. This is a young and growing university, but it has already fulfilled Bishop Hurst's enlightened hope for the study of history and public affairs in a city devoted to the making of history and to the conduct of the public's business. By sponsoring this institution of higher learning for all who wish to learn, whatever their colour or their creed, the Methodists of this area and the Nation deserve the Nation's thanks, and I commend all those who are today graduating.

Professor Woodrow Wilson once said that every man sent out from a university should be a man of his nation as well as a man of his time, and I am confident that the men and women who carry the honour of graduating from this institution will continue to give from their lives, from their talents, a high measure of public service and public support.

'There are few earthly things more beautiful than a university,' wrote John Masefield in his tribute to English universities—and his words are equally true today. He did not refer to towers or to campuses. He admired the splendid beauty of a university because it was he said, 'a place where those who hate ignorance may strive to know, where those who perceive truth may strive to make others see.'

I have, therefore, chosen this time and place to discuss a topic on which ignorance too often abounds and the truth, too rarely perceived—and that is the most important topic on earth: world peace.

What kind of a peace do I mean, and what kind of a peace do we seek? Not a Pax Americana enforced on the world by American weapons of war. Not the peace of the grave or the security of the slave. I am talking about genuine peace, the kind of peace that makes life on earth worth living, the kind that enables men and nations to grow and to hope and build a better life for their children—not merely peace for Americans but peace for all men and women—not merely peace in our time but peace in all time.

I speak of peace because of the new face of war. Total war makes no sense in an age where great powers can maintain large and relatively invulnerable nuclear forces and refuse to surrender without resort to those forces. It makes no sense in an age where a single nuclear weapon contains almost ten times the explosive force delivered by all the allied air forces in the Second World War. It makes no sense in an age when the deadly poisons produced by a nuclear exchange would be carried by wind and water and soil and seed to the far corners of the globe and to generations yet unborn.

Today the expenditure of billions of dollars every year on weapons acquired for the purpose of making sure we never need to use them is essential to the keeping of peace. But surely the acquisition of such idle stockpiles—which can only destroy and never create—is not the only, much less the most efficient, means of assuring peace.

I speak of peace, therefore, as the necessary rational end of rational men. I realize the pursuit of peace is not as dramatic as the pursuit of war—and frequently the words of the pursuers fall on deaf ears. But we have no more urgent task.

Some say that it is useless to speak of peace or world law or world disarmament—and that it will be useless until the leaders of the Soviet Union adopt a more enlightened attitude. I hope they do. I believe we can help them do it. But I also believe that we must re-examine our own attitudes—as individuals and as a nation—for our attitude is as essential as theirs. And every graduate of this school, every thoughtful citizen who despairs of war and wishes to bring peace, should begin by looking inward—by examining his own attitude towards the possibilities of peace, towards the Soviet Union, towards the course of the Cold War and towards freedom and peace here at home.

First: Examine our attitude toward peace itself. Too many of us think it is impossible. Too many think it is unreal. But that is a dangerous, defeatist belief. It leads to the conclusion that war is inevitable—that mankind is doomed—that we are gripped by forces we cannot control.

We need not accept that view. Our problems are manmade—therefore, they can be solved by man. And man can be as big as he wants. No problem of human destiny is beyond human beings. Man's reason and spirit have often solved the seemingly unsolvable—and we believe they can do it again.

I am not referring to the absolute, infinite concept of universal peace and good will of which some fantasies and fanatics dream. I do not deny the value of hopes and dreams but we merely invite discouragement and incredulity by making that our only and immediate goal.

Let us focus instead on a more practical, more attainable peace—based not on a sudden revolution in human nature but on a gradual evolution in human institutions—on a series of concrete actions and effective agreements which are in the interest of all concerned. There is no single, simple key to this peace—no grand or magic formula to be adopted by one or two powers. Genuine peace must be the product of many nations, the sum of many acts. It must be dynamic, not static, changing to meet the challenge of each new generation. For peace is a process—a way of solving problems.

With such a peace, there will still be quarrels and conflicting interests, as there are within families and nations. World peace, like community peace, does not require that each man love his neighbour—it requires only that they live together in mutual tolerance, submitting their disputes to a just and peaceful settlement. And history teaches us that enmities between nations, as between individuals, do not last forever. However fixed our likes and dislikes may seem, the tide of time and events will often bring surprising changes in the relations between nations and neighbours.

So let us persevere. Peace need not be impracticable, and war need not be inevitable. By defining our goal more clearly, by making it seem more manageable and less remote, we can help all peoples to see it, to draw hope from it, and to move irresistibly towards it.

Second: Let us re-examine our attitude towards the Soviet Union. It is discouraging to think that their leaders may actually believe what their propagandists write. It is discouraging to read a recent authoritative Soviet text on Military Strategy and find, on page after page, wholly baseless and incredible claims—such as the allegation that American imperialist circles are preparing to unleash different types of war; that there is a very real threat of a preventive war being unleashed by American imperialists against the Soviet Union, and that the political aims, and I quote, 'of the American imperialists are to enslave economically and politically the European and other capitalist countries and to achieve world domination by means of aggressive war,' unquote.

Truly, as it was written long ago: 'The wicked flee when no man pursueth.' Yet it is sad to read these Soviet statements—to realize the extent of the gulf between us. But it is also a warning—a warning to the American people not to fall into the same trap as the Soviets, not to see only a distorted and desperate view of the other side, not to see conflict as inevitable, accommodation as impossible, and communication as nothing more than an exchange of threats.

No government or social system is so evil that its people must be considered as lacking in virtue. As Americans, we find communism profoundly repugnant as a negation of personal freedom and dignity. But we can still hail the Russian people for their many achievements—in science; in space; in economic and industrial growth; in culture; in acts of courage.

Among the many traits the peoples of our two countries have in common, none is stronger than our mutual abhorrence of war. Almost unique among the major world powers, we have never been at war with each other. And no nation in the history of battle ever suffered more than the Soviet Union in the Second World War. At least twenty million lost their lives. Countless millions of homes and families were burned or sacked. A third of the nation's territory, including two thirds of its industrial base, was turned into a wasteland—a loss equivalent to the destruction of this country east of Chicago.

Today, should total war ever break out again—no matter how—our two countries will be the primary target. It is an ironic but accurate fact that the two strongest powers are the two in the most danger of devastation. All we have built, all we have worked for, would be destroyed in the first twenty-four hours. And even in the Cold War, which brings burdens and dangers to so many countries, including this Nation's closest allies—our two countries bear the heaviest burdens. For we are both devoting massive sums of money to weapons that could be better devoted to combat ignorance, poverty, and disease. We are both caught up in a vicious and dangerous cycle with suspicion on one side breeding suspicion on the other, and new weapons begetting counter-weapons.

In short, both the United States and its allies, and the Soviet Union and its allies, have a mutually deep interest in a just and genuine peace and in halting the arms race. Agreements to this end are in the interests of the Soviet Union as well as ours—and even the most hostile nations can be relied upon to accept and keep those treaty obligations, and only those treaty obligations, which are in their own interest.

So, let us not be blind to our differences—but let us also direct attention to our common interests and the means by which those differences can be resolved. And if we cannot end now our differences, at least we can help make the world safe for diversity. For, in the final analysis, our most basic common link is that we all inhabit this small planet. We all breathe the same air. We all cherish our children's futures. And we are all mortal.

Third: Let us re-examine our attitude towards the Cold War, remembering that we are not engaged in a debate, seeking to pile up debating points. We are not here distributing blame or pointing the finger of judgment. We must deal with the world as it is, and not as it might have been had the history of the last eighteen years been different.

We must, therefore, persevere in the search for peace in the hope that constructive changes within the Communist Bloc might bring within reach solutions which now seem beyond us. We must conduct our affairs in such a way that it becomes in the Communists' interest to agree on a genuine peace. And above all, while defending our own vital interests, nuclear powers must avert those confrontations which bring an adversary to a choice of either a humiliating retreat or a nuclear war. To adopt that kind of course in the nuclear age would be evidence only of the bankruptcy of our policy—or of a collective death wish for the world.

To secure these ends, America's weapons are non-provocative, carefully controlled, designed to deter, and capable of selective use. Our military forces are committed to peace and disciplined in self-restraint. Our diplomats are instructed to avoid unnecessary irritants and purely rhetorical hostility.

For we can seek a relaxation of tensions without relaxing our guard. And, for our part, we do not need to use threats to prove we are resolute. We do not need to jam foreign broadcasts out of fear our faith will be eroded. We are unwilling to impose our system on any unwilling people—but we are willing and able to engage in peaceful competition with any people on earth.

Meanwhile, we seek to strengthen the United Nations, to help solve its financial problems, to make it a more effective instrument for peace, to develop it into a genuine world security system—a system capable of resolving disputes on the basis of law, of insuring the security of the large and the small, and of creating conditions under which arms can finally be abolished.

At the same time we seek to keep peace inside the non-communist world, where many nations, all of them our friends, are divided over issues which weaken Western unity, which invite Communist intervention or which threaten to erupt into war. Our efforts in West New Guinea, in the Congo, in the Middle East, and the Indian subcontinent, have been persistent and patient despite criticism from both sides. We have also tried to set an example for others—by seeking to adjust small but significant differences with our own closest neighbours in Mexico and Canada.

Speaking of other nations, I wish to make one point clear. We are bound to many nations by alliances. These alliances exist because our concern and theirs substantially overlap. Our commitment to defend

Western Europe and West Berlin, for example, stands undiminished because of the identity of our vital interests. The United States will make no deal with the Soviet Union at the expense of other nations and other peoples, not merely because they are our partners, but also because their interests and ours converge.

Our interests converge, however, not only in defending the frontiers of freedom, but in pursuing the paths of peace. It is our hope—and the purpose of allied policy—to convince the Soviet Union that she, too, should let each nation choose its own future, so long as that choice does not interfere with the choices of others. The Communist drive to impose their political and economic system on others is the primary cause of world tension today. For there can be no doubt that if all nations could refrain from interfering in the self-determination of others, the peace would be much more assured.

This will require a new effort to achieve world law—a new context for world discussions. It will require increased understanding between the Soviets and ourselves. And increased understanding will require increased contact and communication. One step in this direction is the proposed arrangement for a direct line between Moscow and Washington, to avoid on each side the dangerous delays, misunderstandings, and misreadings of the others' actions which might occur at a time of crisis.

We have also been talking in Geneva about our first-step measures of arm controls designed to limit the intensity of the arms race and reduce the risk of accidental war. Our primary long range interest in Geneva, however, is general and complete disarmament—designed to take place by stages, permitting parallel political developments to build the new institutions of peace which would take the place of arms. The pursuit of disarmament has been an effort of this government since the 1920s. It has been urgently sought by the past three administrations. And however dim the prospects are today, we intend to continue this effort—to continue it in order that all countries, including our own, can better grasp what the problems and possibilities of disarmament are.

The only major area of these negotiations where the end is in sight, yet where a fresh start is badly needed, is in a treaty to outlaw nuclear tests. The conclusion of such a treaty, so near and yet so far, would check the spiralling arms race in one of its most dangerous areas. It would place the nuclear powers in a position to deal more effectively with one of the greatest hazards which man faces in 1963, the further spread of nuclear arms. It would increase our security—it would decrease the prospects of war. Surely this goal is sufficiently important to require our steady pursuit, yielding neither to the temptation to give up the whole effort nor the temptation to give up our insistence on vital and responsible safeguards.

I am taking this opportunity, therefore, to announce two important decisions in this regard.

First: Chairman Khrushchev, Prime Minister Macmillan, and I have agreed that high-level discussions will shortly begin in Moscow looking toward early agreement on a comprehensive test ban treaty. Our hope must be tempered . . . Our hopes must be tempered with a caution of history—but with our hopes go the hopes of all mankind.

Second: To make clear our good faith and solemn convictions on this matter, I now declare that the United States does not propose to conduct nuclear tests in the atmosphere so long as other states do not do so. We will not . . . We will not be the first to resume. Such a declaration is no substitute for a formal binding treaty, but I hope it will help us achieve one. Nor would such a treaty be a substitute for disarmament, but I hope it will help us achieve it.

Finally, my fellow Americans, let us examine our attitude toward peace and freedom here at home. The quality and spirit of our own society must justify and support our efforts abroad. We must show it in the dedication of our own lives—as many of you who are graduating today will have an opportunity to do, by serving without pay in the Peace Corps abroad or in the proposed National Service Corps here at home.

But wherever we are, we must all, in our daily lives, live up to the age-old faith that peace and freedom walk together. In too many of our cities today, the peace is not secure because freedom is incomplete.

It is the responsibility of the executive branch at all levels of government—local, State, and National—to provide and protect that freedom for all of our citizens by all means within our authority. It is the responsibility of the legislative branch at all levels, wherever the authority is not now adequate, to make it adequate. And it is the responsibility of all citizens in all sections of this country to respect the rights of others and respect the law of the land.

All this . . . All this is not unrelated to world peace. 'When a man's way please the Lord,' the Scriptures tell us, 'he maketh even his enemies to be at peace with him.' And is not peace, in the last analysis, basically a matter of human rights—the right to live out our lives without fear of devastation—the right to breathe air as nature provided it—the right of future generations to a healthy existence?

While we proceed to safeguard our national interests, let us also safeguard human interests. And the elimination of war and arms is clearly in the interest of both. No treaty, however much it may be to the advantage of all, however tightly it may be worded, can provide absolute security against the risks of deception and evasion. But it can—if it is sufficiently effective in its enforcement and it is sufficiently in the interest of its signers—offer far more security and far fewer risks than an unabated, uncontrolled, unpredictable arms race.

The United States, as the world knows, will never start a war. We do not want a war. We do not now expect a war. This generation of Americans has already had enough—more than enough—of war and hate and oppression. We shall be prepared if others wish it. We shall be alert to try to stop it. But we shall also do our part to build a world of peace where the weak are safe and the strong are just. We are not helpless before that task or hopeless of its success. Confident and unafraid, we labour on—not towards a strategy of annihilation but toward a strategy of peace.

# 29

## Ich Bin Ein Berliner

★ ★ ★ ★ ★ ★ ★

John F. Kennedy
Berlin, Germany
26 June 1963

*The title of the speech translates to 'I am a Berliner.'*

*In 1961, millions of people migrated from East Germany to West Germany. The people of East Germany were suffering under the repressions of the Communist Party while democracy flourished in West. Life in West Germany seemed promising. It had managed to rope in financial help through the Marshall Plan of the U.S.A.*

*The Eastern government did what they could to prevent further migration to their western counterpart—they closed the border by erecting the Berlin Wall. This move separated families and robbed the citizens of their freedom.*

*Kennedy delivered the following speech to the citizens of West Berlin, making it clear that the Wall was a mark of failure of the communist system.*

I am proud to come to this city as the guest of your distinguished Mayor, who has symbolized throughout the world the fighting spirit of West Berlin. And I am proud to visit the Federal Republic with your distinguished Chancellor who for so many years has committed Germany to democracy and freedom and progress, and to come here in the company of my fellow American, General Clay, who has been in this city during its great moments of crisis and will come again if ever needed.

Two thousand years ago the proudest boast was *civis Romanus sum*. Today, in the world of freedom, the proudest boast is *Ich bin ein Berliner*.

I appreciate my interpreter translating my German!

There are many people in the world who really don't understand, or say they don't, what is the great issue between the free world and the Communist world. Let them come to Berlin. There are some who say that communism is the wave of the future. Let them come to Berlin. And there are some who say in Europe and elsewhere we can work with the Communists. Let them come to Berlin. And there are even a few who say that it is true that communism is an evil system, but it permits us to make economic progress. Lass' sie nach Berlin kommen. Let them come to Berlin.

Freedom has many difficulties and democracy is not perfect, but we have never had to put a wall up to keep our people in, to prevent them from leaving us. I want to say, on behalf of my countrymen, who live many miles away on the other side of the Atlantic, who are far distant from you, that they take the greatest pride that they have been able to share with you, even from a distance, the story of the last eighteen years. I know of no town, no city, that has been besieged for eighteen years that still lives with the vitality and the force, and the hope and the determination of the city of West Berlin. While the wall is the most obvious and vivid demonstration of the failures of the Communist system, for all the world to see, we take no satisfaction in it, for it is, as your Mayor has said, an offense not only against history but an offense against humanity, separating families, dividing husbands and wives and brothers and sisters, and dividing a people who wish to be joined together.

What is true of this city is true of Germany—real, lasting peace in Europe can never be assured as long as one German out of four is denied the elementary right of free men, and that is to make a free choice. In eighteen years of peace and good faith, this generation of Germans has earned the right to be free, including the right to unite their families and their nation in lasting peace, with goodwill to all people. You live in a defended island of freedom, but your life is part of the main. So let me ask you as I close, to lift your eyes beyond the dangers of today, to the hopes of tomorrow, beyond the freedom merely of this city of Berlin, or your country of Germany, to the advance of freedom everywhere, beyond the wall to the day of peace with justice, beyond yourselves and ourselves to all mankind.

Freedom is indivisible, and when one man is enslaved, all are not free. When all are free, then we can look forward to that day when this city will be joined as one and this country and this great Continent of Europe in a peaceful and hopeful globe. When that day finally comes, as it will, the people of West Berlin can take sober satisfaction in the fact that they were in the front lines for almost two decades.

All free men, wherever they may live, are citizens of Berlin, and, therefore, as a free man, I take pride in the words *Ich bin ein Berliner.*

# 30

## I Have a Dream

★ ★ ★ ★ ★ ★ ★

Martin Luther King Jr.
Washington, D.C., U.S.A.
28 August 1963

*Slavery had been abolished, voting rights had been gained, and still African-Americans faced a struggle of their own in the white society of America. The following speech was delivered at such a time, in front a crowd gathered to demand equal civil and political rights for blacks.*

*The greatest, the most iconic, the profoundly inspirational speech given by Martin Luther King Jr, on the steps of the Lincoln Memorial, poignantly paints his vision, his dream of living in a world of racial harmony.*

I am happy to join with you today in what will go down in history as the greatest demonstration for freedom in the history of our nation.

Five score years ago, a great American, in whose symbolic shadow we stand today, signed the Emancipation Proclamation. This momentous decree came as a great beacon light of hope to millions of Negro slaves who had been seared in the flames of withering injustice. It came as a joyous daybreak to end the long night of their captivity.

But one hundred years later, the Negro still is not free. One hundred years later, the life of the Negro is still sadly crippled by the manacles of segregation and the chains of discrimination. One hundred years later, the Negro lives on a lonely island of poverty in the midst of a vast ocean of material prosperity. One hundred years later, the Negro is still languishing in the corners of American society and finds himself an exile in his own land. So we have come here today to dramatize a shameful condition.

In a sense we have come to our nation's capital to cash a check. When the architects of our republic wrote the magnificent words of the Constitution and the Declaration of Independence, they were signing a promissory note to which every American was to fall heir. This note was a promise that all men, yes, black men as well as white men, would be guaranteed the unalienable rights of life, liberty, and the pursuit of happiness.

It is obvious today that America has defaulted on this promissory note insofar as her citizens of color are concerned. Instead of honoring this sacred obligation, America has given the Negro people a bad check, a check which has come back marked 'insufficient funds.' But we refuse to believe that the bank of justice is bankrupt. We refuse to believe that there are insufficient funds in the great vaults of opportunity of this nation. So we have come to cash this check—a check that will give us upon demand the riches of freedom and the security of justice. We have also come to this hallowed spot to remind America of the fierce urgency of now. This is no time to engage in the luxury of cooling off or to take the tranquilizing drug of gradualism. Now is the time to make real the promises of democracy. Now is the time to rise from the dark and desolate valley of segregation to the sunlit path of racial justice. Now is the time to lift our nation from the quick sands of racial injustice to the solid rock of brotherhood. Now is the time to make justice a reality for all of God's children.

It would be fatal for the nation to overlook the urgency of the moment. This sweltering summer of the Negro's legitimate discontent will not pass until there is an invigorating autumn of freedom and equality. Nineteen sixty-three is not an end, but a beginning. Those who hope that the Negro needed to blow off steam and will now be content will have a rude awakening if the nation returns to business as usual. There will be neither rest nor tranquility in America until the Negro is granted his citizenship rights. The whirlwinds of revolt will continue to shake the foundations of our nation until the bright day of justice emerges.

But there is something that I must say to my people who stand on the warm threshold which leads into the palace of justice. In the process of gaining our rightful place we must not be guilty of wrongful deeds. Let us not seek to satisfy our thirst for freedom by drinking from the cup of bitterness and hatred.

We must forever conduct our struggle on the high plane of dignity and discipline. We must not allow our creative protest to degenerate into physical violence. Again and again we must rise to the majestic heights of meeting physical force with soul force. The marvelous new militancy which has engulfed the Negro community must not lead us to a distrust of all white people, for many of our white brothers, as evidenced by their presence here today, have come to realize that their destiny is tied up with our destiny. They have come to realize that their freedom is inextricably bound to our freedom. We cannot walk alone.

As we walk, we must make the pledge that we shall always march ahead. We cannot turn back. There are those who are asking the devotees of civil rights, 'When will you be satisfied?' We can never be satisfied as long as the Negro is the victim of the unspeakable horrors of police brutality. We can never be satisfied, as long as our bodies, heavy with the fatigue of travel, cannot gain lodging in the motels of the highways and the hotels of the cities. We cannot be satisfied as long as the Negro's basic mobility is from a smaller ghetto to a larger one. We can never be satisfied as long as our children are stripped of their selfhood and robbed of their dignity by signs stating 'For Whites Only.' We cannot be satisfied as long as a Negro in Mississippi cannot vote and a Negro in New York believes he has nothing for which to vote. No, no, we are not satisfied, and we will not be satisfied until justice rolls down like waters and righteousness like a mighty stream.

I am not unmindful that some of you have come here out of great trials and tribulations. Some of you have come fresh from narrow jail cells. Some of you have come from areas where your quest for freedom left you battered by the storms of persecution and staggered by the winds of police brutality. You have been the veterans of creative suffering. Continue to work with the faith that unearned suffering is redemptive.

Go back to Mississippi, go back to Alabama, go back to South Carolina, go back to Georgia, go back to Louisiana, go back to the slums and ghettos of our northern cities, knowing that somehow this situation can and will be changed. Let us not wallow in the valley of despair.

I say to you today, my friends, so even though we face the difficulties of today and tomorrow, I still have a dream. It is a dream deeply rooted in the American dream.

I have a dream that one day this nation will rise up and live out the true meaning of its creed: 'We hold these truths to be self-evident: that all men are created equal.'

I have a dream that one day on the red hills of Georgia the sons of former slaves and the sons of former slave owners will be able to sit down together at the table of brotherhood.

I have a dream that one day even the state of Mississippi, a state sweltering with the heat of injustice, sweltering with the heat of oppression, will be transformed into an oasis of freedom and justice.

I have a dream that my four little children will one day live in a nation where they will not be judged by the color of their skin but by the content of their character.

I have a dream today.

I have a dream that one day, down in Alabama, with its vicious racists, with its governor having his lips dripping with the words of interposition and nullification; one day right there in Alabama, little black boys and black girls will be able to join hands with little white boys and white girls as sisters and brothers.

I have a dream today.

I have a dream that one day every valley shall be exalted, every hill and mountain shall be made low, the rough places will be made plain, and the crooked places will be made straight, and the glory of the Lord shall be revealed, and all flesh shall see it together.

This is our hope. This is the faith that I go back to the South with. With this faith we will be able to hew out of the mountain of despair a stone of hope. With this faith we will be able to transform the jangling discords of our nation into a beautiful symphony of brotherhood. With this faith we will be able to work together, to pray together, to struggle together, to go to jail together, to stand up for freedom together, knowing that we will be free one day.

This will be the day when all of God's children will be able to sing with a new meaning, 'My country, 'tis of thee, sweet land of liberty, of thee I sing. Land where my fathers died, land of the pilgrim's pride, from every mountainside, let freedom ring.'

And if America is to be a great nation this must become true. So let freedom ring from the prodigious hilltops of New Hampshire. Let freedom ring from the mighty mountains of New York. Let freedom ring from the heightening Alleghenies of Pennsylvania!

Let freedom ring from the snowcapped Rockies of Colorado!

Let freedom ring from the curvaceous slopes of California!

But not only that; let freedom ring from Stone Mountain of Georgia!

Let freedom ring from Lookout Mountain of Tennessee!

Let freedom ring from every hill and molehill of Mississippi. From every mountainside, let freedom ring.

And when this happens, when we allow freedom to ring, when we let it ring from every village and every hamlet, from every state and every city, we will be able to speed up that day when all of God's children, black men and white men, Jews and Gentiles, Protestants and Catholics, will be able to join hands and sing in the words of the old Negro spiritual, 'Free at last! free at last! thank God Almighty, we are free at last!'

*Note: This speech was given during the March on Washington for Jobs and Freedom organized by A. Philip Randolph and Bayard Rustin, both of whom were civil rights activists. The crowd at this march was estimated to be 250,000 people.*

# 31

## I Am Profoundly Sorry

★ ★ ★ ★ ★ ★ ★

Bill Clinton
Washington, D.C., U.S.A.
11 December 1998

*Bill Clinton had an illicit relationship with Monica Lewinsky, an intern at the White House, which led to his impeachment. In the following speech, he apologized for it to the members of the Congress and the American people.*

*There had been a debate in the White House over whether Clinton should be allowed to speak at all since anything he said would be dissected and criticized—and it was. The speech was thought lacking and inadequate by many.*

Good afternoon.

As anyone close to me knows, for months I have been grappling with how best to reconcile myself to the American people, to acknowledge my own wrongdoing and still to maintain my focus on the work of the presidency.

Others are presenting my defence on the facts, the law and the Constitution. Nothing I can say now can add to that.

What I want the American people to know, what I want the Congress to know is that I am profoundly sorry for all I have done wrong in words and deeds.

I never should have misled the country, the Congress, my friends or my family. Quite simply, I gave in to my shame. I have been condemned by my accusers with harsh words.

And while it's hard to hear yourself called deceitful and manipulative, I remember Ben Franklin's admonition that our critics are our friends, for they do show us our faults.

Mere words cannot fully express the profound remorse I feel for what our country is going through and for what members of both parties in Congress are now forced to deal with. These past months have been a torturous process of coming to terms with what I did. I understand that accountability demands consequences, and I'm prepared to accept them.

Painful as the condemnation of the Congress would be, it would pale in comparison to the consequences of the pain I have caused my family. There is no greater agony.

Like anyone who honestly faces the shame of wrongful conduct, I would give anything to go back and undo what I did.

But one of the painful truths I have to live with is the reality that that is simply not possible. An old and dear friend of mine recently sent me the wisdom of a poet who wrote, 'The moving finger writes and having writ, moves on. Nor all your piety nor wit shall lure it back to cancel half a line. Nor all your tears wash out a word of it.'

So nothing, not piety, nor tears, nor wit, nor torment can alter what I have done. I must make my peace with that.

I must also be at peace with the fact that the public consequences of my actions are in the hands of the American people and their representatives in the Congress.

Should they determine that my errors of word and deed require their rebuke and censure, I am ready to accept that.

Meanwhile, I will continue to do all I can to reclaim the trust of the American people and to serve them well.

We must all return to the work, the vital work, of strengthening our nation for the new century. Our country has wonderful opportunities and daunting challenges ahead. I intend to seize those opportunities and meet those challenges with all the energy and ability and strength God has given me.

That is simply all I can do—the work of the American people.

Thank you very much.

# 32

## Resigning the Presidency

★ ★ ★ ★ ★ ★ ★

Richard M. Nixon
Washington, D.C., U.S.A.
9 August 1974

*On 17th June 1972, some burglars were arrested at the office of the Democratic National Committee in the Watergate complex of buildings. But this was not a burglary. The men were caught wiretapping phones and devices and were found to be connected to President Nixon.*

*Nixon's role in the conspiracy, unearthed by the journalists of* Washington Post, *was revealed and he resigned before others could ask for his impeachment. He gave this speech to his staff before he left.*

Good evening. This is the thirty-seventh time I have spoken to you from this office, where so many decisions have been made that shaped the history of this Nation. Each time I have done so to discuss with you some matter that I believe affected the national interest.

In all the decisions I have made in my public life, I have always tried to do what was best for the Nation. Throughout the long and difficult period of Watergate, I have felt it was my duty to persevere, to make every possible effort to complete the term of office to which you elected me.

In the past few days, however, it has become evident to me that I no longer have a strong enough political base in the Congress to justify continuing that effort. As long as there was such a base, I felt strongly that it was necessary to see the constitutional process through to its conclusion, that to do otherwise would be unfaithful to the spirit of that deliberately difficult process and a dangerously destabilizing precedent for the future.

But with the disappearance of that base, I now believe that the constitutional purpose has been served, and there is no longer a need for the process to be prolonged.

I would have preferred to carry through to the finish whatever the personal agony it would have involved, and my family unanimously urged me to do so. But the interest of the Nation must always come before any personal considerations.

From the discussions I have had with Congressional and other leaders, I have concluded that because of the Watergate matter I might not have the support of the Congress that I would consider necessary to back the very difficult decisions and carry out the duties of this office in the way the interests of the Nation would require.

I have never been a quitter. To leave office before my term is completed is abhorrent to every instinct in my body. But as president, I must put the interest of America first.

America needs a full-time president and a full-time Congress, particularly at this time with problems we face at home and abroad.

To continue to fight through the months ahead for my personal vindication would almost totally absorb the time and attention of both the president and the Congress in a period when our entire focus should be on the great issues of peace abroad and prosperity without inflation at home.

Therefore, I shall resign the Presidency effective at noon tomorrow. Vice President Ford will be sworn in as president at that hour in this office.

As I recall the high hopes for America with which we began this second term, I feel a great sadness that I will not be here in this office working on your behalf to achieve those hopes in the next two and a half years. But in turning over direction of the government to Vice President Ford, I know, as I told the Nation when I nominated him for that office ten months ago, that the leadership of America will be in good hands.

In passing this office to the vice president, I also do so with the profound sense of the weight of responsibility that will fall on his shoulders tomorrow and, therefore, of the understanding, the patience, the cooperation he will need from all Americans.

As he assumes that responsibility, he will deserve the help and the support of all of us. As we look to the future, the first essential is to begin healing the wounds of this Nation, to put the bitterness and divisions of the recent past behind us, and to rediscover those shared ideals that lie at the heart of our strength and unity as a great and as a free people.

By taking this action, I hope that I will have hastened the start of that process of healing which is so desperately needed in America.

I regret deeply any injuries that may have been done in the course of the events that led to this decision. I would say only that if some of my judgments were wrong, and some were wrong, they were made in what I believed at the time to be the best interest of the Nation.

To those who have stood with me during these past difficult months, to my family, my friends, to many others who joined in supporting my cause because they believed it was right, I will be eternally grateful for your support.

And to those who have not felt able to give me your support, let me say I leave with no bitterness toward those who have opposed me, because all of us, in the final analysis, have been concerned with the good of the country, however our judgments might differ.

So, let us all now join together in affirming that common commitment and in helping our new president succeed for the benefit of all Americans.

I shall leave this office with regret at not completing my term, but with gratitude for the privilege of serving as your president for the past five and a half years. These years have been a momentous time in the history of our Nation and the world. They have been a time of achievement in which we can all be proud, achievements that represent the shared efforts of the Administration, the Congress, and the people.

But the challenges ahead are equally great, and they, too, will require the support and the efforts of the Congress and the people working in cooperation with the new Administration.

We have ended America's longest war, but in the work of securing a lasting peace in the world, the goals ahead are even more far-reaching and more difficult. We must complete a structure of peace so that it will be said of this generation, our generation of Americans, by the people of all nations, not only that we ended one war but that we prevented future wars.

We have unlocked the doors that for a quarter of a century stood between the United States and the People's Republic of China.

We must now ensure that the one quarter of the world's people who live in the People's Republic of China will be and remain not our enemies but our friends.

In the Middle East, hundred million people in the Arab countries, many of whom have considered us their enemy for nearly twenty years, now look on us as their friends. We must continue to build on that friendship so that peace can settle at last over the Middle East and so that the cradle of civilization will not become its grave.

Together with the Soviet Union we have made the crucial breakthroughs that have begun the process of limiting nuclear arms. But we must set as our goal not just limiting but reducing and finally destroying these terrible weapons so that they cannot destroy civilization and so that the threat of nuclear war will no longer hang over the world and the people.

We have opened the new relation with the Soviet Union. We must continue to develop and expand that new relationship so that the two strongest nations of the world will live together in cooperation rather than confrontation.

Around the world, in Asia, in Africa, in Latin America, in the Middle East, there are millions of people who live in terrible poverty, even starvation. We must keep as our goal turning away from production for war and expanding production for peace so that people everywhere on this earth can at last look forward in their children's time, if not in our own time, to having the necessities for a decent life.

Here in America, we are fortunate that most of our people have not only the blessings of liberty but also the means to live full and good and, by the world's standards, even abundant lives. We must press on, however, toward a goal of not only more and better jobs but of full opportunity for every American and of what we are striving so hard right now to achieve, prosperity without inflation.

For more than a quarter of a century in public life I have shared in the turbulent history of this era. I have fought for what I believed in. I have tried to the best of my ability to discharge those duties and meet those responsibilities that were entrusted to me.

Sometimes I have succeeded and sometimes I have failed, but always I have taken heart from what Theodore Roosevelt once said about the man in the arena, 'whose face is marred by dust and sweat and blood, who strives valiantly, who errs and comes short again and again because there is not effort without error and shortcoming, but who does actually strive to do the deed, who knows the great enthusiasms, the great devotions, who spends himself in a worthy cause, who at the best knows in the end the triumphs of high achievements and who at the worst, if he fails, at least fails while daring greatly.'

I pledge to you tonight that as long as I have a breath of life in my body, I shall continue in that spirit. I shall continue to work for the great causes to which I have been dedicated throughout my years as a congressman, a senator, a vice president, and president, the cause of peace not just for America but among all nations, prosperity, justice, and opportunity for all of our people.

There is one cause above all to which I have been devoted and to which I shall always be devoted for as long as I live.

When I first took the oath of office as president five and a half years ago, I made this sacred commitment, to 'consecrate my office, my energies, and all the wisdom I can summon to the cause of peace among nations.'

I have done my very best in all the days since to be true to that pledge. As a result of these efforts, I am confident that the world is a safer place today, not only for the people of America but for the people of all nations, and that all of our children have a better chance than before of living in peace rather than dying in war.

This, more than anything, is what I hoped to achieve when I sought the Presidency. This, more than anything, is what I hope will be my legacy to you, to our country, as I leave the Presidency.

To have served in this office is to have felt a very personal sense of kinship with each and every American. In leaving it, I do so with this prayer: May God's grace be with you.

# 33

## Tear Down This Wall

★ ★ ★ ★ ★ ★ ★

Ronald Reagan
Berlin, Germany
12 June 1987

*The Berlin Wall, built in 1961, had become a powerful symbol of the Cold War. During this war, communism in East Germany propelled 2.5 million people to flee to West Germany. To curb this migration, the Eastern government decided to seal the free passage from East to West, and set up a wall.*

*Twenty-six years later, Ronald Reagan stood at the Brandenburg Gate and delivered the following speech, clearly conveying America's backing to Germany's efforts to unify their country.*

Thank you. Thank you very much. Chancellor Kohl, Governing Mayor Diepgen, ladies and gentlemen: Twenty-four years ago, President John F. Kennedy visited Berlin, speaking to the people of this city and the world at the City Hall. Well, since then two other presidents have come, each in his turn, to Berlin. And today I, myself, make my second visit to your city.

We come to Berlin, we American presidents, because it's our duty to speak, in this place, of freedom. But I must confess, we're drawn here by other things as well: by the feeling of history in this city, more than five hundred years older than our own nation; by the beauty of the Grunewald and the Tiergarten; most of all, by your courage and determination. Perhaps the composer Paul Lincke understood something about American presidents. You see, like so many presidents before me, I come here today because wherever I go, whatever I do: *Ich hab noch einen Koffer* in Berlin. [I still have a suitcase in Berlin.] Our gathering today is being broadcast throughout Western Europe and North America. I understand that it is being seen and heard as well in the East. To those listening throughout Eastern Europe, I extend my warmest greeting and the goodwill of the American people. To those listening in Eastern Berlin, a special word: Although I cannot be with you, I address my remarks to you just as surely as to those standing here before me. For I join you, as I join your fellow countrymen in the West, in this firm, this unalterable belief: *Es gibt nur ein Berlin.* [There is only one Berlin.]

Behind me stands a wall that encircles the free sectors of this city, part of a vast system of barriers that divides the entire continent of Europe. From the Baltic, south, those barriers cut across Germany in a gash of barbed wire, concrete, dog runs, and guard towers. Farther south, there may be no visible, no obvious wall. But there remain armed guards and checkpoints all the same—still a restriction on the right to travel, still an instrument to impose upon ordinary men and women the will of a totalitarian state. Yet it is here in Berlin where the wall emerges most clearly; here, cutting across your city, where the news photo and the television screen have imprinted this brutal division of a continent upon the mind of the world. Standing before the Brandenburg Gate, every man is a German, separated from his fellow men. Every man is a Berliner, forced to look upon a scar. President Von Weizsacker has said, 'The German question is open as long as the Brandenburg Gate is closed.' Today I say: As long as the gate is closed, as long as this scar of a wall is permitted to stand, it is not the German question alone that remains open, but the question of freedom for all mankind. Yet I do not come here to lament. For I find in Berlin a message of hope, even in the shadow of this wall, a message of triumph.

In this season of spring in 1945, the people of Berlin emerged from their air-raid shelters to find devastation. Thousands of miles away, the people of the United States reached out to help. And in 1947, Secretary of State—as you've been told—George Marshall announced the creation of what would become known as the Marshall Plan. Speaking precisely forty years ago this month, he said: 'Our policy is directed not against any country or doctrine, but against hunger, poverty, desperation, and chaos.' In the Reichstag a few moments ago, I saw a display commemorating this fortieth anniversary of the Marshall Plan. I was struck by the sign on a burnt out, gutted structure that was being rebuilt. I understand that Berliners of my own generation can remember seeing signs like it dotted throughout the western sectors of the city. The sign read simply: 'The Marshall Plan is helping here to strengthen the free world.' A strong, free world in the West, that dream became real. Japan rose from ruin to become an economic giant. Italy, France, Belgium—virtually every nation in Western Europe saw political and economic rebirth; the European Community was founded. In West Germany and here in Berlin, there took place an economic miracle, the Wirtschaftswunder. Adenauer, Erhard, Reuter, and other leaders understood the practical importance of liberty—that just as truth can flourish only when the journalist is given freedom of speech, so prosperity can come about only when the farmer and businessman enjoy economic freedom. The German leaders reduced tariffs, expanded free trade, lowered taxes. From 1950 to 1960 alone, the standard of living in West Germany and Berlin doubled.

Where four decades ago there was rubble, today in West Berlin there is the greatest industrial output of any city in Germany—busy office blocks, fine homes and apartments, proud avenues, and the spreading lawns of parkland. Where a city's culture seemed to have been destroyed, today there are two great universities, orchestras and an opera, countless theaters, and museums. Where there was want, today there's abundance—food, clothing, automobiles—the wonderful goods of the Ku'damm. From devastation, from utter ruin, you Berliners have, in freedom, rebuilt a city that once again ranks as one of the greatest on earth. The Soviets may have had other plans. But my friends, there were a few things the Soviets didn't count on—*Berliner Herz, Berliner Humor, ja, und Berliner Schnauze.* [Berliner heart, Berliner humor, yes, and a Berliner Schnauze.]

In the 1950s, Khrushchev predicted: 'We will bury you.' But in the West today, we see a free world that has achieved a level of prosperity and well-being unprecedented in all human history. In the Communist world, we see failure, technological backwardness, declining standards of health, even want of the most basic kind—too little food. Even today, the Soviet Union still cannot feed itself. After these four decades, then, there stands before the entire world one great and inescapable conclusion: Freedom leads to prosperity. Freedom replaces the ancient hatreds among the nations with comity and peace. Freedom is the victor.

And now the Soviets themselves may, in a limited way, be coming to understand the importance of freedom. We hear much from Moscow about a new policy of reform and openness. Some political prisoners have been released. Certain foreign news broadcasts are no longer being jammed. Some economic enterprises have been permitted to operate with greater freedom from state control. Are these the beginnings of profound changes in the Soviet state? Or are they token gestures, intended to raise false hopes in the West, or to strengthen the Soviet system without changing it? We welcome change and openness; for we believe that freedom and security go together, that the advance of human liberty can only strengthen the cause of world peace. There is one sign the Soviets can make that would be unmistakable, that would advance dramatically the cause of freedom and peace.

General Secretary Gorbachev, if you seek peace, if you seek prosperity for the Soviet Union and Eastern Europe, if you seek liberalization: Come here to this gate! Mr. Gorbachev, open this gate! Mr. Gorbachev, tear down this wall!

I understand the fear of war and the pain of division that afflict this continent—and I pledge to you my country's efforts to help overcome these burdens. To be sure, we in the West must resist Soviet expansion. So we must maintain defenses of unassailable strength. Yet we seek peace; so we must strive to reduce arms on both sides. Beginning ten years ago, the Soviets challenged the Western alliance with a grave new threat, hundreds of new and more deadly SS-20 nuclear missiles, capable of striking every capital in Europe. The Western alliance responded by committing itself to a counter-deployment unless the Soviets agreed to negotiate a better solution; namely, the elimination of such weapons on both sides. For many months, the Soviets refused to bargain in earnestness. As the alliance, in turn, prepared to go forward with its counter-deployment, there were difficult days—days of protests like those during my 1982 visit to this city—and the Soviets later walked away from the table.

But through it all, the alliance held firm. And I invite those who protested then—I invite those who protest today—to mark this fact: Because we remained strong, the Soviets came back to the table. And because we remain strong today, we have within reach the possibility, not merely of limiting the growth of arms, but of eliminating, for the first time, an entire class of nuclear weapons from the face of the earth.

As I speak, NATO ministers are meeting in Iceland to review the progress of our proposals for eliminating these weapons. At the talks in Geneva, we have also proposed deep cuts in strategic offensive weapons. And the Western allies have likewise made far-reaching proposals to reduce the danger of conventional war and to place a total ban on chemical weapons.

While we pursue these arms reductions, I pledge to you that we will maintain the capacity to deter Soviet aggression at any level at which it might occur. And in cooperation with many of our allies, the

United States is pursuing the Strategic Defense Initiative—research to base deterrence not on the threat of offensive retaliation, but on defenses that truly defend; on systems, in short, that will not target populations, but shield them. By these means we seek to increase the safety of Europe and all the world. But we must remember a crucial fact: East and West do not mistrust each other because we are armed; we are armed because we mistrust each other. And our differences are not about weapons but about liberty. When President Kennedy spoke at the City Hall those twenty-four years ago, freedom was encircled, Berlin was under siege. And today, despite all the pressures upon this city, Berlin stands secure in its liberty. And freedom itself is transforming the globe.

In the Philippines, in South and Central America, democracy has been given a rebirth. Throughout the Pacific, free markets are working miracle after miracle of economic growth. In the industrialized nations, a technological revolution is taking place—a revolution marked by rapid, dramatic advances in computers and telecommunications.

In Europe, only one nation and those it controls refuse to join the community of freedom. Yet in this age of redoubled economic growth, of information and innovation, the Soviet Union faces a choice: It must make fundamental changes, or it will become obsolete. Today, thus, represents a moment of hope. We in the West stand ready to cooperate with the East to promote true openness, to break down barriers that separate people, to create a safe, freer world. And surely there is no better place than Berlin, the meeting place of East and West, to make a start. Free people of Berlin: Today, as in the past, the United States stands for the strict observance and full implementation of all parts of the Four Power Agreement of 1971. Let us use this occasion, the seven hundred and fiftieth anniversary of this city, to usher in a new era, to seek a still fuller, richer life for the Berlin of the future. Together, let us maintain and develop the ties between the Federal Republic and the Western sectors of Berlin, which is permitted by the 1971 agreement.

And I invite Mr. Gorbachev: Let us work to bring the Eastern and Western parts of the city closer together, so that all the inhabitants of all

Berlin can enjoy the benefits that come with life in one of the great cities of the world. To open Berlin still further to all Europe, East and West, let us expand the vital air access to this city, finding ways of making commercial air service to Berlin more convenient, more comfortable, and more economical. We look to the day when West Berlin can become one of the chief aviation hubs in all central Europe.

With our French and British partners, the United States is prepared to help bring international meetings to Berlin. It would be only fitting for Berlin to serve as the site of United Nations meetings, or world conferences on human rights and arms control or other issues that call for international cooperation.

There is no better way to establish hope for the future than to enlighten young minds, and we would be honoured to sponsor summer youth exchanges, cultural events, and other programs for young Berliners from the East. Our French and British friends, I'm certain, will do the same. And it's my hope that an authority can be found in East Berlin to sponsor visits from young people of the Western sectors.

One final proposal, one close to my heart: Sport represents a source of enjoyment and ennoblement, and you may have noted that the Republic of Korea—South Korea—has offered to permit certain events of the 1988 Olympics to take place in the North. International sports competitions of all kinds could take place in both parts of this city. And what better way to demonstrate to the world the openness of this city than to offer in some future year to hold the Olympic games here in Berlin, East and West? In these four decades, as I have said, you Berliners have built a great city. You've done so in spite of threats—the Soviet attempts to impose the East-mark, the blockade. Today the city thrives in spite of the challenges implicit in the very presence of this wall. What keeps you here? Certainly there's a great deal to be said for your fortitude, for your defiant courage. But I believe there's something deeper, something that involves Berlin's whole look and feel and way of life—not mere sentiment. No one could live long in Berlin without being completely disabused of illusions. Something instead, that has seen the difficulties of life in Berlin but chose to accept them, that continues to build this good and proud city in contrast to a surrounding totalitarian presence that refuses to release human energies or aspirations. Something that speaks with a powerful voice of affirmation, that says yes to this city, yes to the future, yes to freedom. In a word, I would submit that what keeps you in Berlin is love—love both profound and abiding.

Perhaps this gets to the root of the matter, to the most fundamental distinction of all between East and West. The totalitarian world produces backwardness because it does such violence to the spirit, thwarting the human impulse to create, to enjoy, to worship. The totalitarian world finds even symbols of love and of worship an affront. Years ago, before the East Germans began rebuilding their churches, they erected a secular structure: the television tower at Alexander Platz. Virtually ever since, the authorities have been working to correct what they view as the tower's one major flaw, treating the glass sphere at the top with paints and chemicals of every kind. Yet even today when the sun strikes that sphere—that sphere that towers over all Berlin—the light makes the sign of the cross. There in Berlin, like the city itself, symbols of love, symbols of worship, cannot be suppressed.

As I looked out a moment ago from the Reichstag, that embodiment of German unity, I noticed words crudely spray-painted upon the wall, perhaps by a young Berliner: 'This wall will fall. Beliefs become reality.' Yes, across Europe, this wall will fall. For it cannot withstand faith; it cannot withstand truth. The wall cannot withstand freedom.

And I would like, before I close, to say one word. I have read, and I have been questioned since I've been here about certain demonstrations against my coming. And I would like to say just one thing, and to those who demonstrate so. I wonder if they have ever asked themselves that if they should have the kind of government they apparently seek, no one would ever be able to do what they're doing again.

Thank you and God bless you all.

# 34

## Yes We Can

★ ★ ★ ★ ★ ★ ★

Barack Obama
Chicago, U.S.A.
4 November 2008

*After days of anticipation, the verdict was out—Barack Obama emerged victorious in the election and became the first black President of the United States. The public's jubilation was through the roof.*

*Everyone doubted that a black man would be able to win the presidential election, though most of them hoped he would. Obama delivered the following speech after he won, indicating that his success was proof of social and political emancipation in America's attitude.*

Hello, Chicago.

If there is anyone out there who still doubts that America is a place where all things are possible, who still wonders if the dream of our founders is alive in our time, who still questions the power of our democracy, tonight is your answer.

It's the answer told by lines that stretched around schools and churches in numbers this nation has never seen, by people who waited three hours and four hours, many for the first time in their lives, because they believed that this time must be different, that their voices could be that difference.

It's the answer spoken by young and old, rich and poor, Democrat and Republican, black, white, Hispanic, Asian, Native American, gay, straight, disabled and not disabled. Americans who sent a message to the world that we have never been just a collection of individuals or a collection of red states and blue states. We are, and always will be, the United States of America.

It's the answer that led those who've been told for so long by so many to be cynical and fearful and doubtful about what we can achieve to put their hands on the arc of history and bend it once more toward the hope of a better day.

It's been a long time coming, but tonight, because of what we did on this day, in this election, at this defining moment, change has come to America.

A little bit earlier this evening, I received an extraordinarily gracious call from Senator McCain.

Senator McCain fought long and hard in this campaign. And he's fought even longer and harder for the country that he loves. He has endured sacrifices for America that most of us cannot begin to imagine. We are better off for the service rendered by this brave and selfless leader.

I congratulate him; I congratulate Governor Palin for all that they've achieved. And I look forward to working with them to renew this nation's promise in the months ahead.

I want to thank my partner in this journey, a man who campaigned from his heart, and spoke for the men and women he grew up with on the streets of Scranton . . . and rode with on the train home to Delaware, the vice president-elect of the United States, Joe Biden.

And I would not be standing here tonight without the unyielding support of my best friend for the last sixteen years . . . the rock of our family, the love of my life, the nation's next first lady . . . Michelle Obama.

Sasha and Malia . . . I love you both more than you can imagine. And you have earned the new puppy that's coming with us . . . to the White House.

And while she's no longer with us, I know my grandmother's watching, along with the family that made me who I am. I miss them tonight. I know that my debt to them is beyond measure.

To my sister Maya, my sister Auma, all my other brothers and sisters, thank you so much for all the support that you've given me. I am grateful to them.

And to my campaign manager, David Plouffe . . . the unsung hero of this campaign, who built the best—the best political campaign, I think, in the history of the United States of America.

To my chief strategist David Axelrod . . . who's been a partner with me every step of the way.

To the best campaign team ever assembled in the history of politics . . . you made this happen, and I am forever grateful for what you've sacrificed to get it done.

But above all, I will never forget who this victory truly belongs to. It belongs to you. It belongs to you.

I was never the likeliest candidate for this office. We didn't start with much money or many endorsements. Our campaign was not hatched in the halls of Washington. It began in the backyards of Des Moines and the living rooms of Concord and the front porches of Charleston.

It was built by working men and women who dug into what little savings they had to give five dollars and ten dollars and twenty dollars to the cause. It grew strength from the young people who rejected the myth of their generation's apathy; who left their homes and their families for jobs that offered little pay and less sleep. It drew strength from the not-so-young people who braved the bitter cold and scorching heat to knock on doors of perfect strangers, and from the millions of Americans who volunteered and organized and proved that more than two centuries later a government of the people, by the people, and for the people has not perished from the Earth. This is your victory.

And I know you didn't do this just to win an election. And I know you didn't do it for me. You did it because you understand the enormity of the task that lies ahead. For even as we celebrate tonight, we know the challenges that tomorrow will bring are the greatest of our lifetime—two wars, a planet in peril, the worst financial crisis in a century.

Even as we stand here tonight, we know there are brave Americans waking up in the deserts of Iraq and the mountains of Afghanistan to risk their lives for us.

There are mothers and fathers who will lie awake after the children fall asleep and wonder how they'll make the mortgage or pay their doctors' bills or save enough for their child's college education.

There's new energy to harness, new jobs to be created, new schools to build, and threats to meet, alliances to repair.

The road ahead will be long. Our climb will be steep. We may not get there in one year or even in one term. But, America, I have never been more hopeful than I am tonight that we will get there. I promise you, we as a people will get there.

There will be setbacks and false starts. There are many who won't agree with every decision or policy I make as president. And we know the government can't solve every problem.

But I will always be honest with you about the challenges we face. I will listen to you, especially when we disagree. And, above all, I will ask you to join in the work of remaking this nation, the only way it's been done in America for two hundred and twenty-one ye-ars—block by block, brick by brick, calloused hand by calloused hand.

What began twenty-one months ago in the depths of winter cannot end on this autumn night.

This victory alone is not the change we seek. It is only the chance for us to make that change. And that cannot happen if we go back to the way things were.

It can't happen without you, without a new spirit of service, a new spirit of sacrifice.

So let us summon a new spirit of patriotism, of responsibility, where each of us resolves to pitch in and work harder and look after not only ourselves but each other.

Let us remember that, if this financial crisis taught us anything, it's that we cannot have a thriving Wall Street while Main Street suffers.

In this country, we rise or fall as one nation, as one people. Let's resist the temptation to fall back on the same partisanship and pettiness and immaturity that has poisoned our politics for so long.

Let's remember that it was a man from this state who first carried the banner of the Republican Party to the White House, a party founded on the values of self-reliance and individual liberty and national unity.

Those are values that we all share. And while the Democratic Party has won a great victory tonight, we do so with a measure of humility and determination to heal the divides that have held back our progress.

As Lincoln said to a nation far more divided than ours, we are not enemies but friends. Though passion may have strained, it must not break our bonds of affection.

And to those Americans whose support I have yet to earn, I may not have won your vote tonight, but I hear your voices. I need your help. And I will be your president, too. And to all those watching tonight from beyond our shores, from parliaments and palaces, to those who are huddled around radios in the forgotten corners of the world, our stories are singular, but our destiny is shared, and a new dawn of American leadership is at hand.

To those—to those who would tear the world down: We will defeat you. To those who seek peace and security: We support you. And to all those who have wondered if America's beacon still burns as bright:

Tonight we proved once more that the true strength of our nation comes not from the might of our arms or the scale of our wealth, but from the enduring power of our ideals: democracy, liberty, opportunity and unyielding hope.

That's the true genius of America: that America can change. Our union can be perfected. What we've already achieved gives us hope for what we can and must achieve tomorrow.

This election had many firsts and many stories that will be told for generations. But one that's on my mind tonight is about a woman who cast her ballot in Atlanta. She's a lot like the millions of others who stood in line to make their voice heard in this election except for one thing: Ann Nixon Cooper is one hundred and six years old.

She was born just a generation past slavery; a time when there were no cars on the road or planes in the sky; when someone like her couldn't vote for two reasons—because she was a woman and because of the colour of her skin.

And tonight, I think about all that she's seen throughout her century in America—the heartache and the hope; the struggle and the progress; the times we were told that we can't, and the people who pressed on with that American creed:

Yes we can.

At a time when women's voices were silenced and their hopes dismissed, she lived to see them stand up and speak out and reach out for the ballot.

Yes we can.

When there was despair in the dust bowl and depression across the land, she saw a nation conquer fear itself with a New Deal, new jobs, a new sense of common purpose.

Yes we can.

When the bombs fell on our harbour and tyranny threatened the world, she was there to witness a generation rise to greatness and a democracy was saved.

Yes we can.

She was there for the buses in Montgomery, the hoses in Birmingham, a bridge in Selma, and a preacher from Atlanta who told a people that we shall overcome.

Yes we can.

A man touched down on the moon, a wall came down in Berlin, a world was connected by our own science and imagination.

And this year, in this election, she touched her finger to a screen, and cast her vote, because after one hundred and six years in America, through the best of times and the darkest of hours, she knows how America can change.

Yes we can.

America, we have come so far. We have seen so much. But there is so much more to do. So tonight, let us ask ourselves—if our children should live to see the next century; if my daughters should be so lucky to live as long as Ann Nixon Cooper, what change will they see? What progress will we have made?

This is our chance to answer that call. This is our moment.

This is our time, to put our people back to work and open doors of opportunity for our kids; to restore prosperity and promote the cause of peace; to reclaim the American dream and reaffirm that fundamental truth, that, out of many, we are one; that while we breathe, we hope. And where we are met with cynicism and doubts and those who tell us that we can't, we will respond with that timeless creed that sums up the spirit of a people:

Yes, we can.

Thank you; God bless you, and may God bless the United States of America.

# 35

## Who You Are and What You Stand For

★ ★ ★ ★ ★ ★ ★

Michelle Obama
Columbus, Ohio, U.S.A.
5 May 2012

*Six months before presidential election of 2012, Michelle Obama delivered the following speech to the Ohio State University students.*

Oh, wow. Thank you guys. Wow. It sounds like you all are already fired up and ready to go. This is amazing. It is truly amazing. And you know what? Being here with all of you today . . . let me tell you: I'm feeling pretty fired up and ready to go myself. I really am. But there is a reason why we're here today. And—

[Man in crowd: We love you!]

And we love you too! And it's not just because we support one extraordinary man. Although I'll admit I'm a little biased, because I think our president is awesome. And it's not just because we want to win an election. We are here because of the values we believe in. We're here because of the vision for this country that we all share. We're here because we want all our children to have a good education, right? Schools that push them, and inspire them; prepare them for good jobs. We want our parents and our grandparents to retire with dignity, because we believe that after a lifetime of hard work, they should enjoy their golden years.

We want to restore that basic middle-class security for our families, because we believe that folks shouldn't go bankrupt because they get sick. They shouldn't lose their home because someone loses a job. We believe that responsibility should be rewarded, and hard work should pay off. And, truly, these are basic American values. They're the same values that so many of us were raised with, including myself. You see, my father was a blue-collar city worker at the city water plant, and my family lived in a little-bitty apartment on the South Side of Chicago. And neither of my parents had the chance to go to college.

But let me tell you what my parents did do. They saved. They sacrificed. I mean, they poured everything they had into me and my brother. They wanted us to have the kind of education they could only dream of. And, while pretty much all of my college tuition came from student loans and grants, my dad still paid a little-bitty portion of that tuition himself. And let me tell you: every semester, my dad was determined to pay that bill right on time, because he was so proud to be sending his kids to college. And he couldn't bear the thought of me or my brother missing that registration deadline because his check was late.

Like so many people in this country, my father took great pride in being able to earn a living that allowed him to handle his responsibility to his family, to pay all of his bills, and to pay them on time. And, truly, more than anything else, that is what's at stake. It's that fundamental promise, that no matter who you are or how you started out, if you work hard, you can build a decent life for yourself and, yes, an even better life for your kids. And it is that promise that binds us together as Americans. It's what makes us who we are. And whether it's equal pay for women, or health care for our kids; whether it's tax cuts for middle-class families, or student loans for our young people; that is what my husband has been fighting for every single day as president. Every single day.

And let me tell you something: as First Lady, I have had the chance to see, up-close and personal, what being president looks like. Right? I have seen how the issues that come across a president's desk are always the hard ones.

[Woman in crowd: You're beautiful, Michelle!]

But in all seriousness. These problems: they're always the hard ones. The problems with no clear solutions. The judgment calls where the stakes are so high and there's no margin for error. And as president, you can get all kinds of advice from all kinds of people, but at the end of the day, when it comes time to make that decision, all you have to guide you are your life experiences. Your values. And your vision for this country. That's all you have. In the end, when you're making those impossible choices, it all boils down to who you are and what you stand for.

And we all know what Barack Obama is. Who he is. We all know what our president stands for, right? He is the son of a single mother who struggled to put herself through school, and pay the bills. That's who he is. He's the grandson of a woman who woke up before dawn every day to catch a bus to her job at the bank. And even though Barack's grandmother worked hard to help support his family—and she was good at her job—like so many women, she hit that glass ceiling, and men no more qualified than she was were promoted up the ladder ahead of her. So believe me: Barack knows what it means when a family struggles. He knows what it means when someone doesn't have a chance to fulfill their potential. And what you need to know, America: those are the experiences that have made him the man and the president he is today.

But I have said this before, and I will say it again and again: Barack cannot do this alone. And fortunately, he never has. We have always moved this country forward together. And today, more than ever before, Barack needs your help. He needs your help. He needs your help. He needs every single one of you. Every single one of you to give just a little part of your life each week to this campaign. He needs you to register those voters, right? And to all of the college students out there, all of you: if you're going to be moving over the summer, remember to register at your new address in the fall, you got that? Get that done!

Barack needs you to join one of our neighbourhood teams, and start organizing in your community. And just let me say: if there have ever been any doubts about the difference that you can make, I just want you to remember that in the end, this all could come down to those few thousand people who register to vote. Think about it. It could all come down to those last few thousand votes who get out to the polls on November the sixth. And when you average that out over this entire state, it might mean registering just one more person in your town. It might mean helping just one more person in your community get out and vote on election day.

So know this—with every door you knock on, with every call you make, with every conversation you have—I want you to remember that this could be the one that makes the difference. This could be the one. Remember that. That is exactly the kind of impact that each of you can have. Now, I am not going to kid you: this journey is going to be long, and it is going to be hard. But know that that is how change always happens in this country. And if we keep showing up, if we keep fighting the good fight, then eventually we get there. We always do. Maybe not in our lifetimes, but maybe in our children's lifetimes. Maybe in our grandchildren's lifetimes.

Because in the end, that's what this is all about. That is what I think about when I tuck my girls in at night. I think about the world I want to leave for them, and for all of our sons and our daughters. I think about how I want to do for them what my dad did for me. I want to give them a foundation for their dreams. I want to give them opportunities worthy of their promise. I want to give them that sense of limitless possibility, that belief that here in America, there is always something better out there if you're willing to work for it. So we just cannot turn back now, right?

We have come so far, but we have so much more to do. And if we want to keep on moving forward, then we need to work our hearts out for the man that I have the pleasure of introducing here today. Are you ready? It is my privilege to introduce my husband, and our president. President Barack Obama!